AF725841

At the Schoolhouse Gate

Stakeholder Perceptions of First Amendment Rights and Responsibilities in U.S. Public Schools

A Volume in Teaching and Learning Social Studies

Series Editor:
William B. Russell III, *University of Central Florida*

Teaching and Learning Social Studies

William B. Russell III, Series Editor

At the Schoolhouse Gate: Stakeholder Perceptions of First Amendment Rights and Responsibilities in U.S. Public Schools (2022)
Edited by Nancy C. Patterson and Prentice T. Chandler

Real Classrooms, Real Teachers: The C3 Inquiry in Practice (2021)
Edited by Kristy A. Brugar and Kathryn L. Roberts

Education for Democracy: A Renewed Approach to Civic Inquiries for Social Justice (2021)
By Steven P. Camicia and Ryan Knowles

Movies and Moral Dilemma Discussions: A Practical Guide to Cinema Based Character Development (2020)
By Stewart Waters and William B. Russell III

Marking the "Invisible": Articulating Whiteness in Social Studies Education (2020)
Edited By Andrea M. Hawkman and Sarah B. Shear

Extending the Ground of Public Confidence: Teaching Civil Liberties in K–16 Social Studies Education (2019)
Edited by Janie Hubbard

More Like Life Itself: Simulations as Powerful and Purposeful Social Studies (2018)
Edited by Cory Wright-Maley

No Reluctant Citizens: Teaching Civics in K–12 Classrooms (2018)
Edited by Cory Wright-Maley

(Re)Imagining Elementary Social Studies: A Controversial Issues Reader (2018)
Edited by Sarah B. Shear, Christina M. Tschida, Elizabeth Bellows, Lisa Brown Buchanan, and Elizabeth E. Saylor

The Global Education Movement: Narratives of Distinguished Global Scholars (2018)
Edited by Toni Fuss Kirkwood-Tucker

Digging Deeper: Activities for Enriching and Expanding Social Studies Instruction K–12 (2017)
Edited by M. Gail Hickey and Jeremiah C. Clabough

Teaching and Learning Social Studies
(Continued)

Race Lessons: Using Inquiry to Teach About Race in Social Studies (2017)
Edited by Prentice T. Chandler and Todd S. Hawley

Cinematic Social Studies: A Resource for Teaching and Learning Social Studies With Film (2017)
Edited by William B. Russell III and Stewart Waters

Social Justice Education, Globalization, and Teacher Education (2015)
Edited by Lydiah Nganga and John Kambutu

Unpuzzling History With Primary Sources (2015)
Edited by Jeremiah Clabough, Thomas N. Turner, and William B. Russell III

Doing Race in Social Studies: Critical Perspectives (2015)
Edited by Prentice T. Chandler

Getting at the Core of the Common Core With Social Studies (2014)
Edited by Thomas N. Turner, Jeremiah Clabough, and William Cole

Digital Social Studies (2013)
Edited by William B. Russell III

Integrative Strategies for the K–12 Social Studies Classroom (2013)
Edited by Timothy Lintner

Let the Music Play! Harnessing the Power of Music for History and Social Studies Classrooms (2012)
Edited by Anthony M. Pellegrino and Christopher Dean Lee

Contemporary Social Studies: An Essential Reader (2012)
Edited by William B. Russell III

Reel Character Education: A Cinematic Approach to Character Development (2010)
By William B. Russell III and Stewart Waters

Teaching Social Issues With Film (2009)
By William B. Russell III

Review Board

John P. Broome	*University of Mary Washington*
Diann Brown	*Bowling Green State University*
Nancy Brownell	*Bowling Green State University*
Kristy A. Brugar	*University of Oklahoma*
Prentice Chandler	*Austin Peay State University*
Beth Corrigan	*Notre Dame Academy*
Jason Endacott	*University of Arkansas*
Joe Edens	*Bowling Green State University*
John M. Fischer	*Bowling Green State University*
Clayton Kalaf-Hughes	*Bowling Green City Schools*
Cheryl Lambert	*Austin Peay State University*
Jeffery D. Nokes	*Brigham Young University*
Nancy C. Patterson	*Bowling Green State University*
Jared Reitz	*Ohio Council for the Social Studies*
Jeanne Vidoni	*Bowling Green State University*
Joanna Weaver	*Bowling Green State University*

Acknowledgment: The editors would like to offer a special thank you to Nancy Brownell, our copy editor, for providing hours of professional expertise.

At the Schoolhouse Gate

Stakeholder Perceptions of First Amendment Rights and Responsibilities in U.S. Public Schools

Edited by

Nancy C. Patterson
Bowling Green State University

and

Prentice T. Chandler
Austin Peay State University

IAP

Information Age Publishing, Inc.
Charlotte, North Carolina • www.infoagepub.com

Library of Congress Cataloging-in-Publication Data

CIP data for this book can be found on the Library of Congress website:
http://www.loc.gov/index.html

Paperback: 978-1-64802-724-6
Hardcover: 978-1-64802-725-3
eBook: 978-1-64802-726-0

Copyright © 2022 IAP–Information Age Publishing, Inc.

All rights reserved. No part of this publication may be reproduced, stored in a retrieval system, or transmitted in any form or by any electronic or mechanical means, or by photocopying, microfilming, recording or otherwise without written permission from the publisher.

Printed in the United States of America.

CONTENTS

PART III: CHOICES TO ACT

FOREWORD

Mikayla Hernandez and Wesley Wagner

Our names are Wesley Wagner, a forensics/biochemistry major at Duquesne University in Pittsburgh, Pennsylvania, and Mikayla Hernandez, an interior design major at The Ohio State University in Columbus, Ohio. In the spring of 2018, we both graduated from Van Wert High School, located in a small town of just under 11,000 people in Northwest Ohio. There, we were introduced to the *At the Schoolhouse Gate* project through Dr. Nancy Patterson, when she visited our high school with the intent of recruiting seniors to participate in focus groups that discussed students' views on their First Amendment rights. Every member of our class met with Dr. Patterson during our respective government class periods, a graduation-required class for all seniors, to gain information about the project and begin thinking about whether or not we wanted to participate. Initially, this was a totally new, strange thing: a college professor coming to our middle-of-nowhere town and asking us about rights we had barely even thought about before that year. Seeing an opportunity to get out of class for a while, of course we agreed to participate; however, the more we listened to Dr. Patterson describe her project and the book she intended to write with her colleagues, the more interested we became, and this was only intensified when we actually took part in the focus groups.

A little over halfway through our second semester of college, we were contacted by our high school government teacher—Mr. Jeff Kallas—with the opportunity to write the foreword for the book highlighting not only our high school's focus groups, but a number of other studies conducted

At the Schoolhouse Gate: Stakeholder Perceptions of First Amendment Rights and Responsibilities in U.S. Public Schools, pp. ix–xiii
www.infoagepub.com
Copyright © 2022 by Information Age Publishing
All rights of reproduction in any form reserved.

to investigate the same topics we discussed. The chance to write a few pages about our experiences in an actual *published* book seemed like a once-in-a-lifetime opportunity, and we were greatly honored to be selected to take on the task. Needless to say, we excitedly agreed to collaborate on this project and spent the next several months emailing back and forth with Dr. Patterson, as well as meeting together in a video conference to touch base with what exactly needed to be done and to discuss experiences we have had post-high school graduation regarding our First Amendment rights.

Since we are both still students, though now studying at universities 3 hours away from one another, we still care deeply about this particular subject and continue to observe how our rights impact us on a regular basis at school. We often think back to how we felt in our high school classrooms when the chance arose to speak our minds and share our opinions. It is our view that being informed about our First Amendment rights in the school setting is critical for growth and civic engagement as we transition into the "real world." We also realize that unfortunately many students like us are unaware of how to apply and completely understand these rights. If you do not know your rights, it can be intimidating, or even scary, to test them. We want to be heard and respected when we honestly give our input during a discussion about something controversial, and we want to be taken seriously when we exercise our rights in nationwide protests and walkouts. We know these desires are not always easy to accomplish when the opinions we hold are unorthodox, when it seems like everyone around us strongly disagrees with us, or when we are not completely sure we have the right to say or do what we desire to and therefore fear potential consequences.

My name is Mikayla Hernandez and I am a sophomore at The Ohio State University. During my time in Columbus, my experiences with my First Amendment rights have differed dramatically from the ones I had in high school; moving from a small, generally conservative town to a huge urban city was quite a transition in all areas of my life. During the beginning of my senior year of high school, I kept my mouth shut in class when anything remotely controversial was mentioned, because I knew what I would have to say would likely be unpopular among my classmates. Over the course of the year, seeing various posts by student activists on social media regarding school shootings made me realize I was hindering myself and my education by not speaking up. I participated in the walkout following the tragic shooting at Marjory Stoneman Douglas High School in Parkland, Florida in March 2018, mainly to challenge myself to express how I felt about the issues surrounding gun rights despite being unsure if I would have to face some sort of disciplinary consequences as a result. Getting reassurance from my teachers that I would not be punished if I decided to leave class to participate gave me the confidence I needed to join my peers in the event, and by taking part, I learned that feeling supported and understood by my educators made it easier to exercise my rights.

Now that I am in a completely different academic setting in Columbus and have experience with my rights, I have noticed it no longer feels like I am debating with others in my classes or that I am saying something wrong when I share how I feel because I know I have the right to speak my mind, just like everyone around me does. Occasionally, a protestor will come onto campus and stand in a largely populated area to speak about the sinful lives of college students and to tell passersby that they will be condemned. There is always a group of students crowded around these people, arguing with them and telling them how wrong they are, but seeing this reminds me of all the times I have felt very strongly about my views and wanted someone to hear them. These notable events in particular are the events that teach me the most about accepting the validity of opposition and listening intently even though I disagree.

My name is Wesley Wagner, a sophomore at Duquesne University. During my time at college, the transition from a quiet, conservative town to downtown of a large city was also abrupt. In high school, my experiences with First Amendment rights were limited to two memorable examples. First was taking part in the walkout following the tragic events at Marjory Stoneman Douglas High School. While our administration and teachers assured us of the lack of negative consequences, my experience was still mildly awkward. The day of the walkout was the same day as a group presentation in my class, with none of my group members participating in the walkout. This put supporting my group and doing my part at odds with my beliefs and wanting to express my First Amendment rights; however, I chose to participate in the walkout. My second experience was through the teacher's union protests that occurred throughout our senior year. Most of the teachers wore pins and T-shirts that called for contract renegotiations for the teachers in the district. This helped to open my eyes to the fact that teachers' First Amendment rights are even more precarious than the students' rights, as I learned of guidelines and rules that had to be followed to avoid negative repercussions from discussions with my teachers.

On my college campus, dialogue between those of different beliefs is a crucial part of Duquesne's mission, with different round table and panel discussions on various topics, like race and religion, occurring about once a month. Being directly in the city has also exposed me to some outside, citywide protests, such as the student walkout for climate change and protests involving police brutality—protests I would have only seen on TV when I was in high school. This could have been attributed to the small size of our school and town, or the fact that we very rarely took advantage of our First Amendment rights.

Taking part in this project brought to our attention that we were not as educated about our rights as we should have wanted to be leading up to the end of our final year of high school. While we extensively discussed and studied famous court cases regarding First Amendment rights, we rarely stopped to apply them to our lives. Cases like *Tinker v. Des Moines* (1969) and *Hazelwood School District v. Kuhlmeier* (1988) seemed far too distant and removed from us as students, because we were letting ourselves slip by believing our issues with First Amendment rights had already been handled by the Supreme Court in the past. In reality, the two of us were just hoping that if we played it safe and stuck with what we knew was allowed, we would be fine when speaking in class and in the hallways. The truth is, First Amendment rights in the academic setting are extremely complicated for everyone involved and they change over time. We began thinking more about how our educators have also faced plenty of struggles with rights themselves. We barely had considered this, so reading several teachers' perspectives on their rights in the chapters of this book allowed us to see their experiences are not too different from our own and provided insight that we may have never had the chance to consider otherwise. The book additionally places great emphasis on the importance of educating students of all ages on their First Amendment rights. Now, we realize just how important it is for even young children in elementary school to advocate for themselves, and there are an abundance of ways to integrate this into their education, including student-led conferences and democratic classroom settings. The narratives in the chapters included here also accurately communicate, through students' words, what it is like to be a student now, particularly in dealing with the problems of First Amendment rights that arise through social media use, proving just how complicated the limitations of our rights can get as we progress, technology advances, and media grows.

Overall, the importance of this book and the research that contributed to it are amplified by the many perspectives presented. We truly believe everyone can learn something from this book, whether it is a student trying to understand a teacher's perspective, a teacher trying to understand a student's perspective, or even someone outside of the school trying to learn more about the environment of the educational system, like current or future parents and guardians. This book can also inform school and community members about the extent of their rights in school, regardless of whether that person is a student or a teacher. This collection of stories is a unique singular source that fulfills the need for a clear explanation of these complex rights and their potential.We are honored to have been able to play a role in its production. While First Amendment rights can and are threatened through court cases, such as *Hazelwood School District v. Kuhlmeier*, through which student's freedom of press rights are limited, or *Garcetti v. Ceballos*, which has been used to strip teachers of their First Amendment rights regarding both curriculum choice and how that curriculum is taught, an even more serious threat is people being uninformed or misinformed about what is and is not protected speech.

REFERENCES

Garcetti v. Ceballos, 547 U.S. 410 (2006).
Hazelwood School District v. Kuhlmeier, 484 U.S 260 (1988).
Tinker v. Des Moines Independent Community School District, 393 U.S. 503 (1969).

INTRODUCTION

The objective of this volume is to shed light upon K–12 perspectives of various school stakeholders in the current context of increasing political polarization and heightened teacher and student activism. It is grounded in academic freedom case law and the majority opinion of the Supreme Court in the *Tinker v. Des Moines Independent Community School District* (1969) that held that certain forms of expression are protected by the First Amendment. Justice Fortas wrote in the majority opinion that "it can hardly be argued that either students or teachers shed their constitutional rights to freedom of speech or expression at the schoolhouse gate."

This volume is timely and instructive, as protections afforded by the First Amendment are a topic of enduring concern, with such freedoms requiring vigilant advocacy and protection from each generation. Paulo Freire stated, "Citizenship is not obtained by chance: It is a construction that, never finished, demands we fight for it" (1998, p. 90). There is confusion and much debate in and outside of schools about how and when these and other rights described in the First Amendment may or may not be limited, and the time is now to clarify the place of such rights in public education.

The 10 chapters included in *At the Schoolhouse Gate* are divided into three sections: "Foundations," "The State of Rights in Schools," and "Choices to Act." The Foundations section presents the case law pertaining to the rights of both teachers and students, setting the tone for what presently is permissible and chronicling the ongoing struggle with defining rights in schools. In Chapter 1, Nancy Patterson and Prentice Chandler present an overview of the state of academic freedom in our schools. This work highlights relevant case law and offers suggestions of how to exercise academic freedom in school settings. In Chapter 2, "A More

At the Schoolhouse Gate: Stakeholder Perceptions of First Amendment Rights and Responsibilities in U.S. Public Schools, pp. xv–xviii
Copyright © 2022 by Information Age Publishing
All rights of reproduction in any form reserved.

Complicated Story: Student Free Speech in Public K–12 Education" Ryan Suskey examines 80 years of case law, providing insight into areas that are likely to be resolved by the courts in the future. This work is instructive in that it highlights future trends and contours for First Amendment issues.

In Part II, "The State of Rights in Schools," various authors examine teacher and student interactions with rights in schools, including the interest of students in participating with their teachers in the democratic experiment of schooling. In the first entry in this section, Nancy Patterson, Diann Brown, and Jeanne Vidoni's chapter "Taking Action and Taking Offense in Our Their Little Democracy" uses case study reports from public high school students to understand their thoughts on 1st Amendment Rights and their limits. Findings in this study point to the importance of freedom of speech and the desire of students to build more authentic relationships with adults. In Chapter 4, Cheryl Lambert discusses "student-led conferences" as a way to allow students to incorporate democratic practices in schools. In this chapter, Lambert highlights relevant literature and offers guidance for school leaders. This chapter is followed by Jeffrey Nokes' chapter that details components of "democratic classrooms," including classroom organization, management tactics, and instructional shifts. This work includes the experiences of a first-year teacher attempting to make these structural and philosophical shifts in her classroom. In Chapter 6, Sarah Kaka's qualitative study examines student views of technology and expression. Findings from Kaka's work include students' use of alternative news sources, limitations of students' rights, and thoughts on administrators' censorship of digital information.

The "Choices to Act" section includes portraits of student and teacher activism as well as advice for teachers for availing themselves of their rights. In Chapter 7, Kristy Brugar and Dalton Savage describe the experiences of four secondary social studies teachers as they participated in the Oklahoma teacher walkout in the spring of 2018. In this portraiture research, the roles of teacher, citizen, public employee, and community member are examined across teachers with different levels of experience. In Chapter 8, we offer a reprinted article from a special issue on academic freedom in *Social Education*, a flagship journal of the National Council for the Social Studies. This piece, "Defending Academic Freedom: Advice from Teachers" (Simpson, 2010), provides sound and still timely advice for teachers in the field as they navigate First Amendment issues. This chapter addresses teacher rights, parental rights, district rights, and culminates with "lessons" for teachers in the field. This chapter is followed by "They Speak for Themselves: Students Name the Phenomenon of Civic Education and Freedom of Speech." In this chapter, Donna Philips investigates the lived experience of democratic civic education for middle school students through the *We the People: The Citizen and the Constitution*

(WTP) Simulated Congressional Hearing program. Lastly, in Chapter 10, Elise Boyle, Leo Bucks, and Clay Kalaf-Hughes' chapter "Real Choices to Act: Waking Up to Charlottesville and Testing the First Amendment" includes two vignettes crafted by students in Bowling Green City Schools (Ohio). The context for this chapter is the Charlottesville "Unite the Right Rally," ongoing National Football League player protests, and the Stoneman Douglas High School shooting. The stories and reasoned actions of these two young people offer up the argument that high school students can indeed avail themselves responsibly of their rights and suggest that adults attend to the education of young people about their rights.

The chapters contained here clarify the often-misunderstood responsibilities associated with the First Amendment and how they operate in the context of American schools. It is clear that in order to train children for participation in a democracy, democratic ideals and practices should be a fundamental part of that education. It is not an add-on to democratic education—it *is* democratic education. Our First Amendment rights are the bedrock of our system of government and the lived experiences of our citizens. Without these rights, there is no America—there is no We the People. We also believe that this volume is coming at a unique time in the history of our nation and our schools. The presidency of Donald Trump is over, the yearlong battle with COVID-19 is ongoing, racial inequity persists, and economic uncertainty looms. The mission of our schools is to prepare young people for entry into this world as it is.

Justice Fortas, who wrote for majority in the *Tinker* case, frequently cited Robert Jackson's majority opinion from the 1943 *West Virginia v. Barnette* case, in which the Supreme Court held it was unconstitutional to coerce schoolchildren into saluting the U.S flag. Jackson argued the following: "That [schools] are educating the young for citizenship is reason for scrupulous protection of Constitutional freedoms of the individual." Fortas and Jackson are making the point that John Dewey made long before and that many educational researchers have made since, that if schools are where students learn about the value of constitutional freedoms of the individual, then schools must be places in which those values are embedded and modeled.

As for what this might look like in schools, who better to consult than Mary Beth Tinker herself? In a recent Constitution Day virtual session she delivered at Bowling Green State University on the power of youth voices, Ms. Tinker fielded a question about her views on the ongoing challenges school administrators face, including whether to ban such things as student displays of various flags on the football field. Ms. Tinker stated very simply that what we need is more conversation and less censorship. We the co-authors of this volume concur and laud the precedent in our courts as well as the voices of stakeholders represented in these chapters to uphold such values within the schoolhouse gates.

REFERENCES

Freire, P. (1998). *Teachers as cultural workers: Letters to those who dare to teach*. Westview.

Simpson, M. (2010). Defending academic freedom: Advice for teachers. *Social Education, 74*(6), 310–315.

Tinker v. Des Moines Indep. Community School District, 393 U.S. 503 (1969).

West Virginia v. Barnette, 319 U.S. 624 (1943).

PART I

FOUNDATIONS

CHAPTER 1

ACADEMIC FREEDOM IN THE BALANCE

What We Know About the Rights of Public School Teachers

Nancy C. Patterson
Bowling Green State University

Prentice T. Chandler
Austin Peay State University

This chapter presents an overview of what we have learned about the state of academic freedom in the public schools. It includes a rationale for the place of academic freedom in social studies classrooms, a perspective on the court system as recourse for teachers, and a call for action to protect our freedoms by alternative means. Based on a National Council for the Social Studies presentation by American Civil Liberties Union lawyer Fritz Mulhauser, the paper provides a thematic summary of case law and precedent as they stand at present, including speech outside of school, classroom materials and content, classroom discussion, and expression through dress. Finally, the paper offers suggestions of how to exercise academic freedom successfully in the classroom.

At the Schoolhouse Gate: Stakeholder Perceptions of First Amendment Rights and Responsibilities in U.S. Public Schools, pp. 3–20
www.infoagepub.com
Copyright © 2022 by Information Age Publishing
All rights of reproduction in any form reserved.

When we ask our students—prospective secondary social studies teachers—where they get their right to free speech, they inevitably respond that the U.S. Constitution guarantees it. The majority attests we have it because it is an inviolable part of the Bill of Rights as written in the First Amendment. There is no small degree of misunderstanding—or perhaps a simple forgetting—among these prospective teachers about the origins of their rights, both that the rights they currently enjoy were hard-won and that these important rights are at risk and/or the subject of ongoing debate. Paulo Freire stated, "Citizenship is not obtained by chance: It is a construction that, never finished, demands we fight for it" (1998, p. 90). Entwined with the struggle for citizenship is the ongoing fight for academic freedom in K–12 education. It continues in this generation and has implications for preservice teacher education.

United States Supreme Court Justice David H. Souter recently recalled the court's words 46 years earlier, which stated, "the vigilant protection of constitutional freedoms is nowhere more vital than in the community of American schools" (in *Garcetti v. Ceballos*, 2006, quoting *Shelton v. Tucker*, 1960). It is the need for this vigilant protection that has motivated us to write this review. We provide some background for the place of academic freedom in K–12 classrooms and summarize what we have learned about the state of academic freedom in the public schools, including a perspective on the court system as recourse for teachers and a call for action to protect our freedoms by alternative means. Finally, we offer suggestions of how to exercise academic freedom successfully in the classroom.

This freedom allegedly protects teachers' rights to make instructional and curricular decisions in the best interest of their students and is a hotly contested right in the courts. The National Council for the Social Studies has defined academic freedom over the years, with the original position statement published in 1968 and revised in 2007 and 2018. The 2018 statement, entitled "Academic Freedom and Social Studies Educator," states: with the current position statement reading in a 1968 position statement (revised in 2007 and 2018) entitled "Academic Freedom and the Social Studies Teacher," which states:

> Academic freedom means that both social studies educators and students have the opportunity to engage in intellectual debate without fear of censorship or retaliation. Academic freedom gives both social studies educators and students the right to express their views—in speech, writing, and/or through electronic communication without fear of sanction. Academic freedom for social studies educators and students includes the right and responsibility to study, investigate, present, interpret, discuss, and debate relevant facts, issues, and ideas.

Academic freedom is an element of social studies teaching so essential that our governing national organization has not only published this document but also has endorsed, along with other national organizations, the 1940 American Association of University Professors' "1940 Statement of Principles on Academic Freedom and Tenure."

Thoughtful teachers of all grade levels and around the world want to be able to plan their own lessons (including goals and materials), speak to students as they think best, and encourage free-ranging discourse in their classes unfettered by interference from authorities within their institutions or beyond. In higher education (apart from sectarian schools), a cultural consensus establishes norms to protect professors at both public and private schools. For their part, public school K–12 teachers have long argued that protections in the U.S. Constitution for free expression should cover them and yield similar protection.

The difficulty is that teachers are public employees, and as such, the government, with responsibility both for education and as an employer, also has important rights. The balance has been contested in the courts for decades. This balance and the measure of it was first articulated in the landmark case, *Pickering v. Board of Education* (1968), wherein a public school teacher was dismissed for having written a sarcastic letter to a local paper about school district financing. Pickering sued and won his case in the Supreme Court. Writing for the majority, Justice Thurgood Marshall wrote:

> The problem in any case is to arrive at a balance between the interests of the teacher, as a citizen, in commenting upon matters of public concern and the interest of the State, as an employer, in promoting the efficiency of the public services it performs through its employees.

The test of balance has been whether the teacher's right to discuss matters of public concern outweighed the school's interest in efficiency and avoiding disruption. As described in the case studies that follow, the *Pickering* balancing test has been used to weigh numerous free speech cases.

For K–12 social studies educators, the fact that courts balance individual and government rights makes for uncertain outcomes. Exploring this tension and assessing its implications for teachers are the purposes of this paper. We are writing as members of the Academic Freedom Committee of National Council for the Social Studies and as professors of social studies education to summarize what we have learned about the tenuous state of academic freedom. Both of us have served on this committee in varying capacities and have worked with numerous prospective teachers at our respective institutions. We have been unnerved upon learning of the challenges teachers across all grade levels and content areas face when they try to implement issues-based curriculum or engage with controversial issues. We have learned of many ways in which teacher expression and professional judgment in general can be at risk: Conflicts may arise over choices of broad topics (e.g., peace, war in Iraq, or the Arab-Israeli conflict), choices of interpretive frameworks (i.e., teaching backward from the present, using revisionist narratives, choosing materials like specific readings and plays or films with adult content), or even small-scale choices (i.e., classroom language which allows vernacular and "street" terms). Since the landmark decision of *Tinker v. Des Moines Independent Community School District* (1969) that upheld students' rights of nondisruptive expression at school, our students' cheerful assumption that "the Constitution protects us" may actually be truer of their own speech than that of their teachers.

The Context for Academic Freedom in Social Studies

Academic freedom is the cornerstone of democratic citizenship in the public system and thus deserves a privileged place in social studies. The story line for social studies instruction has been penned in the National Council for the Social Studies position statement, *A Vision of Powerful Teaching and Learning in the Social Studies* (2016), where it is stated that social studies builds "skills that students will use in their roles as student, employee, and most importantly as informed and engaged citizen of the world" and furthermore, "an excellent education in social studies is essential to civic competence and the maintenance and enhancement of a free and democratic society" (p. 180).

In other words, the social studies, as the most inclusive of all of the school disciplines (Ross, 2001), is the academic discipline in which teachers engender the growth of competent democratic citizens who can carry on the democratic traditions and institutions of the American state. It is evident that, while citizenship and training of people to play productive roles in society is a mission of the schooling at large, it is a mission that is uniquely suited to social studies.

Debate persists over the exact nature of that mission, perhaps because the meaning of "democratic citizen" is contested, giving rise to an irresolvable dialectical tension. On one end of the spectrum is the citizen who disrupts and resists all forms and systems of oppression. On the other end of the spectrum is the more traditional, conservative citizen who accepts a given sociocultural position and provides unquestioned support to those leaders perceived as capable of preserving America's role in the grand march of history. Westheimer and Kahne (2004) have described a continuum of citizenship orientations from personally responsible (traditional) to participatory (somewhere in the middle) to justice-oriented (revisionist philosophical). They argue that the decisions that people make as to what sort of citizen each will be as an individual have critical political implications for social studies education.

We argue that, indeed, the description of "citizen" espoused in the guiding documents of our national organization is one that aligns with the justice-oriented citizen. This citizen is not only well informed, as a personally responsible citizen might be, or simply active, as the participatory citizen might be, but active for the common good, acknowledging cultural diversity and interdependence in this citizenship role. Teachers such as these have opportunities to "analyze and understand the interplay of social economic and political forces" and bring attention to "matters of injustice and to the importance of pursuing social justice" (Westheimer & Kahne, 2004, p. 4).

This teacher-citizen is equipped and enabled to teach about controversy, offering consideration of multiple perspectives on any issue and calling students to active participation based on these understandings. They have great need of free speech protections described in the First Amendment and subsequently defined in the courts as academic freedom. The tension lies herein to transmit the shared knowledge of the larger cultural narrative of America by way of history, political science, sociology, geography, psychology, economics, and so forth in a context of academic freedom. Such freedom is a prerequisite to developing a citizenry who can act upon the world to change and reform it by resisting oppressive and inequitable antidemocratic conditions (Stanley & Nelson, 1994).

The tensions inherent in the discussion of whether or not a social studies teacher is justice-oriented is but one marker along a complicated continuum of ways of conceptualizing the social studies. Since the inception of social studies in the early 1900s, the expressed/overt goal of the social studies has been that of *citizenship* education. From the founding of the American republic until the founding of social studies more than a century later, public education was created and developed to serve the civic purpose of creating a strong electorate, one whose citizens would fulfill their civic duty to the United States (Shaver, 1981). Ross (2001) highlights the foundational concept of "Social studies, in the broadest sense," as "the preparation of young people so that they possess the knowledge, skills, and values necessary for active participation in society" (p. 21). Of course, this expressed goal can be shaped and formed to mean different things to different people in different historical eras. The meaning and mission of social studies shifts with the times. The basic dilemma outlined by Shaver (1981) in defining, teaching, learning, and thinking about social studies is "How can the school contribute to the continuity of the society by preserving and passing on its traditions and values while also contributing to appropriate social change by helping youth to question current social forms and solutions?" (p. 125).

In this reconceptualization of good citizenship, "educators should be given the opportunities to analyze and understand the interplay of social, economic, and political forces" and bring attention to "matters of injustice and to the importance of pursing social justice" (Westheimer & Kayne, 2004, p. 4). Freire (1998) probably best conceptualizes citizenship in ways that differ from the modernist notions of citizenship as given, fixed, and neutral:

> Yes, citizenship—above all in a society like ours, of such authoritarian and racially, sexually, and class-based discriminatory traditions—is really an invention, a political production. In this sense, one who suffers any (or all) of the discriminations ... does not enjoy the full exercise of citizenship as a peaceful and recognized right. On the contrary, it is a right to be reached and whose conquest makes democracy grow substantively. Citizenship implies freedom.... It demands commitment, political clarity, coherence, and decision. For this reason, a democratic education cannot be realized apart from an education of and for citizenship. (p. 90)

Amidst the debate, we choose to frame citizenship education in terms of social justice—a social justice whose mission is to interrupt oppressive discourses not merely celebrating the heroic meta-narrative of the past. In reference to the Shaver (1981) quote above, social studies would lean in favor of "contributing to appropriate social change by helping youth to question current social forms and solutions" more than "preserving and passing on traditions" (p. 125). This would involve a break from the way that social studies education has taken place in American schools and would have as its focus, not the creation of passive students, but active, change-oriented students.

This is not to suggest that all teachers should adopt the social justice orientation, but rather that teachers taking this stance are more likely to encounter challenges related to academic freedom. Teachers who find their pedagogical strategies, content, and/or opinions about schooling to be different from the accepted schooling discourses can be reprimanded; one need not be a justice-oriented teacher to face issues of academic freedom—one need only to disagree with accepted practice and/or policy. Academic freedom is meant to protect all individuals across the continuum of citizenship, but as the following review of case law suggests, it is rare that teachers are reprimanded or disciplined for teaching in traditional ways or covering accepted content in social studies classes. Its advocacy has been marshaled in great part by teachers who challenge the status quo.

Citizenship education in justice-oriented classrooms can be the basis for the healthy development of students who learn to analyze facts and values and reach well-grounded positions that guide their conduct as democratic citizens of the future. It is also within this context that academic freedom teeters in the balance. Evidence of the current status of academic freedom in the service of democracy is detailed in the following account of court actions related to academic freedom over the past quarter century.

THE REALITY OF ACADEMIC FREEDOM IN THE BALANCE

Each year, our committee has sponsored a panel discussion at the annual meeting to explore yet again the contested terrain of teachers' rights in instruction and how teachers may best avail themselves of their rights. While our understanding of the challenges many teachers face comes from engaging with teachers and reading their case transcripts, our understanding of recourse they may have has been built from talking with National Education Association (NEA) and American Civil Liberties Union (ACLU) lawyers. Both NEA and ACLU speakers at our sessions over the years, while joining us in enthusiasm about the goal of academic freedom, have warned that in any specific court test of a teacher's instructional decisions, the results will rest on inherently unpredictable balancing of competing values and the outcome thus is never certain. At the December 2006 conference in Washington, DC, much of what we have been learning over the last few years became clearer as we listened to our guest from the ACLU present an overview of case law concerning academic freedom. From this and other sources, we have constructed our understanding of the present state of academic freedom in the public schools. It is a complicated, murky story of this generation's struggle and a starting point for planning future courses of action.

Fritz Mulhauser (2006), staff attorney at the ACLU in Washington, DC, opened our December panel discussion with the statement that there is little certainty of a winning decision for teacher academic freedom in the courts. Mulhauser began his career in the 1960s as a social studies teacher and curriculum developer, including a period on the staff of the Harvard Social Studies Project led by Professors Donald Oliver and Fred Newmann, creating materials for teaching controversial issues in high schools. He noted that 2006 was the 40th anniversary of *Teaching Public Issues in the High School* (1966) by Oliver and James P. Shaver, and he dedicated his remarks to Oliver. Though noting that teachers retain the protection of their expression as citizens in general outside of school, he warned of the uncertainty of success in court in a fight with officials involving teaching, so he urged educators to build alternative bases of support that can be relied upon in troubled times. His rationale is built upon the following overview of salient court cases. He built the argument thematically, beginning with cases dealing with speech outside of school, then moving to cases concerning teachers' choices regarding content of instruction, followed by teachers' right of expression in the classroom discussion, and closing with teachers' expression in their dress. We conclude the case law overview with a discussion of a recent pivotal Supreme Court case that appears to tip the balance against academic freedom.

TEACHERS' SPEECH OUTSIDE OF SCHOOL

Public employees do not forfeit the right to comment publicly on matters of public concern, such that, in general, teachers cannot be fired or disciplined for statements out of school unless it can be demonstrated that speech created a substantial adverse impact on school functioning. For example, the Supreme Court held that it could be a violation of the First Amendment if an untenured Cincinnati teacher was not rehired just because he called a radio station to pass on information about an internal memo setting a dress code for teachers to spruce up the schools' image at tax time (*Mt. Healthy City School District Board of Education v. Doyle*, 1977). Applying what has come to be called "*Pickering* balancing," the court rejected discipline for a teacher who wrote a letter to the newspaper about a proposed tax increase for school funding—a letter that was critical of board priorities—because there was no evidence that it affected his classroom work or interfered with the operation of the school system generally.

The court explained in a 1983 decision that there are limits to the definition of speech on matters of public concern. A city prosecutor in New Orleans challenged her being fired after circulating a "survey" to other attorneys about morale and other internal topics as part of her own protest of a proposed transfer. In *Connick v. Myers* (1983), the Supreme Court held that her questions were "mere extensions of [her] dispute over her transfer" and hence of only personal interest. Under these rules, a teacher's off-campus statements regarding such things as war and/or participation in an off-campus political demonstration would not be a constitutionally acceptable basis for job discipline or termination. The right to comment publicly on such matters of public importance is protected.

TEACHER EXPRESSION IN CHOOSING THE CONTENT OF INSTRUCTION

Once inside the school, the teacher at work in the classroom is an employee of the state; therefor, choices of content and methods of teaching highlight the classic questions of *Pickering* balancing—the contending interests of the teacher and the employer. The longstanding claim of educators as "professionals" in the way of doctors or lawyers, entitled by training and specialized knowledge to teach as they know best, has not been consistently accepted by the courts. Courts sometimes protect the academic freedom of college and university professors to lecture as they wish, as in the *Sweezy* case cited above, or to pursue novel curricula or teaching methods. In *Hardy v. Jefferson Community College* (2001), vulgar language was protected, where discipline was reversed on grounds that the professor's street talk was relevant to instruction in his communications class.

These principles do not apply with equal force to K–12 teachers, creating an artificial separation between levels of education and roles they should play in the marketplace of ideas. Classroom speech rulings in precollege education generally follow the principle that a teacher "appears to speak for the state when he or she [sic] teaches," and accordingly, the state has a strong interest in determining the content of the message its teachers will deliver (*Tucker v. California Board of Education,* 1996). The critical question is at what level the teacher has some professional autonomy. In general, there would be no quarrel that a teacher must teach in the assigned subject area. It does not violate a teacher's free speech rights when the district insists, for example, that a teacher hired in the science department teach physics and not political science or that he or she should not lead students in prayer—even though both have the result of limiting what the teacher says in the classroom; however, the employer's right to prescribe reaches further. For example, a court in Washington state, 20 years ago, summarized the case law in general as holding that "a school district has authority to prescribe both course content and teaching methods" (*Millikan v. Board of Directors of Everett School District,* 1980). In that case, two social studies teachers challenged the school's refusal to let them team teach an alternative global studies course in place of a regular history class after a pilot period showed little student interest. When the court reviewed their claim that denying them their chosen content and approach was a First Amendment violation, it began by acknowledging that the two "utilized unconventional but professionally recognized methods designed to teach the student to think," and that this was a "worthy objective." Even so, the court upheld the administration, reasoning that "an educational institution may require some conformity in teaching methods.... The board's requirement that petitioners teach history classes in a conventional manner contrary to their own preferred teaching philosophy is not violative of their rights" (p. 417). *Millikan* essentially removes the suggestion that a teacher "appears" to speak for the state and instead mandates that teachers *are* agents of the state.

On even smaller scale curriculum decision making, courts have denied teachers a right of expression that includes unilateral choice of materials. A teacher in North Carolina unsuccessfully challenged her transfer following controversy over her choice of a play with mature themes about dysfunctional families. In *Boring v. Buncombe County Board of Education* (1998), the court of appeals held the teacher's selection of the play did not involve a matter of public concern and so was not protected speech, and even if her selection of the play was protected speech, school officials had a legitimate pedagogical interest in regulating that speech. In *Kirkland v. Northside Independent School District* (5th Cir., 1989), the court turned away a challenge by a teacher denied reappointment for what he said was assigning a supplementary reading list that had not been approved. He argued that nonconforming views were being squelched, but the court of appeals saw no First Amendment issue, stating that "although the concept of academic freedom has been recognized in our jurisprudence, the doctrine has never conferred upon teachers the control of public school curricula."

TEACHERS' EXPRESSION IN THE CLASSROOM AS PART OF CLASSROOM DISCUSSION

Although the boundaries are not precise, there is an outer limit to a school district's ability to control teachers' supposedly controversial speech in the classroom, and some speech has been protected, namely, as follows: (a) if there is no pedagogical purpose for the ban, (b) if the restriction is considered to be gross, or (c) if the restriction harmed students' ability to receive important ideas relevant to the curriculum. Courts have sometimes ruled that schools may not punish teachers for uttering particular concepts or words in class that are otherwise consistent with the school curriculum. In *Epperson v. Arkansas* (1968), the court overturned the state's ban on teaching about evolution, arguing that the restriction harmed students' ability to receive important ideas relevant to the curriculum. In *Hosford v. School Committee of Sandwich* (1996), the Massachusetts Supreme Court upheld a special education teacher's brief classroom discussion of vulgar words. Her superiors first suspended her and then denied her contract renewal on grounds her brief lesson was "pedagogically inappropriate" for 13-year-old boys in a special education class, but the court reviewed the facts in detail and disagreed. The case is unusual, however, and teachers cannot count on every court taking a close look at the details of a lesson that superiors deem out of bounds.

If a teacher faces some discipline for speech in the classroom on a matter of public concern, a court would apply the *Pickering* balancing test, reviewing the teacher's rights along with the government interest in effective and efficient fulfillment of responsibilities to the public. A difference of opinion with a school's administration that does not interfere with school operations or discipline would probably not be a sufficient government interest to overcome teacher First Amendment rights. In *Piver v. Pender County Board of Education* (1987), a high school social studies teacher successfully challenged a punitive transfer after he allowed discussion in his classroom of the firing of the principal. The discussions were not considered propagandizing; the retention of a principal was a matter of public concern and administration fears of disruption were insubstantial and of little weight in the balancing test.

Similarly, in *Cockrel v. Shelby County School District* (2001), the court of appeals upheld a fifth-grade teacher's invitation to the television series *Cheers* star, actor Woody Harrelson to speak to her class about the environmental benefits of industrial hemp, an illegal substance in Kentucky, holding that the invitation was a form of protected expression as it touched on a matter of public concern—the environmental benefits of different crops in Kentucky. In analyzing the *Pickering* balance, the court of appeals dismissed the school's concerns about a bit of public controversy afterwards—especially as the principal had approved the speaker—and found the teacher's interest in her choice of topic and speaker paramount.

The courts of appeals have thus reached diverse conclusions in applying *Pickering* balancing to teachers' expression at work. Compare the 6th Circuit findings in favor of the teacher's expression touching on a "public concern" in *Cockrel* with those in the other direction by the 4th Circuit in *Boring* or by the 5th Circuit in *Kirkland.* A California court in 2001 held the law so unclear that it gave no effective guidance to educators as to when they might lawfully limit teachers' speech, hence making them immune from any lawsuit for incorrect action (see *Debro v. San Leandro Unified School District,* 2001). Following parent opposition to a Gay Straight Alliance, an honors English teacher discussed tolerance of gay students in class, and a few students, whose parents formed the opposition group, walked out. The school reprimanded the teacher, who sued. The court noted the general principle that teacher comments on matters of public concern are not only protected, but also there is no clear authority for the proposition a teacher may depart from classroom instruction in order to initiate discussion on such matters. The court declined to let the case against the school go forward, holding that no reasonable administrator would have clearly understood the teacher's rights.

It may be a small consolation that limits regarding teacher expression must be clearly set forward. Thus, courts have overturned discipline for speech in violation of school or board rules where there has not been clear prior notice. In *Ward v. Hickey* (1993), the court of appeals noted that a school is "not entitled to retaliate against speech that it never prohibited." The court continued, stating that "few subjects lack controversy. If teachers must fear retaliation for every utterance, they will fear teaching." For technical reasons, the *Ward* court never reached the question whether a ninth-grade, untenured, biology teacher could be fired for discussing abortion in class where the board had given no warning such discussion was prohibited.

TEACHERS' EXPRESSION THROUGH THEIR DRESS

Student dress was at issue when in December 1965, when John and Mary Beth Tinker were suspended for wearing black armbands to school in Des Moines, Iowa, to protest the war in Vietnam. The most famous of all student rights cases, *Tinker v. Des Moines Independent Community School District* (1969), established that public school students may wear armbands in class as an expression of their views on topics of public concern: a right that may be limited only if there is good reason to believe that the speech would cause a substantial and material disruption to education or violate the rights of others.

The courts have differed over whether teachers have the same right as students to display personal political messages on their clothing. In *James v. Board of Education* (1972), the court of appeals held that a New York teacher could not be fired for wearing a black armband in protest of the Vietnam War, since the armband had caused no classroom disruption (while he taught poetry to his 11th-grade English class), was not perceived as an official statement of the school, did not interfere with instruction, and did not coerce or "arbitrarily inculcate doctrinaire views in the minds of the students" (p. 573). As conflict was building over the Vietnam War, the court embraced at least this symbolic level of teacher dissent within the schoolhouse walls, pointing out that "we cannot countenance school authorities arbitrarily censoring a teacher's speech merely because they do not agree with the teacher's political philosophies or leanings" and that to uphold the discipline would create the "danger that the school, by power of example, would appear to the students to be sanctioning the very pall of orthodoxy … which chokes freedom of dissent" (pp. 573–574).

Twenty-five years later, at the height of a California statewide campaign concerning school vouchers, a school district prohibited any political activity by teachers at work, including wearing buttons in class. The court upheld the rule against a challenge by teachers in *California Teachers Association v. San Diego Unified School District* (1996), reasoning that school districts have legitimate authority to "dissociate themselves from matters of political controversy."

In summary, depending on the precise form of message displayed on the teacher's clothing, a school may have legitimate concern that a teacher's right to display a political message is more likely than a student's right to disrupt the school's intended educational message. For example, a school intending to educate students about the benefits of racial tolerance would find its message disrupted by a teacher wearing a Nazi-style armband with swastika.

GARCETTI V. CEBALLOS AND TIPPING THE *PICKERING* BALANCE

We close with a review of one additional case regarding free speech and the *Pickering* balance. The recent Supreme Court case, *Garcetti v. Ceballos* (2006) is emblematic of an ongoing balancing act and has tipped the scales against academic freedom for teachers. The case is a whistleblower case in which the plaintiff—a district attorney—claimed that he had been passed up for a promotion for criticizing the legitimacy of a warrant. In a slim 5–4 majority, the court upheld the power of the government to impose discipline for public employees' statements made as part of their official duties, arguing that because Ceballos' statements were made pursuant to his position as a public employee rather than as a private citizen, his speech had no First Amendment protection.

While this case had no direct connection to academic freedom, it is notable that Justice Souter, writing in dissent, expressed a concern that the ruling would be used as precedent in academic freedom cases. He expressed his hope that "today's majority does not mean to imperil First Amendment protection of academic freedom in public colleges and universities, whose teachers necessarily speak and write 'pursuant to official duties.'" Perhaps to emphasize that *Garcetti* should have the least implication for higher education, Justice Souter also quoted from *Sweezy v. New Hampshire* (1957), an even older case from the days when states investigated "subversive" professors, in which the court held that a governmental inquiry into the contents of a scholar's lectures at a state university "unquestionably was an invasion of [his] liberties in the areas of academic freedom and political expression—areas in which government should be extremely reticent to tread" (p. 13). Justice Stevens warned that the majority's decision in *Garcetti* was "misguided" (Hudson, 2007).

Beyond the passage Justice Souter quoted, the *Sweezy* court affirmed the need for free inquiry and expression because of the following:

> To impose any straitjacket upon the intellectual leaders in our colleges and universities would imperil the future of our nation. No field of education is so thoroughly comprehended by man that new discoveries cannot yet be made. Particularly is that true in the social sciences, where few, if any, principles are accepted as absolutes. Scholarship cannot flourish in an atmosphere of suspicion and distrust. Teachers and students must always remain free to inquire, to study, and to evaluate, to gain new maturity and understanding; otherwise, our civilization will stagnate and die. (*Sweezy v. New Hampshire,* 1957)

More recent developments with *Garcetti* (2006) have given cause for concern, confirming Justice Souter's prediction (Hudson, 2007). The case has been used as precedent in numerous cases to strike down plaintiffs in free speech cases, such as in several cases dealing with academic freedom in public schools (*Houlihan v. Sussex Technical School District Board of Education* and *Mayer vs. Monroe County Community School Corp., 06-1657).* It is reported to be having a palpable effect on public employee speech, and First Amendment expert Robert M. O'Neil, founder of the Thomas Jefferson Center for the Protection of Free Expression explains:

> I'm not surprised that Garcetti has such an effect. We specifically warned in our amicus brief in the Garcetti case that its implications were potentially far reaching. The central flaw in Garcetti is the failure to recognize that often great public interest lies in giving government employees broad latitude to speak in the areas of their expertise. In a sense Garcetti got it backwards. (see Hudson, 2007, p. 3)

CONCLUSION

This review of case law presents a patchwork of rulings that situate academic freedom in the balance, with the scales tipping by turns for and against. To summarize, the Constitution is commonly held to protect a teacher's speech outside the classroom on matters of public concern. At school, teachers' rights of expression have inconsistently been extended to individual choice of curriculum and materials. Courts have divided in their analysis of teachers' rights when speaking in class, some broadly defining topics of public concern that at least merit analysis against the school's asserted interest. Others have found no public concern in the content or overpowering government interest in regulating classroom speech.

In short, when a teacher speaks in the classroom on matters of public concern and the court applies the *Pickering* balancing analysis (teacher rights versus government interest in effective and efficient fulfillment of responsibilities to the public), the outcome is difficult to predict. One constant that runs through the above rulings is that they seek to control and suppress the inevitable messiness of controversy. In this way, they are supporting educational philosophies that are at odds with the purpose of social studies to develop young citizens as defined in the literature (Westheimer & Kahne, 2004).

It appears that courts are calling for teachers to remain neutral in the classroom. Our review of the call for citizenship education in social studies and the current unfavorable context for enacting this mandate led us to question the consistency with which the courts have argued for such neutral thought and action on the part of teachers. Rulings from cases such as *California Teachers' Association,* wherein teachers were required to "dissociate themselves from matters of political controversy" convey confusion on the part of the courts about the nature of schooling and social studies writ large. This line of thinking is (again) the product of the modernist myth of objectivity and neutrality. There is no argument in philosophical or scholarly circles about the notion of being neutral in schooling in the 21st century. Everything is value laden, including the widely accepted purpose for social studies education as defined by National Council for the Social Studies.

IMPLICATIONS AND RECOMMENDATIONS

The outlook may seem bleak for a teacher who would embrace controversy and open the classroom to vigorous engagement with issues of the day. Conservative majorities in many of the U.S. Courts of Appeals and a closely divided Supreme Court will apply a body of legal doctrine on the speech rights of public employees—including teachers—that includes the inherently unpredictable balancing test from *Pickering* and dozens of cases supporting state power to control materials and teaching. It is no surprise that legal experts advise teachers not to expect protection from the courts if they face discipline for being experimental, unorthodox, or outspoken.

The following recommendations about how to fight for academic freedom outside the court system are practical ways to work toward fulfilling the mission of the democratic classroom in the current context. The source for most of these recommendations is Michael Simpson, general counsel for the NEA, who has worked in legal advocacy with teachers in defense of academic freedom for many years and has had several articles published in *NEA Today* that are relevant to this topic. His recommendations include the following:

1. Address your state tenure laws: Each state has tenure laws designed to protect teachers from frivolous or political-related dismissal. Contact your local and/or state teachers' union to determine how your state deals with academic freedom. If your state's laws relative to academic freedom are weak, it is imperative that a collective effort is made to strengthen these laws (Simpson, 1998).
2. Look at your district's collective bargaining agreement and due process procedures: When your teachers' union negotiates the next contract or collective bargaining agreement, make sure that the negotiating team presses for explicit protections for academic freedom. Note that solid contract language gives a teacher facing discipline important authority to rely on in the grievance and arbitration stages. "Arbitrators—who interpret and enforce collective bargaining agreements— are much more sympathetic to teachers' claims of academic freedom than state and federal courts" (Simpson, 1998).
3. Carefully review your school/district policies covering additions to the curriculum, readings, outside speakers, and controversial issues in the classroom. Challenge ambiguous or biased policies and ask for new policy to be drafted by legal counsel, who can do so thoughtfully and in line with precedent if there are hidden "rules" not reduced to clear language. It can cost tens of thousands of dollars to take a case through the courts to get discipline overturned because it was based on a vague or unpublished rule. Knowing and following the rules for advance approval of unusual material or teaching by the department head, principal, or subject matter specialist can also get school officials on your side when a student or parent complains.
4. Avoid certain "red flags" that may bring negative attention to your teaching: This is essentially self-censorship. Although this is not attractive to many teachers who teach for social justice in schools, avoiding explicitly obscene or sexual content can save you a lot of trouble (Simpson, 1998).
5. Work with your local school board to incorporate academic freedom and teaching about controversial issues language in board policies. Form a coalition to support these values by enlisting members of the faculty at any local college or university in such advocacy, as well as ministers and members of progressive churches

and staff and members of statewide organizations such as People for the American Way or the ACLU.

6. Keep legal battles at the local level. While decisions at the higher courts have been sometimes counterproductive, lower level courts have a more favorable record on academic freedom (Mulhauser, 2006).

We call on teachers to assume a new role relative to academic freedom and social justice within the social studies—that of the "oppositional intellectual" (Giroux, 2001). In this reconceptualization of teaching, teachers do not reject authority outright; they interrogate and engage it to help students learn to govern themselves and assume the role of active and critical citizens. This active, informed, justice-oriented citizen stands in stark contrast to the personally responsible, traditional citizen. Without academic freedom in schools, the mission of social studies is dead. Without academic freedom and the ability to challenge the status quo and its "common sense" (Bourdieu, 2005) explanations of the world, society, from the standpoint of knowledge, is in trouble. It is our hope that this review will help to strengthen ways in which teachers can protect themselves in an environment in which academic freedom is in the balance.

AUTHORS' NOTE

Correspondence concerning this chapter should be addressed to Nancy C. Patterson, Bowling Green State University, Bowling Green, Ohio, 43402. Contact: ncpatte@bgsu.edu. This manuscript was first published in July of 2008 in *Social Studies Research and Practice* and is being reprinted here with minor revisions and permission of the editor.

REFERENCES

American Association of University Professors. (n.d.). *1940 statement of principles on academic freedom and tenure.* http://aaup.org/report/1940-statement-principles-academic-freedom-and-tenure

Boring v. Buncombe County Bd. of Education, 136 F.3d 364 (4th Cir. 1998).

Bourdieu, P. (2005). *Outline of a theory of practice.* Cambridge University Press.

California Teachers Association v. San Diego Unified School District (Cal. Ct. App. 1996).

Cockrel v. Shelby County School District, 270 F.3d 1036 (6th Cir. 2001).

Connick v. Myers, 461 U.S. 138 (1983).

Debro v. San Leandro Unified School District, WL 1329605 (N.D. Cal. 2001).

Epperson v. Arkansas, 393 U.S. 97 (1968).

Freire, P. (1998). *Teachers as cultural workers: Letters to those who dare to teach.* Westview.

Garcetti v. Ceballos, 547 U.S. 410 (2006).

Giroux, H. A. (2001). *Theory and resistance in education: Towards pedagogy for the opposition.* Bergin & Garvey.

Hardy v. Jefferson Community College, 260 F.3d 671 (6th Cir. 2001).

Houlihan v. Sussex Technical School District Board of Education, 461 F Sup. 2d 252 (D. Del. 206).

Hosford v. School Committee of Sandwich, 659 N.E. 2nd 1178 (Mass. 1996).

Hudson, D. (2007, May). Garcetti's palpable effect on public employee speech. https://www.freedomforuminstitute.org/2007/05/29/garcettis-palpable-effect-on-public-employee-speech/

James v. Board of Education, 461 F.2d 566 (2nd Cir. 1972).

Kirkland v. Northside Independent School District, 890 F.2d 794, 800-01 (5th Cir. 1989).

Mayer vs. Monroe County Cmty. Sch. Corp. 06-1993 (7th Cir. 2007).

Millikan v. Board of Directors of Everett Sch. Dist., 611 P.2d 414, 416 (Wash. 1980).

Mulhauser, F. (2006, December). What case law says about academic freedom [Panel discussion]. National Council for the Social Studies Conference, Washington, DC.

Mt. Healthy City Sch. Dist. Board of Education v. Doyle, 429 U.S. 274 (1977).

National Council for the Social Studies. (2016). Academic freedom and the social studies educator. *Social Education, 80*(3), 186.

National Council for the Social Studies (2016). A vision of powerful teaching and learning in the social studies. *Social Education, 80*(3), 180–182.

Oliver, D., & Shaver, J. P. (1966). *Teaching public issues in the high school.* Houghton Mifflin Company.

Pickering v. Board of Education, 391 U.S. 563 (1968).

Piver v. Pender County Board of Education, 835 F.2d 1076 (4th Cir. 1987).

Ross, E. W. (Ed.). (2001). *The social studies curriculum: Purposes, problems, and possibilities* (Rev. ed.). State University of New York Press.

Shaver, J. P. (1981). Citizenship, values, and morality in the social studies. In H. Mehlinger & O. L. Davis (Eds.), *The social studies: The eightieth yearbook of the national society for the study of education* (pp. 105–125). University of Chicago Press.

Shelton v. Tucker, 364 U.S. 479, 487 (1960).

Simpson, M. (1998, November). Academic freedom takes a hit [Electronic version]. *NEA Today,* 1–3.

Stanley, W. B., & Nelson, J. L. (1994). The foundations of social education in historical context. In R. Martusewicz & W. Reynolds (Eds.), *Inside/out: Contemporary critical perspectives in education* (pp. 266–284). St. Martin's.

Sweezy v. New Hampshire, 354 U. S. 234, 250 (1957).

Tinker v. Des Moines Indep. Community School District, 393 U.S. 503 (1969).

Tucker v. California Board of Education, 97 F.3d 1204, 1213 (9th Cir. 1996).

Ward v. Hickey, 996 F.2d 448, 453 (1st Cir. 1993).

Westheimer, J., & Kahne, J. (2004). What kind of citizen? The politics of educating for democracy. *American Education Research Journal, 41*(2), 1–30.

CHAPTER 2

A MORE COMPLICATED STORY

Student Free Speech in Public K–12 Education

Ryan Suskey
The Ohio Center for Law-Related Education

This chapter provides an overview of U.S. Supreme Court precedent on the issue of student speech, and forecasts areas of tension that the court will likely resolve in the future. Taking a historical and categorical approach, this chapter seeks to build an organizational framework for 80 years of case law. Special attention is given to the needs of a lay audience through the inclusion of explanatory sections on American jurisprudence.

> It can hardly be argued that either students or teachers shed their constitutional rights to freedom of speech or expression at the schoolhouse gate.
>
> —Justice Abe Fortas
> (*Tinker v. Des Moines Independent Community School Dist.*, 1969)

Among educators, these immortal words are possibly the most well-known statement by a Supreme Court justice. Indeed, these words are so famous

At the Schoolhouse Gate: Stakeholder Perceptions of First Amendment Rights and Responsibilities in U.S. Public Schools, pp. 21–45
www.infoagepub.com
Copyright © 2022 by Information Age Publishing
All rights of reproduction in any form reserved.

that they grace the cover of this volume, and even a recent book about student rights generally.[1] But how many educators truly know what follows? How many educators can so readily recall the elaboration that Justice Fortas gives in the 11-page opinion to hedge in and limit the application of this ostensibly sweeping declaration?

When taken on its own, Justice Fortas' clarion call for the free speech rights of students in schools seems to be a "full stop." Do students have free speech rights in schools? Yes. With this statement, Justice Fortas vindicated the rights of Mary Beth Tinker and her fellow students, correcting the deprivation of their right to free speech almost 4 years earlier when they were suspended for wearing a black armband in protest of the Vietnam War.

Dive deeper, however, and the reality is more nuanced. The statement makes for a great sound bite, but it is hardly an accurate guide for deciding when and how schools can limit student speech. The *Tinker* court does not give students *carte blanche* to unlimited free speech in schools, nor do the limiting decisions handed down since that decision afford schools an unlimited ability to stifle student speech. A full understanding of student free speech rights must be teased out from *Tinker* and from the multiple cases in which courts have considered the issue since. Peeling back the layers of the onion, a more complicated story emerges about the free expression rights (or lack thereof) of students in public schools.

This chapter will attempt to elucidate the most important signposts of 8 decades of Supreme Court history on the topic. In doing so, we hope to place Justice Fortas' statement in the proper context and provide the basis for a deeper understanding of the special relationship between schools and the pupils under their charge. We will begin with a preliminary discussion of how Supreme Court jurisprudence functions, focusing especially on how the Supreme Court reaches its decisions. With a better understanding of the function of the judicial branch, we will then work categorically through the different areas of free speech that the court has, to this point, resolved. To conclude, we will take a brief look at how free speech rights are likely (or need) to evolve in the coming years, as courts grapple with new technology and new forums for communication.

PRECEDENT AND STARE DECISIS

The majority of this article will deal with the U.S. Supreme Court and its decisions. To a lay audience, this may seem like a counterintuitive mission for an issue as personal and mundane as what students can and cannot say in schools. Surely such a local issue should be dealt with by local government. Why not look to school policies or state legislatures? The answer is, unsurprisingly, more complicated.

When it comes to a discussion of "rights," we typically look to the Bill of Rights in the U.S. Constitution. The reason the Constitution is relevant goes right to the heart of why the Founding Fathers included the Bill of Rights to begin with. The Constitution did not *create* a set of rights that the people could have, rather, it limited the power of the government to intrude on rights that already existed, and still do. Among these rights is the right to free speech, as found in the First Amendment. The Constitution prevents the government from abridging the freedoms that *all* persons in the United States enjoy.

In the First Amendment, we see unequivocally that "*Congress* shall make no law ... abridging the freedom of speech" (U.S. Const. amend. I, emphasis added). Taking these words at face value, it would appear that, as long as the United States Congress does not pass a law that would limit what an individual can and cannot say, there is no Constitutional violation. How, then, do we get from this reading of the text to understanding what happened to Mary Beth Tinker and her classmates when they were suspended for wearing black armbands? How does a school board policy fall under the prohibition of laws passed by Congress?

Although initially drafted as a limitation on Congress, the right to free speech was gradually seen by courts as so fundamental that it deserved protection from intrusion by the state governments as well. In the 1925 case *Gitlow v. New York,* the U.S. Supreme Court held that the due process clause of the Fourteenth Amendment created an obligation on the States to respect the fundamental right to free speech. If an individual has a right to free speech, the Fourteenth Amendment has come to be seen as ensuring that the right to free speech should persist regardless of the state in which the individual is resident, or even down to the school district the individual might attend.

This process of enforcing specific rights guaranteed by the Bill of Rights against the states is known as *selective incorporation*. The reason it is "selective" is that the Supreme Court has found only some of the rights in the First through Eighth Amendments to be so fundamental that they should be incorporated (enforced against state governments), but have found others to be *less* fundamental, and therefore not incorporated.[2]

The next question that comes from this discussion is why courts, and not U.S. Congress, have the power to determine what laws are (or are not) applicable to the states. This question provides an opportunity to dust off and revisit the textbooks from Civics 101, prompting a review of the "jobs" of each of the three branches, specifically, the job of the judicial branch. The simple answer that all of us should know from our school days is that the judiciary is tasked with "interpreting the law."[3] What this actually means, however, is less well known. Chief Justice John Marshall codified the duty of the judiciary in 1803 in the majority opinion in *Marbury v. Madison*: "It is emphatically the province and duty of the Judicial Department to say what the law is" (*Marbury v. Madison*, 1803). This does not mean that the judiciary infringes on the legislative power to create law, rather that they are tasked with taking the words of the law and settling their meaning.

To fulfill their obligation of interpreting the law, judges routinely employ a variety of logical tools (called "canons") to determine what the law means in a particular situation.[4] Each of these canons has a rich tradition within the law, which helps to add predictability and stability to the outcomes of legal disputes. For example, one such canon is known as in pari materia (on the same subject), which instructs that a judge encountering an ambiguous term in a statute should look to other statutes on the same subject to decide the meaning of the word in the statute in question. The canons have evolved over time based on logical assumptions about how the law works. In the instance of in pari materia, the canon rests on the assumption that legislatures are not intentionally contradictory or inconsistent.

Canons of construction, however, are not the only limitation on the practice of interpreting the law. In instances where the law is unclear, the justices cannot simply make up an answer based on whatever canon of construction they might favor. They must follow the well-worn path of precedent. Judges are trained to search prior cases to discover analogous situations, drawing out similarities and differences from situations in the present case to situations they have dealt with in the past.

The job of judges (and by extension lawyers) can in some ways be boiled down to using their creativity and imagination to decide cases based on a limited set of prior examples. This practice of applying precedent to decide novel questions is known as "stare decisis." The Latin phrase means to "stand by what is decided." For the courts, this means that they should draw upon past decisions (precedent) to decide similar situations similarly (i.e., do not make decisions without regard to what has been decided in the past). The Supreme Court notes that "stare decisis promotes the evenhanded, predictable, and consistent development of legal principles, fosters reliance on judicial decisions, and contributes to the actual and perceived integrity of the judicial process" (*Payne v. Tennessee,* 1991).

The "predictability" highlighted in *Payne* means that lower courts (trial courts, intermediate appellate courts, etc.) will rely on past rulings to find the situation that most closely matches the case in front of them; then, apply the rules from that case to their present situation. This practice ensures that situations can be resolved under the law without the need of the highest court in the land weighing in on every unique issue. Indeed, very few cases ever make it all the way to the Supreme Court. Each term the justices of the Supreme Court must wade through over 7,000 petitions for review, of which approximately 70 are accepted. For the other 99% of reviewed cases, litigants must live with the outcome handed to them by the lower courts.

Among the factors that the Justices weigh when deciding whether or not to accept a case is whether the case's question has already been suitably resolved in prior cases, or not (i.e., whether the case presents a novel question of law). Making this determination requires the justices (or more accurately their law clerks) to search case precedent for clear analogies from past rulings to the present situation. This is how we make the leap from armbands (*Tinker*, 1969) to a T-shirt whose political message was offensive to the president (*Marineau*, 2007), certiorari denied). In both cases, the students were sanctioned by the school for attire that was intended to convey some form of symbolic speech (antiwar in *Tinker*, and critique of drug policy in *Guiles*). The Second Circuit, which heard the *Guiles* case before its final appeal to the Supreme Court, found enough guidance in the *Tinker* case to conclude that the T-shirt should not be treated any differently than the student armbands, and that the school could not sanction the student for a nondisruptive act of symbolic speech.

When the school district petitioned the Supreme Court for review, their petition was denied. Although an explanation of why a petition was denied is not given, we can reasonably infer the court denied certiorari, at least in part, because their precedent provided enough guidance to lower courts (and/or because no lower courts had yet disagreed on the way to interpret their prior rulings to that end).

Although this lengthy discussion of legal principles may seem superfluous, it is a necessary antecedent to the murky waters in which this chapter must wade. Student free speech rights are not always clear. The judiciary has taken a somewhat circuitous path to the present moment, so understanding how they make decisions about student free speech rights is helpful.

Once the reader understands the role that stare decisis plays in all legal issues before the court, the question next occurs as to what the Supreme Court has already decided in the area of student free expression. How has the Supreme Court ruled on the issue of student speech in the past, and what does this mean about student free speech in the future?

SUPREME COURT PRECEDENT ON STUDENT FREE SPEECH

Having begun our exploration of the concept of free speech with its general principles, as outlined in the First Amendment, our consideration of *student* free speech must be more narrowly tailored. Students, owing to their immaturity and special status as being "under the care" of the school,[5] are in many contexts seen to have different rights than adults. As such, a review of free speech case law generally will not *necessarily* be instructive. Each time a case involves students, a judge must determine whether there is a reason to treat juveniles differently from adults, and if so, it is necessary to tease apart the differences to determine what rule(s) should apply. Unsurprisingly, limitations that would otherwise be unconstitutional for nonstudent adults are often permitted. The terminology of "nonstudent adult" may seem overly pedantic, however, the reality is that even students aged eighteen fall into a special category. Because students are under the care of teachers, and schools are seen by the law as being a special environment outside normal public settings, the law grants more leeway in the extent to which state actors (i.e., school employees) can regulate the conduct of students. This being the case, most of the precedent that follows will deal directly with students.

Before considering this decades long process, it is important to note at the outset the confines and limits of our exploration. First and foremost, what follows is an exploration of free speech in *public* schools. Private schools, as nonstate actors, are not bound by the same restrictions or precedent, and therefore will not be a part of this discussion. Also inherent in the preceding is this chapter's focus on the *free speech* rights of students. This chapter will not deal with the First Amendment Establishment and Free Exercise clauses.

It is also important to note that the terminology used by the Supreme Court in outlining student rights has not always been "clean." There are times when the court refers to a collective right to free expression (including speech, press, assembly, and petition) and other times when they specifically mention speech. This chapter will predominantly refer to the right to "free speech." In some instances, direct citations from Supreme Court opinions will reference a right to "free expression," in which a right to free speech is included. In such instances, care will be given to clarify the language.

In considering the progression of the court's case law on student free speech, it is helpful to group the holdings into categories. Although by no means an exact science (due to the frequent overlap and mixing of tests in novel scenarios), the cases can broadly be understood to fall into the following categories: compelled speech, political/opinion speech, school sponsored speech, offensive/crude speech, speech promoting illegal drug use, and off-campus speech.

COMPELLED SPEECH: *GOBITIS* AND *BARNETTE*

Although possibly the most well-known of cases, *Tinker v. Des Moines Independent Community School District* (1969) was not the *first* indicator that the law was prepared to recognize the free speech rights of students. The earliest articulation of student free speech rights came in 1940 at a slightly different angle than might be expected when talking about free speech. Rather than focusing on students' right *to* speak, the Supreme Court was tasked with deciding whether students had a right *not* to "speak." In a rare situation for the court, the answer was first "no" followed only 3 years later by "yes."

In a time when Americans were occupied with thoughts of World War, and fears that the United States would soon join its allies in the conflict, the Supreme Court was tasked with considering whether a public school could expel students who refused to pledge allegiance to the flag. William and Lillian Gobitas, Jehovah's Witnesses living in a predominantly Catholic Pennsylvania town, refused to comply with a school board policy mandating that all students salute and pledge to the flag each morning. For their failure to comply, the siblings were expelled from their public school and forced to attend a private institution. In the 1940 Supreme Court Case, *Minersville School District v. Gobitis*,[6] an 8–1 majority held that "national unity is the basis of national security," and that the quest for unity could even outweigh individual liberty. Justice Frankfurter went even further, declaring that policies like those of Minersville School District were soundly within the police powers of the states, and that courts should therefore practice restraint in questioning their validity.

Only 3 years later, after the United States entered World War II, a 6–3 court voted to directly overrule their prior decision, finding that schools *cannot* compel students to salute the flag. In the 1943 case *West Virginia State Board of Education v. Barnette*,[7] the "mistake," made by Justice Frankfurter such a short time earlier was overturned by Justice Robert Jackson, who wrote,

> If there is any fixed star in our constitutional constellation, it is that no official, high or petty, can prescribe what shall be orthodox in politics, nationalism, religion, or other matters of opinion, or force citizens to confess by word or act their faith therein. If there are any circumstances which permit an exception, they do not now occur to us. (*West Virginia State Board of Education v. Barnette,* 1943)

Although somewhat entangled with religion, owing to the fact that the plaintiffs in the case were Jehovah's Witnesses objecting to the pledge on religious grounds, the court ultimately ruled on a broader issue that dealt with freedom of speech, rather than free exercise of religion. In ruling for the students, the court was not vindicating the religious views held by the students (although that was certainly a secondary outcome), they were vindicating the right of the students to make a "statement" through their choice to be silent. In so doing, we can reasonably infer that a similar outcome would result if the choice not to participate in the pledge was motivated by any number of justifications, both religious and secular.

Releasing their opinion on *Barnette* on Flag Day, June 14, 1943, the Supreme Court sent a signal about the fundamentality of the freedoms in the Bill of Rights and opened the door to future challenges when an individual student's rights were in conflict with the views of the state.

POLITICAL/OPINION SPEECH: *BURNSIDE, BLACKWELL, TINKER,* AND *PICO*

More than 20 years passed before the Supreme Court again took up the issue of free speech so directly. Having previously considered whether students had a right *not* to speak, the time had come when the courts would have to grapple with whether a student had an affirmative right *to* speak. Although *Tinker* (1969) would be the most famous case to come out of this period, it was certainly not the only case of its era to deal with the question of student free speech.

In almost every scenario, cases that come before the Supreme Court of the United States have already been heard by multiple lower courts. When it is a federal case being heard, the lower court is typically one of the 13 circuit courts of appeal. For instance, *Tinker* was appealed from a ruling by the U.S. Court of Appeals for the Eighth Circuit.

At the time that the *Tinker* case was working its way through the court system, two other cases were being decided in the U.S. Court of Appeals for the Fifth Circuit, both out of Mississippi. On July 21, 1966, the Fifth Circuit issued two separate rulings, one upholding student speech, and one upholding the ability of schools to limit student speech. The decision in both of these cases would ultimately influence the Supreme Court in the *Tinker* case.

In both cases, the Fifth Circuit was facing a question of whether a school could ban the wearing of "freedom buttons" produced by the Student Nonviolent Coordinating Committee (SNCC). In two different high schools in Mississippi, both all-Black public schools, students wore and distributed the buttons. The manner in which the students distributed the buttons, however, could not have been more different.

The first case, *Burnside v. Byars,* dealt with students at Booker T. Washington High School in Philadelphia, Mississippi who began wearing "Freedom Buttons" in September of 1964.[8] The principal, believing the buttons "didn't have any bearing on their education" and could lead to disruptions and delays in the school day, banned the wearing of the buttons. Four days after the pronouncement, several students wore the buttons and were suspended. They challenged their suspensions in court, ultimately appealing to the Fifth Circuit.

When the circuit court issued their opinion in *Burnside,* it overturned the lower court ruling in favor of the school district, thereby invalidating the principal's ban on the buttons. The court based their decision on the fact that no evidence existed that the buttons caused a disruption or hampered the school in any way. The court was quick to mention, however, that

> if the decorum had been so disturbed by the presence of the 'freedom buttons,' the principal would have been acting within his authority and the regulation forbidding the presence of buttons on school grounds would have been reasonable. (*Burnside*, 1966, p. 748)

This disturbed decorum was not merely a hypothetical scenario, it was exactly the situation the court was confronting in another case decided that same day. In *Blackwell v. Issaquena County Board of Education* (1966), the students were not merely wearing the buttons, but engaged in a number of activities that made learning at the school nigh impossible, including interrupting classes to enlist supporters, throwing the buttons through open windows into the school, and trying to forcibly pin buttons onto students who did not wish to be a part of the protest (*Blackwell*, p. 749). Given the tumultuous environment caused by the students carrying the buttons, the Fifth Circuit found that the principal acted within their authority to prohibit the buttons and discipline the students involved in the *Blackwell* case (*Blackwell,* p. 753).

In differentiating the two cases, the court made reference to *Burnside* "where no disruption of classes or school routine appeared in the evidence" (*Blackwell,* p. 753). The Blackwell case presented a decidedly different environment. By juxtaposing the two, the Fifth Circuit employed what came to be known as an "actual disruption" test for determining whether the school officials could reasonably regulate the speech of students (Driver, 2018).

It was within this context that the U.S. Supreme Court would consider the case of *Tinker v. Des Moines Independent Community School District.* The case had its roots in a decision by a small group of students in Des Moines, Iowa, who decided in December 1965 to wear black armbands to school to spark conversations about their views against the Vietnam War. Among them was 13-year-old Mary Beth Tinker, and her brother John Tinker (age 15). Hearing of the planned protest, the Des Moines Independent Community Schools administrators created a policy that students wearing the armbands would be suspended. In opposition to the policy, several students went ahead with the protest, and were subsequently suspended. The students filed suit, setting in motion a struggle that would take over 3 years to resolve.

Of particular note for teachers working with students, it is helpful to consider a *somewhat* counterintuitive piece of analysis performed by the court. The actions taken by the students in *Tinker*, wearing armbands, is very often spoken of as an act of "protest" against American involvement in the conflict in Vietnam. Additionally, because their expression was silent, the students were not "speaking" in the traditional sense. Students may, understandably, be confused about why this is an issue of student *speech*, rather than petition or assembly. The answer, according to the court, is that the students were engaging in a form of "symbolic speech" (*Tinker*, p. 505). This is the same form of "speech" in which the students in both *Burnside* and *Blackwell* were engaging, namely, the wearing of symbols that are representative of political views. In the *Tinker* case, the armbands were a form of "pure speech," meant to convey the political views of the students, even absent any "spoken" words.

After suffering defeat in two lower courts, the plaintiff students put their fate in the hands of the nine members of the U.S. Supreme Court. In February 1969, a 7–2 court vindicated the rights of the students to express their views in school. Although it declined to expressly adopt the stricter *actual disruption* standard advocated in *Burnside* and *Blackwell*, the court did reference both Fifth Circuit cases in the majority opinion. Justice Fortas, author of the majority opinion, borrowed from the case precedent to articulate a series of tests—ultimately concluding in all instances that the school was unjustified in limiting the students' protest.

Justice Fortas considered whether the students participating in the protests "intrude[d] upon the work of the schools or the rights of other students" (*Tinker*, p. 508). The record established that the protest was a "silent, passive expression of opinion, unaccompanied by any disorder or disturbance" by the student participants.[9] Given this lack of evidence of disruption, the *Tinker* case seems to be more in line with *Burnside* than with *Blackwell*, with a predictable outcome.

However, Justice Fortas went further to explore other potential avenues through which the regulation of speech would have been reasonable. Recognizing that no actual disruption occurred, the court contemplated whether it would have been permissible for a school to limit student expression (including speech) out of the fear that disruption *could* occur. The court was quick to point out a flaw in the fear defense, owing to the ever-present danger that dissident speech often creates discomfort.

The Supreme Court recognized that differences of opinion are almost always uncomfortable, creating tension and unpleasantness. A mere desire to avoid this, however, is antithetical to the purpose of schools. Justice Fortas borrowed from his colleague Justice Brennan's opinion in

Keyishian v. Board of Regents (1967) to label the classroom the "marketplace of ideas" with the strength of our future nation being aided by students' "wide exposure" to a "robust exchange of ideas" (*Tinker*, p. 512). A desire to shut down this marketplace simply because the mainstream may find the views unpleasant would hamper national strength.

In order to curtail free expression (including but not limited to free speech) on the basis of fear of disruption, a school administrator would need to articulate reasonable grounds that "forecast substantial disruption or material interference with school activities" (*Tinker*, p. 514). This language has become known as the "substantial disruption" test and has been the most influential legacy of the *Tinker* case on lower courts. Future court rulings would take the *substantial disruption* test and apply it to many unique situations, creating a reliable metric for school districts in setting new policies. The test has also come to serve as a guidepost for school administrators, who were confronting the reality of a student population that was increasingly active and engaged in the political and social conversations of the day.

The victory for student speech rights has been reasonably celebrated in the 50 years since the court handed down its decision in *Tinker*; but it must be noted that the same court has subsequently hedged in and chipped away at the expansive view of student speech ever since. The intervening years have brought about multiple "defeats" for students, or at the very least, student free speech rights can be seen to pale in comparison to the major victory that was *Tinker*. Some commentators have remarked that *Tinker* was the "high water mark" of student free speech, with the flood never again reaching such great heights (Chemerinsky, 2004).

The next significant case to draw upon the lineage of *Tinker* came about in 1982, when the court was asked to consider whether a school board could vote to remove books from library shelves when it deemed the content to be objectionable. The case stemmed from an incident in Levittown, New York, where in 1975 members of the school board removed nine books from the shelves of the local schools that they considered to be "anti-American, anti-Christian, anti-Sem[i]tic, and just plain filthy" (Driver, 2018, p. 112). After the removal, several students filed suit, alleging that the removal of the books was a violation of their right to free speech.

In what can hardly be considered a win (although not explicitly a loss) a divided Supreme Court authored six different opinions as to how to handle the issue in *Board of Education, Island Trees Union Free School District No. 26 v. Pico by Pico*. A plurality of three concluded that the *removal* of books was the determinative factor, which led them to conclude that the school board's banning of the books violated the students' right to free speech.

The court was clear that its opinion said nothing about *acquisition* of books by a library. In ordering that preexisting books be removed, merely because they disapproved of the content, the school board was operating similarly to the administrators in *Tinker* who sought to disallow nondisruptive speech with which they disagreed.

SCHOOL SPONSORED/CURRICULAR SPEECH: *KUHLMEIER*

Not long after the decision in *Pico*, the circumstances arose for the next pivotal case, which forced the court to confront the issue of student speech in the context of school sponsored activities or classes. In May of 1983 at Hazelwood East High School in St. Louis, Missouri, students in the *Journalism II* class were finishing up the final issue of their class project, a student newspaper called *Spectrum*. As was customary before the publication, the journalism teacher submitted the paper to the principal for review. During this review, the principal determined that two articles—one about how students are impacted by parental divorce and a second about teen pregnancy—were deemed inappropriate.

Fearing that there was not enough time for the articles to be revised and published before the end of the year, the decision was made to eliminate the two pages that contained the offending articles. The consequence of this decision was that several other articles appearing on those same two pages were also scrapped, despite no objections being raised to their content. Cathy Kuhlmeier, student layout editor of the *Spectrum*, along with two fellow students, filed a lawsuit against the school contending that the censorship of the articles was a violation of the student journalists' right to free speech.

In 1988 the Supreme Court ruled in *Hazelwood School District v. Kuhlmeier* that the school did not violate the students' free speech rights by removing the articles. Writing for a 5–3 majority, Justice Byron White distinguished the case from *Tinker* in finding that the circumstances of the speech were different from the independent marketplace in which *Tinker* and *Pico* were operating.

In distinguishing *Kuhlmeier* from *Tinker*, the court framed the issue in *Tinker* as being "whether the First Amendment requires a school to tolerate particular student speech." In *Kuhlmeier*, they characterized the legal question as "whether the First Amendment requires a school affirmatively to promote a particular student speech" (*Kuhlmeier*, p. 270–1). In separating the two cases, the court opened a new category of legal analysis, in which the *substantial disruption* test would not be controlling.

Because the newspaper was part of a class project, the court held that a different consideration applied to "school-sponsored publications, theatrical productions, and other expressive activities that students, parents, and members of the public might reasonably perceive to bear the imprimatur of the school" (*Kuhlmeier*, p. 271). They further concluded that "Educators are entitled to exercise greater control" in order to "set high standards for the student speech that is disseminated under its auspices ... and may refuse to disseminate student speech that does not meet those standards" (*Kuhlmeier*, p. 272).

By creating the journalism course, the school was effectively creating a different kind of forum, separate and apart from the pseudo-public forum into which prior litigants (e.g., *Tinker*) were engaged. As the creator of this forum, the school had authority to moderate and regulate the forum in order to advance "legitimate pedagogical concerns" (*Kuhlmeier*, pp. 272–273). The majority, therefore, concluded that the principal did not violate the free speech rights of the students in removing the two pages from the newspaper. In separating from *Tinker*, the court carved out a type of student speech ("school sponsored speech") that did not require analysis as to the disruption (real or potential) that occurred as a result of the speech.

The blow to student rights did not go unnoticed, as three justices stood in a powerful dissent against the majority. Justice William Brennan, whose words had been marshaled two decades earlier to uphold the "marketplace of ideas," called the principal's actions "brutal censorship" which were "particularly insidious [coming] from one to whom the public entrusts the task of inculcating... cherished democratic liberties that our Constitution guarantees" (*Kuhlmeier*, p. 290). The three dissenters considered the ruling a loss for constitutional liberties, and a failure of the court's obligations.

OFFENSIVE OR CRUDE SPEECH: *FRASER*

Although the aforementioned cases were not without controversy, the speech made by students in each of the prior instances was difficult to reasonably label as crude or outwardly offensive. The political and opinion-based speech of *Tinker* was distinguished by the Supreme Court from other kinds of speech that could shock and offend. Just such a case would come before the court in 1986 in the form of *Bethel School District v. Fraser* (1986).

In 1983, Matthew Fraser stood in his high school auditorium to throw his support behind a fellow student's bid for student government president. The roughly 1-minute speech supporting his favored candidate would spark a 3-year long controversy. Attentive readers will wonder why, if this particular speech was clearly political in nature, this case does not belong in the previous section. In this instance, it was not the political viewpoint advocated by the student that was problematic, it was his word choice in expressing said political view. Matthew's nominating speech was laced with sexual innuendo, which was not lost upon most of the audience.

In Justice Brennan's concurring opinion, we get to read some of the more choice lines from the speech, including passages like "I know a man who is firm—he's firm in his pants, he's firm in his shirt, his character is firm—but most ... of all, his belief in you, the students of Bethel, is firm" (*Fraser*, p. 687). The reactions of students in the audience were reported to have ranged from elated—hooting, yelling, and gesturing to simulate the acts Fraser referred to in his speech—to embarrassed and bewildered (*Fraser*, p. 678).

The uproar caused by the speech led the principal to issue a 3-day suspension for Fraser, finding that he had violated a school policy that could have been culled directly from the majority opinion in *Tinker* which read: "Conduct which materially and substantially interferes with the educational process is prohibited, including the use of obscene, profane language or gestures" (*Fraser*, p. 678). Fraser later filed suit with his parents against the school district for having violated his First Amendment right to free speech.

A five-justice majority (with two additional justices concurring in the judgment for different reasons) found that the court's ruling in *Tinker* does not prohibit a school from disciplining students for lewd or offensive speech, even if that same speech would be permissible by an adult (*Fraser*, p. 682). Chief Justice Burger, writing for the majority, clearly distinguished *Fraser* from *Tinker*, in that the words of the speech did not contain any political viewpoint (unlike the armbands protesting the war or the SNCC buttons protesting segregation and impediments to suffrage). Justice Burger aptly summarized the court's position stating,

> The First Amendment does not prevent the school officials from determining that to permit a vulgar and lewd speech such as respondent's would undermine the school's basic educational mission. A high school assembly or classroom is no place for a sexually explicit monologue directed towards an unsuspecting audience of teenage students. (*Fraser*, p. 685)

Although the justices took care to distinguish the speech in *Fraser* from that in *Tinker*, arguably their holding could have been decided in keeping with the rule established in that case without requiring any new law to be created.[10] Allowing students to openly engage in lewd or obscene speech could reasonably "forecast substantial disruption or material interference with school activities" (*Tinker*, p. 514), which, under *Tinker*, would allow the administrator to forbid the speech. And, indeed, disruption did occur.

The students in the auditorium for the speeches were visibly rowdier during and after the speech than they had been previously.

Justice Burger, however, did not extend the rule established in *Tinker*, choosing instead to carve out a new exception for speech of a sexual or offensive nature. The rationale for this holding ignores the discomfort that often results from a disputatious society (mentioned in *Tinker*), focusing instead on the need for schools to "teach by example the shared values of a civilized social order" (*Bethel School Dist. v. Fraser*, 1986). In Burger's opinion, speech containing sexual innuendo robbed the listeners of a moral example of polite interactions that would be expected of the students when they enter adult society, although, he simultaneously noted that adults are permitted to speak this way.

Viewed in light of *Tinker*, the *Fraser* decision represents a limiting or hedging in of student speech rights, draining the pool a bit from the "high water mark" of student free speech. By carving out the exception for obscene speech, some commentators saw the court as handing back to educators the ability to discipline students and maintain order. Indeed, 3 years prior to the decision in *Fraser*, President Reagan bemoaned the erosion of order in public society and the "need to restore good old-fashioned discipline" (Reagan, 1983). The decision in *Fraser* fulfills this promise and clarified for administrators that they did not need to remit all authority over pupils, allowing that sometimes student speech in and of itself is the disruption (irrespective of the responses it could or does provoke in the student audience).

PROMOTING DRUG USE: *FREDERICK*

One of the more recent examples of the limiting principle that the court has employed in tackling student free speech rights since *Tinker* occurred in the 2007 case *Morse v. Frederick*. Many who are actually familiar with this case may not *initially* recognize the caption. The case is more popularly referred to by the slogan emblazoned upon the banner that sparked the controversy "BONG HiTS 4 JESUS."

In January of 2002, the students of Juneau-Douglas High School in Juneau, Alaska, were excused from their morning classes to join a crowd observing the Olympic torch parade that would pass through town and in front of their school. Joseph Frederick, an 18-year-old senior had not been in class that morning, but joined the crowd outside, across the street from the school, to participate in the parade. In anticipation of the torch's arrival, he unfurled a banner bearing the phrase "BONG HiTS 4 JESUS." The principal, Deborah Morse, immediately crossed the street and ordered that he take the banner down. Frederick and Morse argued, with

Frederick alleging that he had a First Amendment right to fly the banner. Morse disagreed, confiscated the banner, and suspended Frederick for 10 days. Frederick then brought suit, arguing both that he had a First Amendment right to free speech, and that the speech was off campus and thus outside the school's regulation.

When the case came before the Supreme Court, the majority quickly dispatched the claim that the speech was off campus. Despite being across the street from the school, despite the parade itself not being school sponsored, and despite the fact that Frederick was technically absent from school up to this point, the majority held that the parade was equivalent to a class trip or an assembly (*Morse v. Frederick*, 2007, pg. 400). Chief Justice Roberts, writing for the majority, based this decision on the fact that the parade was during normal school hours, that students had permission to attend, that school administrators were also in attendance, and that the school band was performing in the parade.

Having found that the speech was "on campus" for the purposes of their analysis, they proceeded to employ a pattern not unlike that used in *Fraser*. To reach this line of reasoning, Roberts first needed to conclude that not even Frederick (the student) contended that the banner's message was political.[11] By labeling the speech as nonpolitical, the court could move the speech outside of the *Tinker* analysis. Indeed, the court even took steps to point out that "the rule of *Tinker* is not the only basis for restricting student speech" (*Frederick*, pg. 406).

Following neatly in the footsteps of *Fraser* (recalling the special status of schools as moral educators) Chief Justice Roberts outlined that the court would need to weigh this case "in light of the special characteristics of the school environment" (*Frederick*, p. 405 citing from *Tinker*). The majority goes on to cite other areas in which schools are a special environment where student rights can be more constrained, specifically for the Fourth Amendment, and Fourteenth Amendments. One of the special characteristics identified by Justice Roberts was the need to deter drug use by school age children.

With this narrow approach, the court unsurprisingly wound up with an exceedingly narrow holding. Taking great pains to differentiate schools from the general public (an analysis which would not have been possible if they had concluded Frederick was off-campus) they carved out a slim exception to "allow schools to restrict student expression that they reasonably regard as promoting illegal drug use" (*Frederick*, p. 408). In the court's analysis, Frederick's banner clearly fell within this exception, and was therefore permissibly censored by the school administrator. This same logic could be relied upon by future administrators to stop students from speaking (or wearing T-shirts, making signs, etc.) that are reasonably viewed to be in favor of illegal drug use.

Counsel for the school district advocated for simply finding the speech to be within the realm of *Fraser*'s prohibition on "offensive" speech. Chief Justice Roberts, however, could not square this expansion of offensive speech to categorically include speech like the banner (*Frederick*, p. 409). Several justices, and the lower court judges who considered the case, admitted being confused by the language of the banner (*Frederick*, p. 402). The court concluded that the banner was *at least* confusing gibberish, and at *most* promoting or celebrating drug use. In either case, the speech was not so repugnant as to match the sexual innuendo of *Fraser*. The speech of *Frederick*, therefore, represented a new and unique category of pro-drug speech that was distinct, but likewise within school authority to prohibit.

By taking such pains to ignore the political speech, the court provides no guidance for a situation in which a student uses a pro-drug message to make political statements about drug laws or the potential need for drug sentencing reform. In fact, this was the exact situation described in another case we encountered earlier in this chapter, *Guiles v. Marineau*, in which a student wore a T-shirt depicting then President George W. Bush as being a drug and alcohol addicted "chicken-hawk" whose antidrug policies are hypocritical. Lower courts ruled in favor of the student, relying on *Tinker*, *Fraser*, and *Kuhlmeier* to determine that the school district erred in regulating the student's nondisruptive political speech.

The U.S. Supreme Court denied the school district's certiorari petition only 4 days after issuing their decision in *Frederick*. Again, although no rationale is provided, we must reasonably infer that they felt the question was sufficiently resolved by prior precedent, and that the decision in the lower court was not in conflict with said precedent.

In holding so narrowly in *Morse*, the court missed an opportunity to make a broader statement about the confines of on-campus versus off-campus speech. Indeed, some critics have called *Frederick* a "missed opportunity" because of the extreme narrowness of the opinion and the lack of broader applicability in the school speech context (Hofheimer, 2013). Although school administrators now have clear guidance on whether they can suspend a student for speech that clearly promotes drug use, they are left in the dark about what to do when the student's expression is "pro-drug" only in so far as it is a political viewpoint on drug-law reform.

THE FUTURE OF STUDENT EXPRESSION: ONLINE OFF-CAMPUS SPEECH

Looking to the future of how jurisprudence on student free speech will continue to evolve, it is impossible to reliably predict exactly how the wind will turn. Remembering the guidance of stare decisis, however, some insights can reasonably be gleaned. It is the opinion of the author, that future cases the court will decide will likely be needed around the evolving and expanding territory of "on campus" as defined by new technology.

The explosion of social media and accessible forums for public expression have brought into play entirely new forms of speech that the Supreme Court has not yet addressed. The explosion of social media and accessible forums for public expression have brought into play entirely new forms of speech that the Supreme Court is only beginning to address. How should courts (and ultimately school administrators) handle situations in which students use digital platforms (during or after school hours) to express views that have immediate bearing on the discipline and order of the school day?

Chief Justice Roberts alluded to the possibility of blurry lines of on-campus versus off-campus speech in *Frederick*, admitting "some uncertainty at the outer boundaries as to when courts should apply school speech precedents." The Chief Justice made reference to a Fifth Circuit case in which a student was suspended for having drawn a sketch at home of a violent siege on his high school, which was brought to school accidentally by his younger brother 2 years later. Recognizing that no clear guidance existed on the subject, the Fifth Circuit granted qualified immunity to the principal, meaning they would not need to answer the ultimate question of whether or not the speech could be regulated like school speech (*Porter v. Ascension Parish School Board*, 2004).

Imagine now that the expression is occurring off campus, after school hours, outside the view of teachers, but online in social media platforms like Twitter, Facebook, and TikTok. As some commentators point out, the use of these platforms is not altogether different from the way in which young people have always expressed themselves (Papandrea, 2008). Teenagers have always kept journals, passed notes, and complained about their teachers in mall food courts across America. What is new about the social media age, however, is that what would once have been a shared private conversation between two friends has become a live-streamed vlog on Instagram that is archived, reblogged, and memed into many days worth of content.

How should school administrators handle the social media behavior of their pupils when that online presence creates disruption in the school day? Does the answer change when the expressed views online are a threat to students, teachers, or administrators? Shortly before this book went to press, the Supreme Court finally dipped their toes into these waters with *Mahanoy Area School District v. B.L., 594 U.S.* (2021). This was not, however, their first opportunity to have given clarity on this issue. In 2016, the Supreme Court declined to hear the appeal of an aspiring teenage rapper who recorded a hip-hop song about alleged sexual harassment by school administrators at the school. The rapper's contention was that administrators had mishandled claims of sexual harassment by the coaches at the school. The song was recorded off-campus, after hours, and posted to their Facebook page. The song had explicit lyrics and included boasting about what the student would do to the administrators for their misdeeds.

The Fifth Circuit ruled that the school administrators acted appropriately in suspending the student (*Bell v. Itawamba County School Board*, 2015). By denying the students petition for certiorari, the court left open the question, leaving school administrators to "struggle to appropriately balance the school's interest in safety, order, and discipline against the First Amendment rights of students" (Black, 2015, p. 532).

One of the common claims of the factors weighed by the court in considering whether to take a case is whether there is a "circuit-split" that must be resolved. This term is used to describe a situation in which the lower courts, the federal circuit courts, have ruled differently on an issue. Given the way that jurisdictions work in the United States, a circuit split would mean that the rights of individuals living in one circuit (e.g., the Mississippi student rapper who lives in the Fifth Circuit's territory) would be different from a student living in a different circuit (e.g., the Sixth Circuit which covers Kentucky, Michigan, Ohio, and Tennessee). Traditionally, the Supreme Court has tried to avoid this outcome, to ensure the rule of law and predictability of outcome is uniform (refer back to our discussion in the first section as to why the First Amendment applies to states; due process frowns upon such disparate outcomes). As such, one strong factor encouraging the court to take a case is whether the lower courts have been consistent in their holdings on the issue.

Given this desire to avoid circuit splits, the Supreme Court had every reason to take the rapper's appeal. In the past, the various circuit courts have ruled differently on this issue of off-campus speech. Although not containing the same threats, a case hinging on the same question of whether or not off-campus internet speech could be considered "school speech" for disciplinary issues was answered in the negative by the Third Circuit in *J.S. v. Blue Mountain*, a case in which a student created a satirical MySpace page for her principal (under an alias) (*J.S.*, 2011 at 921). The page included the principal's photograph and was shared with the student's friends, who also attended the school. Although the page did not include the alleged threats that were present in *Bell*, the vulgar claims on the page suggested the principal was a pedophile.

Both courts acknowledge that there is a blurring of lines between on-campus and off-campus activity with the advent of the internet and new forms of communication. Two different cases, arguably similar questions, different results. The distinguishing factor in the two cases could largely be argued to be the threats that existed in one case and not in the other. In fact, in the *Bell* case, the uptick in incidents of violence was cited as one reason to take the speech more seriously than they otherwise might have. The same argument, however, could reasonably be made about allegations of sexual abuse by a school administrator, a serious allegation to make at any time.

The situation becomes even murkier as more and more forms of school communication move into the online space. Classrooms are embracing the potentials of technology to allow communication with and among students and thus, also to expand student collaboration. Many schools are moving to policies that issue each student a device (one to one) or encourage them to bring their own device to school for student use in the classroom. In these spaces, the division between on and off campus, during and after school hours, becomes even more nebulous.

Undoubtedly students have brought a unique set of challenges with them into the classroom since time immemorial. It would be overly simplistic, however, to ignore the uniqueness that new technology and social practices have placed on this eternally challenging environment. As new forms of communication evolve, the old precedents of armbands and student print journalism may not be able to keep up. It is the unenviable task of a school administrator to consider if and how to limit the impact of everything, from a student's Twitter feed to disappearing messages on social media platforms like Snapchat. Principals may find themselves longing for an "easy" question on student speech, like those posed by student T-shirts, when they are staring down a school full of students with mobile internet at their fingertips and ready-made platforms for their voices.

The Supreme Court provided only a bit more clarity in their recent holding in *Mahanoy Area School District v. B.L.*, where they have, at least, concluded that some circumstances exist in which a student's off-campus speech may be regulated by schools. The case presented precisely the challenge listed above, where a student used disappearing Snapchat posts (captured by fellow students) to express her dissatisfaction about not making the varsity cheerleading squad. Although she used language the school would undoubtedly consider coarse, she did not consider her one-year suspension from the squad to be justified, and subsequently brought suit against the school district.

Writing for an 8-1 majority, Justice Stephen Breyer disagreed with a Third Circuit ruling in favor of the student holding that *Tinker* categorically did not apply to off-campus speech. They were not, however, prepared to give schools carte blanche to regulate all off-campus speech. Justice Breyer did little to clarify by saying

> We are uncertain as to the length or content of any such list of appropriate exceptions or carve outs [to a categorical ban on regulation].... Particularly given the advent of computer-based learning, we hesitate to determine precisely which of many school-related off-campus activities belong on such a list. Neither do we now know how such a list might vary, depending upon a student's age, the nature of the school's off- campus activity, or the impact upon the school itself. (Mahanoy Area School District v. B.L.)

Ultimately the court created in *Mahanoy* a series of factors for consideration, amounting to a very fact specific analysis of each individual scenario to be teased out by lower courts. These are factors that they say "diminish" the special characteristics that justify school oversight of student speech, but may not altogether eliminate them. First, the Court notes that schools are rarely (but not *never*) acting in loco pare.

CONCLUSION

Students today are grappling with the same kinds of questions that they have always faced, the challenge of interacting with and responding to a society that does not see them as equal to its adult members. It may, in some ways, feel like we are seeing a new wave of student activism around issues like climate change and gun violence, as the students of Marjorie Stoneman Douglas lead nationwide walkouts, or activists like Greta Thunberg inspire students to organize their own climate protests. Mary Beth Tinker, however, would challenge the assumption that such student activism is "new," and William and Lillian Gobitas would stand at her side to assert that they also stood up for their own rights in their time. The court has responded to student activism for eight decades, and they will continue to be called upon to settle future controversies as well.

To the school administrators hoping this chapter would provide guidance for how to handle the situation confronted just this morning, I offer my apologies that it did not provide the exact answer you may need in this moment. The reality remains that the court's jurisprudence in the area of student free speech is highly fact specific. Disparate outcomes abound when small details are tweaked here and there, sometimes opening entirely new areas of legal precedent. Students pose a unique challenge for the adults tasked with their care, all the more so when we consider the ways in which they are experimenting with their identities and beliefs.

Courts, however, are not unsympathetic to the difficulties faced by school administrators; not only in terms of the exceedingly demanding task of caring for their pupils, but also in determining what the law *is* in a particular situation. Anyone who has spent time caring for students in schools knows to expect the unexpected. Courts recognize that they could never resolve every unique situation that a principal might confront and could not expect individual principals to always make the "right" choice regarding whether or when to limit student speech. School administrators, therefore, are routinely found to have what is known as "qualified immunity," a concept whereby individual government officials are held not to be liable for making choices that are "not objectively unreasonable" given the circumstances.[12] Given how complex and varied the court's precedent has been on student free speech, it is highly likely that a principal making reasonable efforts to follow the law will be spared from individual liability in cases.

Over the last 50 years, the court has chipped away at, and boxed in, the holding of *Tinker* to give "clarity" to how limited student speech rights actually are. The seemingly simple phrase that students do not "shed their constitutional rights ... at the schoolhouse gate" is not so simple after all. However, using the principles articulated in the case law thus far, a clearer picture of *some* kinds of speech rights can be seen. Whether the court has finished weighing in on this issue, is an open question.

This is not to say that the picture of student expression rights will always be so varied and situational. There is a possibility that, in the next few years, the Supreme Court could take up any number of the pending free speech cases that will refine or even overturn their prior rulings. Marty Ginsburg, attorney, professor, and late husband of the late Supreme Court Justice Ruth Bader Ginsburg, would often remark that the true symbol of the United States is not the bald eagle, it is the pendulum. When the pendulum swings too far in one direction, it will inevitably return back to the center over time (Schmidt, 2018). The question that remains, however, is whether *Tinker* represents the center, or if the "high water mark" of student free expression is actually at one end of the pendulum's swing.

The ever-changing world continues to pose challenges to how and when students may express themselves. The evolution of new technologies such as social media, content creation and curation, and self-publishing are opening new horizons with which the courts will need to grapple over the next decade. When asked when and how student expression in schools can be challenged, even savvy administrators or teachers will often cite the *substantial disruption* standard outlined in *Tinker*. Judging from the 50 years since the decision was handed down, however, the true answer is a far more complicated story.

AUTHOR'S NOTE

Correspondence concerning this chapter should be addressed to Ryan Suskey, The Ohio Center for Law-Related Education, 1700 Lake Shore Drive, Columbus, OH 43204. Contact: rsuskey@oclre.org

NOTES

1. Professor Justin Driver's 2018 *The Schoolhouse Gate: Public Education, The Supreme Court, and the Battle for the American Mind* borrows Justice Fortas' phraseology to discuss student rights generally and the way that courts have handled public education through American history.
2. Selective Incorporation as a doctrine has evolved over time and has relied on different avenues for incorporation of rights (i.e., some rights were incorporated via the Privileges or Immunities Clause). The modern iteration of the test as to which amendments should be incorporated via the Due Process Clause is articulated by Justice Benjamin Cardozo in *Palko v. Connecticut* (1937) where he argued that the Due Process Clause protects rights that are "of the very essence of a scheme of ordered liberty." To date, many of the rights guaranteed by the Bill of Rights have been incorporated (e.g., free exercise of religion from the First Amendment, right to an impartial jury from the Sixth Amendment, right to keep and bear arms from the Second Amendment, etc.) but others still have not (e.g., the right to a jury in civil trials exceeding $20 in value from the Seventh Amendment).
3. Although this fact is a basic component of many state standards (see, e.g., Ohio High School American Government Standards 7, 14, 15, 16), recent studies suggest that knowledge of civics may be staggeringly lower. The Annenberg Public Policy Center at the University of Pennsylvania completes an annual survey of civic knowledge, the most recent of which was in September of 2018. At least as it applies to knowing the names of the three branches (the role of each branch was not asked), 34% of respondents could not name a single branch. https://cdn.annenbergpublicpolicycenter.org/wp-content/uploads/2018/09/Annenberg_2018_civics_survey_complete.pdf
4. For an extensive overview of judicial canons and the interpretation of the law, see Scalia (2012).
5. The doctrine of in loco parentis is well established in both English common law and American jurisprudence. Justice Clarence Thomas gave a detailed overview of his reading of the doctrine in his concurring opinion in *Morse v. Frederick* (551 U.S. 393, 2007, Thomas concurring 413).
6. The official citation for this case includes a misspelling of the name of the plaintiff children. Although inaccurate (as to the parties) the proper citation for the case should copy the misspelling, replacing the "a" for an "i" in the name of the students.
7. In an odd twist of fate, both the *Gobitis* case and the *Barnette* case misspelled the names of the families involved. Marie and Gathie Barnett (without an "e") were the names of the children in the *Barnette* case. See https://www.thirteen.org/wnet/supremecourt/personality/landmark_minersville.html and https://www.freedomforuminstitute.org/2009/04/29/woman-in-barnette-reflects-on-flag-salute-case/
8. The timing of the appearance of the buttons (and the location of the school) is not insignificant. The civil rights movement playing out across

the south was on the minds of many of the students, especially in August and September of 1964. Earlier that summer, three civil rights activists, members of SNCC, went missing after being released from jail for speeding. Six-weeks after their disappearance, their mutilated bodies were uncovered in Philadelphia, Mississippi. When school resumed that September, students began wearing the SNCC buttons that said "One Man, One Vote." The FBI investigations into the SNCC activists' deaths would eventually lead to indictments for 21 men, several of whom were members of local law enforcement, including the county sheriff. For more on the impact of the Civil Rights movement on the outcome of *Tinker*, see "The Civil Rights Roots of *Tinker*'s Disruption Tests," in *American University Law Review* (2009).

9. The specific mention of the student participants here is relevant, as it will bear upon later analyses and future considerations that the court will likely undertake. The issue of whether disruption caused by nonparticipants, in response to the protestors, can be the valid basis for limiting student speech is still an open question as courts consider what has come to be known as the "heckler's veto," a process by which a rowdy audience can effectively silence disfavored groups by the practice or threat of disruption.
10. Arguably, the justices could also have ruled that this was an example of "school sponsored speech," given that the school had created this forum for expression (a school sponsored student government election) and not disciplining the student would have created the impression that the schools sanctioned such speech. The timeline, however, is important. The concept of "school sponsored speech" as a carve-out from the Substantial Disruption Test was not created until 1988, when *Kuhlmeier* was decided. The *Fraser* case was decided 2 years before this ruling.
11. It is worth noting that Frederick's contention was *not* that the banner was not political. Arguably his continuous claims that the banner represented his First Amendment right *is* a political message. This claim, however, was seriously harmed by his explanation of the banner to be an attempt to be noticed by the television cameras present.
12. Several of the defendants in the cases we have seen were found to have such qualified immunity. See, for example, *Porter v. Ascension Parish School Board* (2004), *Bell v. Itawamba County School Board* (2014).

REFERENCES

Bell v. Itawamba County School Board, 799 F.3d 379 (5th Cir. 2015).

Bethel School District v. Fraser, 478 U.S. 675 (1986).

Black, W. L., Jr. (2015). Omnipresent student speech and the schoolhouse gate: Interpreting *Tinker* in the digital age. *St. Louis University Law Journal, 59*, 531.

Blackwell v. Issaquena County Board of Education, 363 F.2d 749 (5th Cir. 1966).

Board of Education, Island Trees Union Free School District No. 26 v. Pico by Pico, 457 U.S. 853 (1982).

Bowman, K. L. (2009). The civil rights roots of Tinker's disruption tests Tinker turns 40: Freedom of expression at school and its meaning for American democracy—April 16, 2009—Symposium. *American University Law Review, 58*(5), 1129–1165.

Burnside v. Byars, 363 F.2d 744, 748 (5th Cir. 1966).

Chemerinsky, E. (2004). The deconstitutionalization of education. *Loyola University Chicago Law Journal, 36*(1), 101–125.

Driver, J. (2018). *The schoolhouse gate: Public education, the Supreme Court, and the battle for the American mind*. Pantheon Books.

Gitlow v. New York, 268 U.S. 652 (1925).

Hazelwood School District v. Kuhlmeier, 484 U.S. 260 (1988).

Hofheimer, A. (2013). Saved by the bell? Is online, off-campus student speech protected by the First Amendment? *Florida State University Law Review, 40*(4), 971–994.

J.S. v. Blue Mountain, 650 F.3d 915, 921 (3d Cir. 2011).

Keyishian v. Board of Regents, 385 U.S. 589, 603 (1967).

Mahanoy Area School District v. B.L., 594 U.S. (2021).

Marbury v. Madison, 5 U.S. 137 (1803).

Marineau v. Guiles, 127 S. Ct. 3054 (2007).

Minersville School District v. Gobitis, 310 U.S. 586 (1940).

Morse v. Frederick, 551 U.S. 393 (2007).

Palko v. Connecticut, 302 U.S. 319 (1937).

Papandrea, M. (2008). Student speech rights in the digital age. *Florida Law Review, 60*(5), 1028.

Payne v. Tennessee, 501 U. S. 808, 827–828 (1991).

Porter v. Ascension Parish School Board, 393 F.3d 608, 615, n. 22 (CA5 2004).

Reagan, R. (1983, December 8). Remarks at the National Forum on Excellence in Education. *Public Papers of President Ronald W. Reagan*.

Scalia, A. (2012). *Reading law: The interpretation of legal texts*. Thomson/West.

Schmidt, S. (2018, July 30). Ruth Bader Ginsburg says she has 'at least 5 more years' on the Supreme Court. Her fans rejoice. *The Washington Post*. https://www.google.com/url?sa=t&rct=j&q=&esrc=s&source=web&cd=17&ved=2ahUKEwjjo_Gm0qXhAhULLKwKHbaoA3gQFjAQegQIBRAB&url=https://www.washingtonpost.com/news/morning-mix/wp/2018/07/30/ruth-bader-ginsburg-says-she-has-at-least-5-more-years-on-the-supreme-court-her-fans-rejoice/&usg=AOvVaw1EwAcOt45cnHtgz22Z5wME

Tinker v. Des Moines Independent Community School District, 39 U.S. 503 (1969).

U.S. Const. amend. I.

West Virginia State Board of Education v. Barnette, 319 U.S. 634 (1943).

PART II

THE STATE OF RIGHTS IN SCHOOLS

CHAPTER 3

TAKING ACTION AND TAKING OFFENSE IN OUR OWN LITTLE DEMOCRACY

High School Students' Perceptions of First Amendment Rights and Responsibilities

Nancy C. Patterson, Diann Brown, and Jeanne Vidoni
Bowling Green State University

This case study reports the perspectives of public high school students in a Midwestern state on their First Amendment rights and responsibilities in school. The study was conducted during the 2017–2018 school year, when secondary students across the United States were mobilizing and engaging with their First Amendment rights of assembly and petition. The research questions that framed the study were: (1) How important are First Amendment rights to Ohio high school students? and (2) What are Ohio high school students' perspectives of responsibilities related to these rights? Findings show that these students universally value their First Amendment rights, with speech discussed the most. They readily acknowledge that rights often must be tempered by responsibilities and express interest in being more involved in who made the decisions about what was permissible and what was not. Finally, they desire more authentic connections with the adults in their schools, with priority on building rapport and relationships and

At the Schoolhouse Gate: Stakeholder Perceptions of First Amendment Rights and Responsibilities in U.S. Public Schools, pp. 49–77
www.infoagepub.com
Copyright © 2022 by Information Age Publishing
All rights of reproduction in any form reserved.

listening as a central component. They desire increased advocacy and support as well as more meaningful and active classroom learning.

A colleague offered me a warm reception one winter morning at one of our local urban high schools and helped tuck me away in a nice, quiet room off the library. It was anything but quiet times contextually, and mine was anything but a quiet purpose in sitting there, tethering with my phone to gain network access where it was blocked by the district. It was the last day of February 2018, fourteen days after February 14, the Valentine's Day on which ex-student Nikolas Cruz shot and killed 17 people at Marjory Stoneman Douglas High School in Florida. I situate this, because my purpose was to collect students' views of their First Amendment rights in high schools, and high school students across the United States were mobilizing and engaging with their First Amendment rights of assembly and petition.

I was more than halfway through the 29 focus groups I ultimately would conduct with 127 high school students in six schools across northwest Ohio. Time after time, these young people had plenty to say and overwhelmed me with their easy trust and openness. Jakoby (pseudonym of choice) was one of five in my second focus group that morning and was particularly affable in his quick and confident response to how important he thought First Amendment rights were:

Jakoby: My name's Jakoby. I think these are all very important, especially petition. I feel like we're kind of our own (pause) little democracy, and we should be able to agree and fix things as our own government inside here within the bigger program.

Nancy: Oh really? Is that what happens?

Jakoby: No, but I feel like it should.

And there it was—admittedly just what I was hoping to hear—that young people have a clear perception of their rights, that they connect that perception to rights in schools, and that they view themselves as part of a governmental process through which people can communicate, compromise, and make things better in public schools. Jakoby was among the minority of participants who made these connections right off the bat. He also was not the only one who pointed out that there was more to do in schools. His observation forecasts a complicated tale of the messiness, offense, action, and reaction among the Northwest Ohio high school students who volunteered for this case study. The overall research questions that framed it were: (1) How important are First Amendment rights to

Ohio high school students? and (2) What are Ohio high school students' perspectives of responsibilities related to these rights?

REVIEW OF LITERATURE: WHAT HAPPENS WHEN STUDENTS HAVE POWER?

Researchers (Fielding, 2012; Haynes et al., 2003; Mitchell, 2016; Hess & McAvoy, 2020; Pace, 2019; Youniss, 2011) have argued that schools are places uniquely suited to teach about democracy and the rights of its citizens. Walter Parker (2004) described them as places where "diverse children are congregated in a buzzing variety that does not exist in many other places" (p. 160) that can routinely subject students to challenge and stimulus that have the promise of propelling them to new awareness and action. Fielding (2012) argues that "taking participatory traditions of democracy more seriously" (p. 45) in education is key to addressing the contemporary world crises of political, social, and economic polarization. This brief review of the research focuses on the power students should have yet may or may not have over their own rights of expression in classrooms. It lays out what we know about respect for and protection of youth rights and exercise thereof.

A large of volume of research highlights student expression and its value (see Andolina & Conklin, 2018), with Dewey (1916/1966) himself arguing for participation as having the highest value. This body of literature both implies and asserts that students must somehow acquire some power over their own expression and action for such classrooms to work. Ira Shor (1996) discusses the type of classroom that teachers can choose to offer students, describing the "discomforts of democracy" (p. 82) in his experiment with offering a collaborative classroom at the community college level. He made a distinction between his absolute authority (no escaping the fact that he had the authority as the teacher hired to initiate learning experiences assign grades) and the sharable power associated with it. In sharing power with students, he was able to design an experience for his students that transformed his authority, which felt to him like a changing role of "*moving with* instead of pushing, a lightness of *being part of* instead of the weightiness of *being solely in charge of*" (p. 154).

Over 2 decades ago, John J. Patrick (1999) detailed just such knowledge, skills, and dispositions that frame citizenship education. They include "Recognizing the common humanity and dignity of each person" and "Respecting, protecting, and exercising rights possessed equally by each person" (p. 11). Fielding (2004) describes a similar phenomenon in reference to student voice and interaction, which he calls "radical collegiality" (p. 296), whereby he challenges teachers to transform their interactions with students through interdependence and empathetic listening.

We know that the courts have both protected and limited the rights of students in public schools. To date, there have been four Supreme Court cases shaping jurisprudence (*Tinker v. Des Moines Independent School District*, 1969; *Bethel School District v. Fraser*, 1986; *Hazelwood School District v. Kuhlmeier*, 1988; and *Morse v. Frederick*, 2007) that have proscribed limits due to "substantive disruption" variously as vulgar language, unauthorized student use of press rights, and advocating for illegal substances. As Ryan Suskey argues in Chapter 2 of this volume, "The ever-changing world continues to pose challenges to how and when students may express themselves" (p. 33).

We also know that students themselves have high regard for their First Amendment rights, as indicated over time by the Knight Foundation's (2018b) *The Future of the First Amendment: 2018 Survey of High School Students and Teachers*. The aim of this survey is to follow high school students' attitudes toward First Amendment issues, and it has been administered every 2 years since 2004. The most recent administration of the survey (2018) found that high school students' support for the First Amendment continues to hold steady, with only 26% arguing that its protections go too far. This compares to 45% arguing that its protections go too far in the 2006 survey. Regarding limits to free speech, an overwhelming majority supports the right to express unpopular opinions (89%), while only half as many believe people have the right to speech that others consider offensive (45%). The survey establishes increasing positive correlations between student support of First Amendment rights and usage of social media. In the end, it shows that just as jurisprudence continues to settle emerging questions about rights in schools, student themselves struggle to understand their complexity.

Efforts to imbue districts, schools and classrooms with respect for and protection of student rights have proliferated over time and across the spectrum from whole-school reform initiatives to large- and small-scale curricular initiatives. The First Amendment Schools initiative is emblematic of the ambitious path civic education often takes. It spans the school reform spectrum, from structural school reform projects to curricular innovation. The seminal school reform effort on this topic is the 6-year nationwide initiative entitled *First Amendment Schools: Educating for Freedom and Responsibility* (Haynes et al., 2003). One primary goal of the project was to develop school guidelines for "creating and sustaining First Amendment principles in the school community" (p. 17). In a 2016 case study of the project, Cynthia Mitchell details the rise and fall of this effort, which at its height served 22 project schools and 80 affiliate schools that reached 75,426 students. The project continues today through The

National League of Democratic Schools and the McCormick Foundation's Democratic Schools project. Numerous ongoing curricular initiatives continue to be used to fortify civic education in schools, such as varied law-related education programs offered by the Center for Civic Education and its state affiliates (Mock Trial, We the People, and Project Citizen), iCivics, Student Voice (https://www.stuvoice.org/about), and the Mikva Challenge's *Project Soapbox*.

In closing, it is important to note that an argument for students' rights in schools can hardly be made without an argument for teachers' rights in schools. Ira Shor's (1996) classroom in which students have power is impossible without teacher academic freedom. Since *Tinker,* the rights of teachers in public schools have faced more significant legal challenges and afforded fewer protections over time than those for students. While there is yet to be a definitive Supreme Court teacher academic freedom case, *Garcetti v. Ceballos* (2006) has been used in the courts to relegate public servants (with teachers among them) to "agents of the state" status. The majority opinion stated, "When public employees make statements pursuant to their official duties, the employees are not speaking as citizens for First Amendment purposes, and the Constitution does not insulate their communications from employer discipline."

It is in this chilling teacher context that Jack Nelson (2021), long-time scholar and defender of academic freedom, has identified categories of censorship teachers experience:

> Overt censorship, imposed by external regulation or administrative demands, directly blocks teachers, topics of study, and teaching material. Covert censorship happens through slanted and selective coverage in teaching material, curricular manipulation to avoid topics, and parental or organizational interference. Self-censorship occurs when teachers are unwilling to address controversial topics or unnecessarily restrict student investigation. (p. 2)

He further describes the tangible impacts such censorship can have on students, opening them to "indoctrination, incomplete or misleading learning, and citizen ignorance" (p. 2) and urges social studies teachers to be vigilant about pursuing improvement in protections for both themselves and their students.

The research and curricular/program offerings described above make strong cases for why and how to involve students and their teachings in powerful civic education that respects and protects their rights and facilitates the exercise thereof. The study presented here contributes to these ongoing power-sharing efforts by offering an on-the-ground exploration of student perceptions of their experiences with rights in school.

THE STUDY

Case studies are typically used "When the investigator has little control over events, and when the focus is on a contemporary phenomenon within some real-life context" (Yin, 2018, p. 1). Certainly, these two conditions are met with this exploration into high school students' perspectives on their First Amendment rights and responsibilities. No one would deem to be able to control any outcome when talking with older adolescents. The real-life context was the experience of school for 127 Midwestern public high school students during the spring of 2018. There are elements of portraiture research (Lawrence-Lightfoot & Davis, 1997) in this study, such that the narrative reveals the complex nature of ways in which our daily lives are dynamic and varied in their organization. It was my great privilege to enter into relationships with these conscientious young adults for however brief a time and be the willing recorder of their very human experiences, hoping to uncover "dimensions that often go unrecognized by the subjects themselves" (Lawrence-Lightfoot, 1983, p. 6).

Participants

The teachers who facilitated classroom access for this study were colleagues of mine from my years as a secondary social studies methods professor. Beyond the convenience of having an established relationship with all the teachers involved, I chose them purposefully to provide a variety of contexts across the northwest part of the state, from small town (three schools) to suburban (one school) to urban (two schools). Of the six participating schools, students in four schools were designated "high poverty" by this Midwestern state, with the one larger urban area district student population characterized as "very high poverty." See Table 3.1 for an overview of the school typologies and the numbers of focus groups and students in each. School pseudonyms have been provided, and the order in the table is the chronological order in which I visited each school.

Students were recruited for the study through 15-minute classroom visits, during which the study was explained, several scenarios of student course cases were described, and students were asked to be the judge. Cases included *Tinker v. Des Moines Independent School District* (1969); *Bethel School District v. Fraser* (1986); *Hazelwood School District v. Kuhlmeier* (1988); and *Morse v. Frederick* (2007). Individual and parental consent forms were distributed, and students were asked whether they had any

Table 3.1

School Typology Sample and Participant Distribution

Pseudonym	*Typology Designation*	*Focus Groups*	*Total Students*
Ridge	Suburban: Low student poverty and average student population size	9	36
Grove	Small Town 4: High student poverty and average population size	6	28
Hilltop	Urban 8: Very high student poverty and very high student population size	5	21
Lane	Small Town 3: Low student poverty and small student population size	1	5
Ravine	Small Town 4: High student poverty and average population size	6	26
Glade	Urban 7: High student poverty and average student population size	2	11
		29	127

questions. I communicated with each teacher to determine what the deadline would be for return of consent forms and when I might return within the next couple of weeks to conduct focus groups.

Data Collection

I returned to each site within 2 weeks of these information and recruiting sessions to conduct the focus groups. Each session began with students completing a demographic survey and turning in their consent forms. Included in the demographic survey was a request for students to create a pseudonym for themselves, which in all cases were used throughout the study with slight modifications for some requests. A number of students chose to have me use their given name.

To break the ice and to activate students' background knowledge, I began each focus group with a nine-card sorting activity that included the following words/phrases: First Amendment, speech, press, religion, petition, assembly, political/civil rights, and Second Amendment. The cards were spread out on the table when students entered, and they were asked to sort the cards in any order that made sense to them. I gave each group 3–5 minutes and then asked supporting questions to help order the items in a reasonable semblance of order. I explained that the First Amendment included the five rights, and that the Second Amendment was the second in the Bill of Rights and not under discussion today. I explained that the first two amendments of the Bill of Rights are 2 of 10 that afford citizens political and civil rights, and that the First Amendment is all about protecting citizens' rights from governmental overreach. I explained that in that sense, they do not apply to private schools, and that there are other constitutional provisions that do.

Sizes of focus groups ranged from one to six students with the average being four. I asked the same open-ended questions of each group, included in Appendix A. Questions one and two and scenarios four and five were adapted from the Knight Foundation's (2018a) ongoing *Future of the First Amendment survey* (https://knightfoundation.org/reports/the-future-of-the-first-amendment-2018/). Each focus group session was recorded and transcribed.

Out of the 127 students who participated, 73/127 (57%) were from suburban schools, 33/127 (26%) were from rural schools, and 21/127 (17%) were from urban schools. The large majority of participants were high school juniors and seniors who either had taken or were currently enrolled in American Government. Eleven of the urban students were sophomores, who were not yet in American Government, but who were enrolled in Advancement Via Individual Determination (https://www.avid.org/), key components of which are to promote critical thinking and inquiry.

All students in the study volunteered to participate, provided pseudonyms, and consented to be audiotaped. Focus groups were conducted during the school day, except for one conducted after school. Each focus group lasted from 40–50 minutes and began with student completion of a demographic survey on iPads, followed by a brief card sort activity to review human rights and First Amendment rights in particular. All focus group conversations were recorded and then transcribed.

Data Analysis

Three researchers undertook content analysis of all transcripts according to Erikson's (1986) process. They first read through the data and independently identified salient themes. They met as a team to verify and clarify themes and craft warrants for each. They then returned to the transcripts independently to collect warrants for each assertion. They reconvened to discuss the confirming and disconfirming evidence and further define and clarify the assertions.

FINDINGS

The findings are organized around the two research questions:

1. How important are First Amendment rights to Ohio high school students?
2. What are Ohio high school students' perspectives of responsibilities related to these rights?

They flow according to the evolution of focus group conversations, from discussions of student perceptions of the importance of First Amendment rights to limitations and responsibilities related to them. The findings section closes with a discussion of how students view and/or would like to see these rights and responsibilities manifested in schools.

Perspectives on the Importance of Rights

Regarding the research question of how important First Amendment rights are in high school, students report universally valuing their First Amendment rights, with speech mentioned and discussed most. There was unsettled debate about which of the five is most important, with ready acknowledgment that the first five were complex and overlapping.

Multiple students in every group rated the first five as having high importance, just as Jakoby (Hilltop) did. Garrett (Grove) emphasized their overall importance in school, stating it is "extremely necessary that we have these rights, because without these rights—for instance, freedom of speech, freedom of press—we lack the room as people to grow in the high school environment." This enthusiastic advocacy was not unexpected in light of the vivid reminder during the card sort that these rights were theirs as citizens.

Responses became more complicated when students were asked which one was most important, with the majority of students who responded choosing speech as either most important or central to accessing other rights. Arguments for these choices included simple assertions that what young people say has value and represents freedom, as well as more sophisticated assertions of how critical it is in developing skills of expressing opinions, developing skills of discussion, and helping change school environments. Bernice (Ravine) was not alone in her view that after speech, "they all tier down" in importance. Bob L. (Ridge) drilled down beyond the importance of speech rights in school to the importance of having informed classroom conversations: "I think speech is probably the most important in school, simply because education—a lot of education—

relies on discussion, and without some kind of freedom of speech, it's really hard to have an informed or an interesting discussion."

Students ascribed less importance to press, petition, assembly, and religion, with religion the most commonly valued after speech. While discussions of freedom of the press in schools did crop up, they were not started by students and happened primarily when I asked about the news sources in schools. Overall, students had few strong opinions on the issue of free press in school, with an active school newspaper present in only one of the six schools. There were numerous statements of what news was available coming from administration and being more announcement-based than journalistic. There were two groups in which students argued for the need for factual information to inform action. Jennings (Ridge) questioned how democracy could work without a free press: "The way democracy works is if the people are knowledgeable on the issues, so you kind of have to know what you're doing for these to go into effect." The second conversation was an interchange between Seth, Asia, and Sydney (Ravine) about how maybe the press was even more important than speech.

Sydney: Well, it's nice to know what's going on.
Seth: Yeah. If your government is doing stuff you don't know about and then you can't get the word out about it.
Nancy: Yeah, but you have Twitter.
Asia: That stuff is not always right.

Kaka (2022) provides a deeper analysis of the dearth of school newspapers and student views on news sources in Chapter 6: "First Amendment Rights and Expression: News and Views From Students on Information and Social Media in Schools."

Student perspectives on the importance of religious freedom in school centered around how well it appeared to be respected in the school environment and the ways in which it seemed different than other rights. Aaron (Hilltop) saw the need to protect "students coming from all [religious] backgrounds" in his school. One of the small rural schools was located in a traditionally German Catholic county, where religious education still was very closely tied to public education. Lizzie (Lane) described her experience growing up there in a strong religious community culture:

> I think in our school, specifically the freedom of religion is the most important, because when we were in junior high and below, all the way to first grade, we'd go over to religion class in the morning for our first period of class.

Several described the uniqueness of religious freedom as more personal, internal, and values based. Leila (Ridge) reflected that "the right to practice religion is probably the most important out of those to me because, it's something that you can't just leave at the door—it's part of your life." Elizabeth (Ridge) explained why she valued religious freedom above all, stating,

> I think I appreciate the religion one the best.... Because that way we don't have like a set religion in the United States and anyone can think whatever they want about that topic. To me the freedom of religion one is probably respected like the best in school.

Brian (Ridge) concurred, explaining that,

> With religion also comes like personal values and stuff like that. I do think that it's important that we are able to uphold our values no matter where we are, so yeah—I'd say that religion values are like the most important thing that we should be able to maintain.

There was push-back in some groups, with almost as many students arguing for the equal and overlapping standing all of the five as there were assertions of the primacy of speech. Bob M. (Ridge) linked speech, press, and petition: "I think they're all equally important, 'cause if you don't have one of 'em, then a lot of the others don't work, 'cause if you don't have freedom of the press, then you're gonna be fed false information, and then you can't protest the right stuff, or you're not thinking for yourself, necessarily." Mack (Grove) linked petition, press, and religion: "you can't have freedom of petition, 'cause then you, again, can't say what you want, or press, can't say what you want, or religion, can't believe what you want." "They're all very entangled," Sergio (Grove) said, and Jake (Ravine) concurred, stating, "All of these basically give us our freedom as Americans. I mean, they kind of all tie in to each other."

Kathleen (Ridge) explained that because she has always taken them for granted, she found it hard to pick one. Jamie (Grove) also spoke of them as a whole, stating,

> I feel like they're the basic rights that our government grants us (pause). They're what everyone knows and builds off of, so they've just become such an integral part of our society that people don't really think about them as being rights. until they're taken away.

In the end, the question of the most important among the first five was left unresolved, with numerous individuals and groups arguing for their equal and interconnected purpose and overall importance.

Acknowledging Rights and Responsibilities

In each focus group, I transitioned conversations about the importance of rights in schools to the foundational issue of how far these rights should extend. Do the first five freedoms go too far? Are there limits? What, if any, are the responsibilities associated with having these in school? The focus group setting allowed students to push each other on this topic, and as such, enthusiastic early support of a favorite among the five or the five as a whole quickly turned to musings that ranged along a continuum of just how limited rights should be as well as who should limit them. There was confusion and disagreement over some types of action and expression, close consensus for limits on others, and a diversity of views on who should limit student expression and how.

Lack of Consensus on Various Types of Speech and Actions. The scenario that provoked the most within- and cross-group disagreement was that of taking the knee during the National Anthem. During my first focus group of the 29 at Ridge, an intense discussion drew tears. It rolled out in response to my question about whether or not taking a knee during the National Anthem went too far in terms of availing one's self of First Amendment rights:

Marie: I personally think that's way too far.
Nancy: Okay, so tell me about it.
Marie: Personal experience with the situation. I can explain something that happened when I told someone that I didn't agree with it. I played on the soccer team last year.... So pretty much, I voiced that I didn't agree with it.
Nancy: In school?
Marie: No, to them directly, and I got called a racist homophobe by the whole soccer team.

Marie's peers in the group supported her assessment of the incident, weighing in both on students' rights to take the knee as well as Marie's right to voice her offense. They initially backed her assertion that students have the right to protest and argued that protesters should find another way that is not so disrespectful and even embarrassing. Renee stated,

> They should've took [sic] it a different way, though. They shouldn't have done it while the National Anthem was going on, because that offends a lot of people and it's—I don't know. I find that when people do that, I find it wrong because it's not—usually it's what's a tradition. You stand and you put your hand over your heart and for somebody to do that, I just—it doesn't

> make any sense. It's one of those things that are like, why? What's the point? I know you're petitioning, but you could've done it a different way.

Jennie acknowledged that the flag symbolized different things to Maria than it did to the kneeling soccer players and their teammates. She helped summarize the conversation as she grappled with the fact that free expression meant the freedom to disagree and express unpopular opinions, stating,

> I think they should be allowed to because I think if—either way, someone's gonna get offended. You know what I mean? If you stop them from doing it, they're gonna get really offended and say that they're preventing them from expressing all their rights. But if they do it, people are going to be offended because people don't agree with what they're doing. I guess you're always gonna have people disagree with whatever you're doing.

Maria was faced with the dilemma of what she perceived to be necessary limits in both the speech and actions of others while simultaneously desiring respect for her own opinion. This recounting was emblematic of the struggles students were having in everyday life with peer-to-peer school interactions. Students from other focus groups shared Maria's views. Tyler said,

> I don't think they should be able to …, but you're taking a knee during the Pledge of Allegiance. I just think that's not American. I think they should get in trouble for it, personally—high school kids and NFL players both.

Lynne expressed embarrassment about the practice: "I just think that it makes us look bad when we have people from our own country kneeling during that."

A very different conversation rolled out in another group at the same school, with students making various arguments about why we have to permit these types of actions:

> Leila: I whole heartedly agree with that [allowing taking the knee]. It's one of those things it's like it's not something I am personally affected by, but it doesn't mean that it's something people can't do. I have a similar opinion about abortions honestly—like I personally wouldn't get one, but it's not my right to say someone else can't do that same thing.
>
> Kathleen: Yes.
>
> Leila: And because I'm not feeling the same things as some people doing that just doesn't mean they don't get to do it. It's

them expressing their opinion in a different way and I think that's totally reasonable.

Kathleen: And I think with the knee, like taking a knee it's like not an action that's malicious, it's not like—I don't know—I think people take it too seriously. It's just that they're taking knee, and they're standing up for what they believe in.

Nancy: The kneeling down?

Kathleen: Kneeling for what they believe in, I guess. But like I think they're just raising awareness. It's really not that harmful....

Brian: Yeah, I'd say that especially with this issue, I think people's opinions really cloud ... whether or not this is right or not. I feel like—well I personally believe—that the people who choose to do it can do it, and they should be able to do it if they would like too, okay? But I'd say a lot of people think that this is like offending veterans or whatever, but and that's because they think the flag represents veterans, I guess. But I mean like nobody ever said what the flag represents. It means something different to everyone.

Kathleen: Yeah.

Brian: All it really is just a flag, but yeah, I know that my sister knelt during the national anthem at one of her soccer games last year and there was like a lot—and like her and one other or a couple of other players—and there was just like a lot of unnecessary controversy around about it.

Leila's view was that while she may not agree, she supports people's right to express their views, and Brian suggested that we must allow for the fact that any given group of people may see things differently. Students from other groups gave additional arguments in support of this stance. Darnell (from another group) shared Brian's view that we must accept varying perspectives and added his view of taking offense:

> I mean if you want to take a knee—no matter where you go, everybody's gonna get mad. If you don't like it, then don't talk to that person or don't be bothered with them, as simple as that. Everybody is different.... So, if you wanna take a knee, take a knee.

The overall assertion was that we all have the right to controversial and potentially offensive speech, but that we must accept that there may be challenges from others to such speech, and that we have same right to challenge others. Three students from Ravine had similar views. Sydney supported taking the knee, adding "also people should be allowed to say why they don't like it," and James, who disagreed with taking the knee, argued that, nevertheless, "you should be able to voice your opinion with it or against it," but respectfully. His peer in the same group—Seth—agreed with him: "I mean as much as I don't like it or agree with it, they should still be allowed to do that."

Several in addition to Jakoby above, who felt like the right to petition was essential for helping us "be able to agree and fix things," discussed a moral obligation to protest. There were two conversations about taking the knee as a symbolic act to protest systemic racism. Leo (Ridge) discussed how her parents taught her that "there are things wrong with this country, and being quiet is the same as doing the thing ... that if things are wrong, you have to be part of the solution, not just a bystander." He also challenged the argument that the kneeling during the National Anthem is disrespectful:

> I think that since it's symbolic speech. The people who are interpreting it as disrespect of veterans are taking it at face value. For example, the bus boycott. It was a protest of segregation on buses—it wasn't because the African American community hated bussed.

Leila and Jamal from Ridge made similar arguments in support of protest as a historic advocacy tool:

Leila: But I mean just we started at slavery. There's [sic] still people who believe in that sort of racist view, and it's been passed on. I think that's part of the issue I think it's more of a racism more than, "Oh they're disrespecting the flag." I think it's honestly racism ... I think there's a part of those people that think, like they know, whether consciously or not, that it's about racism, and they know that it's wrong, but they're turning it around and making it about the flag and disrespecting the veterans, so they have sort of a basis for their argument or at least in their minds.

Nancy: I've had people argue that if they just didn't do that during the anthem, they'd get more play. Like a failed protest because it's turning half the people off.

Jamal: But then there wouldn't be controversy and without controversy—

Leila: Yeah, I don't think it would have been noticed.

Nancy: That's the nature of protests, right?

Jamal: Without controversy you wouldn't be able to get your point across.

Close Consensus on Certain Speech and Actions. While taking the knee evoked strong emotions and disagreement about limits, there were other speech and actions most students supported, whether in limiting or allowing them. For example, most students supported and/or participated in the spring walkouts, depending on the point at which their focus groups occurred. My interviews at four of the six school happened after the Marjory Stoneman Douglas shootings and were a lively topic of discussion in those groups. There also was agreement about facilitating and allowing for discussion of controversial topics in the classroom (addressed below in the section about what schools should look like) as well as agreement about limits that would ensure the safety of the school and individuals in it.

The subject of school walkouts was a good example of an allowance most students agreed should be made. Walkouts happened in five of the six schools under study here. Most interesting was that in one of the urban schools, I heard from students both before and after the district decision to allow students to observe the planned March 14 national walkout. Prior to this decision, Royal and Jakoby (Hilltop) were asserting their right to take this action but were still thinking through the consequences. The following was in response to my question about whether this should be permitted:

Royal: So, if they didn't [allow the walkout], they would be taking away two of our rights.... Petition. Right to petition.

Jakoby: Petition, speech, assembly.

Royal: And assembly and it basically is a right of speech. So, three of our rights.

Jakoby: Yeah, but in class, you can't just go out and like, "Hey. I'm going to get everybody to sign this petition." You have to kinda do that on your own time. You can't just do it on their [school administrator] time.

Royal: Yeah. You can't petition when you're supposed to be learning in class.

Nancy: So that's what these students are doing. They're going to miss 17 minutes of class.

Jakoby: It's only 17 minutes for 1 day. I would go.

Royal: There probably is—and it probably is excused. If you—you won't get punished if you tell the school what you're doing at that time.

The next week when I went back to meet with different focus groups, the walkout had been sanctioned, and students were discussing how it should be conducted. They were working thought the details in the school student council:

> We were talking about this in student council, freedom of speech and all of these, 'cause that's our way to bring it up so that we can't get in trouble. And then if they do say anything, we would bring up these, and which ones we believe would help represent it, and why we're doing it. (Makayla, Hilltop)

While most students had a favorable response to the walkouts, there were those who had reservations, expressing worries about permission and consequences. Lizzie (Lane) (post-Stoneman Douglas) did not question the hidden rules of the school in regard to protests: "There are some standards that we all know. It's not set in stone, but we know that it's not appropriate to walk out of our high school." Thomas' (Glade) perception was that while there was high interest, "many people did not want to risk a disciplinary action or just miss some of their education." He did not support the walkout for his own reasons:

> I think you really need to do something, walking out of your school isn't going to help anybody. For the people who organize it spend as much time organizing a fundraiser for victims of violence, maybe that would actually help but just skipping out of school for 17 minutes.

Seth (Ravine) was of the opinion that one should be able to have the choice NOT to participate without fear of consequences. Karen and Largo at Glade agreed that some teachers were fine with it and not others, and that some gave pop quizzes or other assignments during the walkout that made it hard for some students to participate.

Others worried about safety. Brian (Ridge) (pre-Stoneman Douglas) could not conceive of how school protests could be safe: "There are certain instances where speech in school should be limited, as well as assembly. Of course, we don't want like a huge protest going on inside our school or anything like that." Lizzie (Lane) argued:

> students shouldn't be allowed to walk out, but they should be allowed to advocate. Because walking out, you're creating more dangers than just staying in school. Walking out, something could've gone terribly wrong. I'm glad it didn't, but something could've happened.

While most students would not have favored limiting walkouts, they had reasonable objections to expression they perceived as causing harm to others and offered few objections to limits. They favored limits that ensured school safety; addressed violent actions of individuals or extreme groups; and addressed face-to-face and cyberbullying, including hate speech. Efie (Hilltop) acknowledged that "There could be some few bad apples and it could be safety issues." Some students (post-Stoneman Douglas) expressed disappointment that their school was not doing enough to put an improved safety plan in place and communicate clearly with students and guardians/parents about it. Anna (Hilltop) was looking for a speedier response from the adults in her building so they could "all feel safe." She continued, "In teacher meetings, they should kinda push it more to where the principal is, like, 'Okay, we should do this.'"

One class had been studying the Westboro Baptist Church history of incendiary pickets that targeted LGBTQ+ communities and other groups. Two focus groups from that class had strong views about expression going too far and the need for limits when there is potential for harm to others. Jennings (Ridge) stated: "Well, I mean, there's the Westboro Baptist Church or whatever. Yeah, I mean, it is subjective, but I think the majority would agree that it was going too far." Joe (Ridge) also discussed violence in terms of inciting such on social media: "Yeah, if—certainly if it's like threatening harm or inciting violence, or any type of that, then those students shouldn't be posting."

The strongest consensus about free expression going too far was the one Joe (Ridge) described above regarding harm caused from one peer to another, whether face-to-face or cyberbullying. Joe S. (Ridge) felt that students should be allowed to express an unpopular opinion but only to a certain extent, drawing "a distinct line when you get into hate speech or blatant racism or whatever." Tyler (Ridge) made the same point, stating, "I feel like if you're down on someone or bullying them on social media and just like harming them, making them feel bad, I think that should be censored." Ruth (Lane) thought it was too far on social media "if you say something threatening." Jennie (Ridge) weighed in on some language she felt went too far in the knee-taking scenario described above. She made the argument that students have a right to voice their opinions and that name-calling in this instance was unwarranted: "just because of the one opinion she has [that taking a knee is wrong] does not mean that she is that [a racist or a homophobe]".

Who Should Limit Expression and How? Embedded in the animated discussions I had with students and they had with each other about limits was the undercurrent of power and enforcement. All groups arrived at varying degrees of agreement that rights and responsibilities go hand in hand, but with acknowledgment of this come a new set of questions: if one argues that rights come along with responsibilities, who is going to do the limiting, and when and how? Who has in fact been setting the limits, and how are they doing? The analysis showed a range of opinions of who is responsible for deciding the limits (adults in the school, the courts, larger culture, one's peers, one's self) and how well they are doing.

Students in a number of groups appeared to accept the embedded authority of the adults in their schools and in larger society, citing their own status as minors and arguing for the importance of adult supervision to ensure safety and order in schools. Largo (Glade) acknowledged that school administrators can limit your practice of religion, for example, "especially if it's affecting other students," and that "Some school contracts prevent you from assembling, and schools censor their internet and media sources." One student from a suburban school acknowledged the important place of oversight that adults have in schools in terms of student newspapers, worrying that there are always students who are "gonna take it too far," and that student writing should "at least be reviewed by a staff member. Maybe not approved, but at least reviewed" (Anonymous, Ridge).

Some described cultural norms that everyone seemed to understand and follow but that were not written down. Royal (Hilltop) explained, "It's not visible, but it's there for you to follow. Even though it's not in the rulebook, you still have to follow the invisible limits, right?" She also said that these limits often make sense, because most students are minors. Lizzie (Lane) gave the example of walking out in protest, stating, "There are some standards that we all know. It's not set in stone, but we know that it's not appropriate to walk out of our high school." Royal (Hilltop) concurred: "You can't petition when you're supposed to be learning in class." Anna argued that both the rules and their consequences are there for a reason, the implication being they are enforced by the adults in the school: "I have the freedom, I have the right to cuss out my teacher, but that doesn't mean that there's not a right that I can't get in trouble for it."

One group from Grove presented a dissenting perspective that these inalienable rights should remain unlimited by government, and that as such any limitations to them should come from self-regulating individuals and communities, meaning not governments or their school administrations. Garrett explained:

> I think an important word to emphasize, especially when these rights were written down for the first time, an important word to emphasize is inalienable, and to me, that word means that you can't limit these rights, that you can't chip away at them, so that's where I draw that from.

Mack agreed with Garrett that "government shouldn't put specific regulations on it ... [speech]" but added the caveat about what she called "professional behavior," which meant regulating one's self so the government doesn't have to. Sergio described the community and its contract with community members as the limiting arbiter:

> I don't see any government regulations suitable to the freedom of speech. I think the freedom of speech should be (linked) to the social contract of each community—each place, different places—because the social contract dictates whether or not you can do something or say something, certain things, do certain things.

A number of students discussed their perceptions that rights are being denied or suppressed in school, acknowledging self-censorship and frustration with overreaching. In a conversation about whether or not the Student Council could advocate for student rights, Makayla and Elena from Hilltop described the school culture as limiting expression:

Makayla: Yeah, but sometimes they [student council] don't always do that. I feel like they're meant for that, but it doesn't always work how we want it to, or how it should, or how it seems to be.

Nancy: What [limits to rights] are you thinking about?

Makayla: All of 'em, really, like, we can do some stuff, but to a certain [degree] restrained, like, we have to stop at some point. Like with speech, with here what we were just talking about, with the teachers, we can't say all of what we want to or what we should.

Elena: Yeah, you can get so far in saying something you wanna say, and then you get stopped, because you're getting told now you can't do it.

Makayla: You don't have your freedom of speech like you're supposed to.

Elizabeth V. (Grove) described the culture of the school as limiting: "But every year, there are rules, on rules, on rules being added and limiting us to what we can do, what we can say." Efie from an urban school (Hilltop) and Jennie from a suburban school (Ridge) both described school contexts in which they felt the need to censor their speech.

Efie: There's teachers in the school that you can go to and talk about anything but then there's some teachers ... I censor myself when I talk to them—keep politics and personal opinions away ... because some teachers had really biased opinions.

Jennie: If a teacher were to overhear you, there's a real fine line that you could say something that might get you in trouble ... depending on who's listening or who finds out, you could possibly get reprimanded for it." One student (anonymous) who transferred and had been at the school only a year described how it felt to him: "I feel that most of those rights aren't accessible to me. I feel that authority within the school looks down on me and thinks that I do not have these rights."

What Does This/Should This Look Like in Schools?

Findings thus far have shown that students place high value on their First Amendment rights in schools and understand their overlapping complexity. They also as a whole accept that various limitations are appropriate and necessary and have questions about how they are being protected and by whom. Focus group discussions rounded out with the question of what the fact of rights and responsibilities might mean for students' school experiences. I asked what advice they had for the adults in their schools pertinent to First Amendment rights and sorted their responses into the following categories: building rapport and relationships, desire for more adult role models, and more active learning classroom environments.

Building Rapport and Relationships. A constant refrain in all groups was the desire for more authentic connections to the adults in their schools. Lucy (Ridge), Royal (Hilltop), Anna (Hilltop), Manuel (Hilltop), Leo (Ravine), Sydney (Ravine), Bradley (Grove), and numerous others started these conversations with simple requests for more listening. Spark (Hilltop) explained:

> outside of school, everything is different. Nobody knows what you're going through ... and sometimes teachers could at least talk to them [before writing them up]. I feel like we should have some more teachers ... that will actually come out and help them—that they want them to succeed, so we can have a lot more students graduating—all of that. A lot of students would really love [it] if teachers cared.

Conversations developed into more nuanced constructions of what "listening" entails and does, beginning with building trust and therefor relationships. As Spark (Hilltop) explained, getting to know who students are and what is going on outside the classroom is key to building trust. Sergio (Grove) noticed when teachers make an effort and are "actually willing to push and willing to get to know their students" that the students will respond in kind. Jania (Glade) discussed how some students in her school seem to be known and heard more than others, describing the privileging of Advanced Placement student voices, stating "we need to recognize who we are, and the position that we're seated at, as students that are AP, like high achieving. The administration is gonna be a lot more prone to hearing what we have to say."

Building trust is not only knowing students and their contexts but also entails affirming that student opinions have value and giving space for that. Bernice (Ravine) thinks that all teachers should push that "Your opinion does matter, and what you say does matter, because in the real world what you say can matter a lot." In discussing press, Aaron (Hilltop) stated he felt teachers should help ensure students have venues for openly expressing their opinions.

Several groups were happy with how well their school environment made room for students' voices. Anastasia (Ravine) said her school has always been "pretty good about that," and Rena (Glade) said "Compared to other schools, the administration is awesome at hearing people out." There also were a number of students who expressed frustration with not getting anywhere with requests for change or of having to worry about consequences for speaking out. Regarding a discussion about a cell phone policy with which the students disagreed, Steve (Lane) explained, "That's the argument, but we can't even have the dialogue in our school anymore with the administration and the teachers. We can't even argue that anymore. It's just shut down right away." Sabrina's (Hilltop) perception was that speech was not very free in her school, because "you get in trouble for basically anything you say here," and Daniel (Grove) had the same experience of feeling like students were not allowed to voice their opinions without consequences.

As for what they feel more rapport and relationships with adults would do for them, a number reinforced Spark's notion that student trust in and rapport with their teachers is motivational and impacts achievement. Edward (Ravine) said that trusting his teachers makes him not want to let them down, that he pays more attention and likes class more. Daniel (Grove) appreciated how rapport with teachers who are "more open" facilitated productive discussions that remained civil: "They'll give you their side, and you can give them your side, and it won't be a big argument." Anna (Hilltop) corroborated this, acknowledging that teachers with whom students shared rapport were more able to undertake discussions of "negative" topics. Jamie (Grove) felt like the best discussion-based classes were those in which she had "an actual connection to the teacher. There's lots of open discussion and everybody gets a say."

In the end, these conversations about desiring more authentic relationships in which they would be heard by the adults in their schools was a desire to be treated more like adults. Asia (Ravine) connected becoming an adult with having a voice in school:

> I feel like most adults don't listen to us, 'cause we're considered children in their eyes ... we're young adults growing up to be adults and we have things that we wanna say that aren't being heard because some of us feel like we can't say it.

Darnell's (Ridge) perception was that the hold on young people was a bit too strong: "It's our generation ... they can hold onto us a little bit, but not that much."

Desire for More Adult Role Models. Overall students share the perspectives that being known and having more freedom of speech would be better and contribute to the building of rapport and relationships in their schools. They also highlighted the kinds of role models they were constantly looking for among the adults in their buildings, discussing the differences they observed between adults and what leaders looked like to them. The implication was that it would enhance the school environment for them if they were able to trust and talk to more teachers in their buildings. Jake (Grove) stated, "Then with freedom of speech, some teachers don't allow you—they tell you to stop talking about this or that. I feel like you can't talk about anything you want to talk about in front of them."

Students sought out teachers who they felt respected their rights and modeled how to use them. One teacher in particular was lauded often for her student advocacy. Sierra (Ravine) described this teacher as "really good at pushing us to use our amendments and use our voice for something" and someone unique in her education who made school important. Anastasia from the same school described how this teacher helped students create a system with school board approval that bridged communication between students and the principal. In her view, that was "a very good thing for the school board to do." She described the school environment as having changed, such that "You feel like you have a teammate, or an advocate, or somebody who cares. We feel like we matter more than we ever have before."

Students from more than one school expressed their admiration for teachers who showed leadership in teaching them civil discourse. Jamie (Grove) described how one of her teachers not only held discussions but helped students develop life-long discussion skills. Garrett (Grove) values teachers like this one who "actually involve themselves with students trying to help benefit the student social experience and have their own personality, whether it's good or bad, it still bonds." Damien (Ravine) had similar admiration for one of his teachers who facilitated classroom civility:

> You can't just go at it just being a hothead and going in complaining about everything you don't like. You've gotta come at it with empathy and see both sides to the story—meet on the middle ground.

More Meaningful and Active Learning. As these students from Grove and Ravine have indicated, how their teachers teach matters as far as student achievement and respect of rights are concerned. The classrooms they most appreciate are those in which the content is meaningful (connected to real life) and teaching is interactive. Isabella (Ravine) appreciated how natural it seemed with one of her teachers who often taught through discussion: "I feel like we learned a lot, it's just that because we have so many discussions, we don't feel like we're learning, but we are."

In these conversations, "meaningful" meant not shying away from controversial topics, connecting content to real life, and not worrying about teaching outside the standards. Anna (Hilltop) felt like "most teachers don't even wanna bring up the subject [something controversial] because it's so negative." The implication is that controversial topics are what's going on and useful for real life. Edward's (Ravine) advice was "teach something we're gonna use." Leila (Ridge) argued that it is "the right of American citizens to talk about controversial topics," and Makayla (Hilltop) corroborated this, stating that "mature conversations about religion, racism, all of that" should be part of a high school education. Royal (Hilltop) made a strong argument for meaning, stating:

> The school should give us more information on what's going on with the world today, because they're preparing us for life outside of high school. They can't prepare us to do that by sheltering us and not telling us enough information.

Discussing discussion is a thread throughout this study, and as indicated above, was valuable to students and central to building rapport and relationships. While the majority favored discussions, they also valued teachers who helped them develop the skill of having civil ones. Several groups in three of the six schools made a point of discussing discussion in terms of how it contributed to learning, arguing for modeling and practice of the skill of civil discourse. Jami (Grove) summarized her teacher's view of the problem of civil discourse in high school. She reported that he spent some time talking about it with government classes:

> [The teacher] "talked about how civil discourse is never taught in school until high school, and at that point, kids have already been told—kids don't want to talk, and when they do talk and voice their opinions, they don't know how to deal with different opinions, and they don't know how to discuss something without arguing.

Steven (Ravine) came from a school in which his teacher modeled and practiced civil discourse with them and described the theory behind it:

> You can't just go at it just being a hothead and going in complaining about everything you don't like. You've gotta come at it with empathy and see both sides to the story—meet on the middle ground.

Aaron (Hilltop) was concerned about his peers having misinformation and wished for teachers to "talk about that stuff with us so that we have the correct information and then we can build [arguments for a discussion]." Mack (Grove) also described a teacher whose approach she appreciated: "He makes it clear he wants us to share, but he also doesn't allow any negativity strictly at another student"; rather, nudging students back on the track of discussing their own opinion and argument behind it. She also made clear that this teacher actively facilitates their discussions, such that he'll help redirect if it "starts to maybe get to be too much."

CONCLUSION AND IMPLICATIONS

Three assertions emerged from the content analysis. First, these students report universally valuing their First Amendment rights and valued and discussed speech the most. Their responses mirror those of students polled over time in the Future of the First Amendment surveys. There was ready acknowledgment that the first five were complex and overlapping. Many discussed the first five as a whole and acknowledged how much they took them for granted.

Second, as evidenced by their thoughtful conversations about the complexity of their rights, students easily acknowledged that rights often must be tempered by responsibilities. There was lack of consensus on various speech and actions and close consensus on others, with more consensus on permissibility of school walkouts than one taking the knee. "Taking the knee" scenarios provoked emotional discussion about whether or not to restrict offensive speech and the interactions of rights and systemic racism. The controversy surrounding some of these issues seems to align with those of the student responses in the *The Future of the First Amendment: 2018 Survey of High School Students and Teachers* regarding whether or not people should be allowed to use speech others consider offensive, where 55% of students stated offensive speech should not be permitted.

Students also discussed limits they want (e.g., the most consensus was on bullying in any form as the limit to speech) and limits they do not want (e.g., limits coming from adults regarding speech and symbolic speech). They also expressed interest in being more involved in who made the decisions about what was permissible and what was not.

Finally, they desire more authentic connections with the adults in their schools. A priority was building rapport and relationships, with listening as a central component; the desire for advocacy and support of more school role models; and more meaningful and active classroom learning. They are keen observers over the 5,000 hours they spend in high schools and have great expectations of and admiration for their schools, particularly for the attentive adults therein.

To some extent, the study bore out my early enthusiasm for Jakoby's comments. These students do have a strong perception of the value of their rights, and many of them readily can connect them to their rights overall in school environments as well as how teachers teach. There were even a number of students who were active in working to make their schools better, although this was not a common thread. This aligns with calls in the research (Fielding, 2012; Haynes et al., 2003; Hess & McAvoy, 2020; Pace, 2019; Parker, 2004; Mitchell, 2016; Youniss, 2011) for schools as places uniquely suited to teach about democracy and the rights of its citizens. Most of these students are some distance away from viewing themselves as part of a governmental process through which people can communicate, compromise, and make things better in public schools. That said, as one can glean from the state of shifting legal limits, this is a common experience, despite age and/or experience.

Like all of us, these young people have more to learn about what their rights are and how to use them. There is more for them to experience in schools in terms of exercising them, as argued by and more power they likely could handle, balanced with a healthy respect for the authority of the adults in their schools. I suspect that this study had an impact on those involved, such that many of these students did recognize some things about themselves and their schools that they had not previously considered (Lawrence-Lightfoot, 1983, p. 6). They take action, and they take offense in their own "little democracy," just like the adults they watch. All of this is to say that these young people are experiencing Schor's "discomforts of democracy" in their peer-to-peer and other school relationships. These 127 students, from diverse backgrounds across six different schools and communities, shared a common and sincere willingness to undertake this journey together with each other and the adults in their schools.

AUTHOR

Correspondence concerning this article should be addressed to Nancy C. Patterson, College of Education and Human Development, Bowling Green State University, Bowling Green, Ohio, 43402. Contact: ncpatte@bgsu.edu

ACKNOWLEDGMENT

This research was funded by Bowling Green State University Institute for the Study of Culture and Society.

REFERENCES

Andolina. M. W., & Conklin, H. G. (2018). Speaking with confidence and listening with empathy: The impact of *Project Soapbox* on high school students, *Theory & Research in Social Education, 46*(3), 374–409. https://doi.org/10.1080/00933104.2018.1435324

Ball, D. L., & Forzani, F. M. (2009). The work of teaching and the challenge of teacher education. *Journal of Teacher Education, 60*, 497–511.

Barton, K. C., & Levstik, L. S. (2013). *Teaching history for the common good*. Routledge.

Bethel School District v. Fraser, 478 U.S. 675 (1986).

Deuchar, R. (2009). Seen and heard, and then not heard: Scottish pupils' experience of democratic educational practice during the transition from primary to secondary school. *Oxford Review of Education, 35*(1), 23–40. https://doi.org/10.1080/03054980802018871

Dewey, J. (1966). *Democracy and education*. Free Press. (Original work published 1916)

Erickson, F. (1986). Qualitative methods in research on teaching. In M. Wittrock (Ed.), *Handbook of research on teaching: A project of the American Educational Research Association* (3rd ed., pp. 119–161). Macmillan.

Fielding, M. (2004). Transformative approaches to student voice: Theoretical underpinnings, recalcitrant realities. *British Educational Research Journal, 30* (2), 295–311. https://doi.org/10.1080/0141192042000195236.

Fielding, M. (2012). Beyond student voice: Patterns of partnership and the demands of deep democracy. *Revista de Educacion, 359*, 45–65. https://doi.org/10.4438/1988-592X-RE-2012-359-195.

Garcetti v. Ceballos 547 US 410 (2006).

Haynes, C. C, Chaltrain, S., Ferguson, J. E., Jr., Hudson, D. L., Jr., & Thomas, O. (2003). *The First Amendment in schools*. ASCD.

Hazelwood School District v. Kuhlmeier, 484 U.S. 260 (1988).

Hess, D., & McAvoy, P. (2015). *The political classroom: Evidence and ethics in democratic education*. Routledge.

Kaka, S. J. (2022). First Amendment rights and speech: Views from students on social media in schools. In N. C. Patterson & P. T. Chandler (Eds.), *At the schoolhouse gate: Stakeholder perceptions of First Amendment rights and responsibilities*. Information Age.

Knight Foundation. (2018a). *Free expression on campus: What college students think about First Amendment issues*. https://knightfoundation.org/reports/free-expression-on-campus-what-college-students-think-about-first-amendment-issues/

Knight Foundation. (2018b). *Future of the First Amendment: 2018 survey of high school students and teachers.* https://kf-site-production.s3.amazonaws.com/media_elements/files/000/000/271/original/Knight-FoFA-HighSchool-18-v2.pdf

Lawrence-Lightfoot, S. (1983). *The good high school: Portraits of character and culture.* Basic Books.

Mitchell, C. (2016) Educating for freedom and responsibility: Lessons from the First Amendment schools project. *Journalism & Mass Communication Educator, 71*(2) 203–219. https://doi.org/10.1177/1077695815587608

Morse v. Frederick, 551 U.S. 393 (2007).

Nelson, J. L. (2021). Academic freedom and issues-based education. In R. W. Evans (Ed.), *Handbook on teaching social issues* (2nd ed.). Charlotte, NC: Information Age Press. Manuscript in preparation.

Pace, J. L. (2019). Contained risk-taking: Preparing preservice teachers to teach controversial issues in three countries. *Theory & Research in Social Education, 47*(2), 228–260. https://doi.org/10.1080/00933104.2019.1595240

Patrick, J. J. (1999). Concepts at the core of education for democratic citizenship. In C. F. Bahmueller & J. J. Patrick (Eds.), *Principles and practices for democratic citizenship: International perspectives and projects* (pp. 1–40). ERIC Clearinghouse for Social Studies/Social Science Education.

Parker, W. C. (2004). Diversity, globalization, and democratic education: Curriculum possibilities. In J. A. Banks (Ed.), *Diversity and citizenship education: Global perspectives* (pp. 433–458). Jossey-Bass.

Shor, I. (1996). *When students have power: Negotiating authority in a critical pedagogy.* University of Chicago Press.

Suskey, R. (2022). A more complicated story: Student free speech in public K–12 education. In N. C. Patterson & P. T. Chandler (Eds.), *At the schoolhouse gate: Stakeholder perceptions of First Amendment rights and responsibilities.* Information Age.

Tinker v. Des Moines Independent Community School District, 39 U.S. 503 (1969).

Villasenior, J. (2017). *Views among college students regarding the First Amendment: A new survey.* http://brook.gs/2h028tD

Yin, R.K. (2018). *Case study research and applications.* SAGE.

Youniss, J. (2011). Civic education: What schools can do to encourage civic identity and action. *Applied Developmental Science, 15*(2), 98–103. https://doi.org/10.1080/10888691.2011.560814

APPENDIX A: FOCUS GROUP PROTOCOL

I will start with a First Amendment rights sorting activity as a reminder, and then open things up with some broad questions such as these, asking for teachers and students to give tangible examples:

1. How important do think these rights are? Is there any one you see as more important than the others?

2. Some argue that the granting of these rights goes too far. Do you agree? Why or why not?
3. What responsibilities do you think you have related to your First Amendment rights?

Should we have time and the issues indicated below have not been addressed, I may propose any among the following scenarios for further discussion, asking participants to discuss whether they agree or disagree and why:

1. People should be allowed to express unpopular opinions.
2. People should be allowed to post their own videos/photographs on the Internet without anyone's permission, including those who are in the videos/pictures.
3. High school students should be allowed to report on controversial issues in their student newspapers without the approval of school authorities.
4. High school athletes should be allowed to take the knee during the anthem.

CHAPTER 4

PRACTICING FREE EXPRESSION IN SCHOOLS THROUGH STUDENT-LED CONFERENCES

A Review of Literature

Cheryl Lambert
Austin Peay State University

As students practice skills of communication, self-evaluation, accountability, and responsibility, the incorporation of student-led conferencing provides a unique format for academic conversations and democratic practices in schools. Allowing students to lead in the conversation offers the pride and sense of accomplishment that accompanies success, encourages the freedom of expressing a defense of their efforts at school, and supports their potential for creative problem-solving. Students are encouraged to self-advocate for their First Amendment right of free speech regarding their academic progress. This review of literature describes student-led conferences, offering guidance for school leaders seeking democratic solutions for students. It argues for student choice and a voice in the presentation of their accomplishments by modifying traditional models of conferencing formats.

At the Schoolhouse Gate: Stakeholder Perceptions of First Amendment Rights and Responsibilities in U.S. Public Schools, pp. 79–98
www.infoagepub.com
Copyright © 2022 by Information Age Publishing
All rights of reproduction in any form reserved.

The communication systems in schools, designed to support teaching and learning, encompass all stakeholders invested in student learning progressions. Students can and should play an integral part in advocating for themselves throughout their educational journey; in reality, they are the most important users of the data produced in classrooms across the country. Students are therefore the best qualified to share their academic strengths and challenges with other stakeholders (Black & Wiliam, 1998). This powerful position affords many opportunities for self-advocacy that empowers students to take charge of their own learning, set goals, and develop insights into themselves as learners. As they practice speaking freely about their own perceptions of their progress in learning, they develop confidence in demonstrating a growth mindset for success (Dweck, 2006).

In our country, schools are expected to foster independence by providing opportunities for student practice of a variety of leadership skills and by facilitating these experiences from a caring, professional vantage point. Are schools supporting such freedom of speech, or are they deterring the understanding of essential democratic skills? Are schools infringing on the rights of students to advocate for a stronger voice in the delivery methods of their own assessment data and academic progress? Student-led conferences (SLC) are intended to give students this voice, thereby promoting freedom of speech as they lead conversations about their own academic growth. A traditional treatment of conferencing is common, but SLC offers another viable option for schools.

In the ever-changing landscape of education, viewing academic conversations through the lens of students' First Amendment rights opens doors of opportunity for students. These conversation opportunities allow practice for students to engage in meaningful free expression. Many schools choose to plan academic calendars to include time for what has traditionally been termed the parent-teacher conference. In this chapter, the usage of parent(s) has been updated to guardian(s) to include nontraditional families. This review of the current literature examines the background of traditional and student-led models of conferencing, the components of implementation, the responses, the benefits and challenges, and the limits to research regarding student-led conferencing.

BACKGROUND: TRADITIONAL VERSUS SLC

The legislation of the Every Student Succeeds Act (114th Congress, 2015) guarantees regular academic communication with guardians. A scheduled academic conference between teachers, guardians, and students is one way to meet this guarantee, whereby stakeholders discuss academic progress, assessment data, and learning goals. These academic discussions are generally conducted in one of two formats—traditional or student led.

The traditional format of a guardian-teacher conference focuses mainly on the teacher's perspective of progress and goals and usually communicates norm-referenced assessment results along with behavioral information about the student. "In a traditional parent[sic]-teacher conference, the adults meet and discuss the child's progress and areas for improvement" (Fuge, 2018, p. 19). This type of conference is conducted in a one-to-one setting with the guardians and the teacher. Traditionally, the format of the meeting is structured as a private conversation between the teacher and guardians, and "the student who is the center of the conversation is not present at the meeting" (Fuge, 2018, p. 1). Students may not be aware of their own assessment scores being shared with their guardians. After the conference, the student receives feedback from the guardians that is filtered, based on the importance assigned to it by the guardians (Fuge, 2018).

In contrast, the format of SLC, allows students to self-advocate using their own work-sample portfolios that showcase skills in multiple applications of the curricular objectives. According to Tuinstra and Hiatt-Michael (2004), the SLC format has these distinct characteristics:

1. The students attend the conference with their guardians. The students are not left at home or out in the hallway of the school, excluded from the conversation that is all about them.
2. The students are given the leading role in the conversation with their guardians instead of being an uninvolved observer. This platform encourages students to explore the freedom of speech about their own learning. The students spend time preparing for the conference by choosing their own work samples, familiarizing themselves with a script (guided language for the conversation), and setting goals for the next steps in learning.
3. The students conduct periodic checkpoints throughout the reporting period to assess their progress in meeting their academic goals for the school year (pp. 68–29).

The teacher serves as the facilitator for the conference between the student and guardians, by moving from a teacher-directed position to a student-support position. At a designated time during the conference, the student signals the teacher to join the conversation. Guardians then ask questions that are directed to the teacher. This SLC format supports family-school communications and offers insight into the student's learning processes, acknowledging the powerful rights of students to voice their learning potential. "The better the communication between the home and school, the less stress the child experiences as he navigates between these two cultures" (Hiatt-Michael, 2001, p. 39). Opportunities for positive interactions between students, guardians, and teachers in the school environment can favorably impact the students' ongoing educational progress. "By listening and evaluating student work through a student-led conference, teachers and parents [sic] can learn a great deal about how to help individual students succeed and excel" (Bailey & Guskey, 2001, p. 11).

COMPONENTS OF SLC

SLC are characterized by several specific components that provide structure for the conference setting. These elements include practicing the dialogue, self-evaluating the work evidence, including guardians in the process, setting goals, and compiling portfolios to present to guardians during the conference. As students, guardians, and teachers develop confidence with these conferencing skills, the effectiveness of SLC becomes evident (Buchino, 2011; Lambert, 2016; Tuinstra & Hiatt-Michael, 2004).

Practice

According to pre- and postsurveys for student-led conferencing (Bailey & Guskey, 2001; Lambert, 2015), students gained confidence by rehearsing conferencing procedures and offering implementation suggestions. Developing a set of guiding documents for students, guardians, and teachers that guided them step by step (Appendix A) proved important for preparing all stakeholders for the SLC conferencing experience. Lambert (2015) noted that students needed support to talk about the rigorous standards and high expectations set forth on instructional rubrics; however, students wanted to lead the discussion. One student commented, "I was glad to be able to talk about my work in my own words" (Lambert, 2015, p. 17).

Self-Evaluation

Self-evaluation involves the process of setting standards and using them for self-judgment (Hattie, 2012). Some of the evidence used for self-evaluation could include formative assessment, summative assessment, academic feedback, and data notebooks. Buchino (2011) implemented SLC with seventh- and eighth-grade students to engage in self-evaluating strengths and challenges. The students were placed in teams, coached with practice and role-playing, and given a packet of information with a sample script. SLC were scheduled during the fall with optional traditional conferences; however, guardians did not take this option.

Guardian Participation

Guardian participation in traditional conferences diminishes as students get older. This decline in guardian participation discourages student ownership of academic proficiency. Tuinstra and Hiatt-Michael (2004) examined the development and effect of SLC at four middle schools across four states including students (N = 524), guardians and administrators, reporting that guardian participation increased significantly to a minimum of 92% participation at all four schools.

Goal Setting

Another aspect of conducting a successful SLC is the goal-setting activity which encourages students to take a closer look at their data and the expected outcomes. Student surveys from one study indicated positive responses toward "assessing their work, reflecting on that work, and setting goals to challenge themselves" (Tuinstra & Hiatt-Michael, 2004, p. 8). Students indicated that they were better students because they set goals. They also felt that their work was better because they spent more time on it. Teaching students to set goals should be intentional and direct. Lambert (2016) included goal setting instruction (Appendix B) in a pilot study with one group of elementary students. Goal setting provides another layer to the students' academic investment in the student-led conference.

Reflection and correction are higher order skills needed to improve and grow academically.

> Conferences with students as participants are a natural extension of learning when students have previously self-assessed and set their own goals. The conferences then provide the opportunity for students to reflect on and share what they know about themselves as learners. (Stiggins et al., 2006, p. 361)

This sharing is a free expression of the students' valued goals. Goals are not predetermined by teachers. Instead, they are developed and discussed with students. This cooperative learning experience has powerful

First Amendment connections, helping students develop their patterns and experiences in a free speech environment.

Portfolios

An academic portfolio of learning experiences provides students with the appropriate tools for demonstrating their performance at school. Academic portfolios should include quality evidence, collected over time, produced by the students for use during the student-led conference to guide student-led discussions. These portfolios may take various forms. Whether paper based or technologically enhanced, the portfolios offer students opportunities to maintain, select, edit, and evaluate quality evidence for presentation during a student-led conference (Bayez, 2013; Chatel, 2003; Duffy & McDonald, 2015). When students "communicate their learning using a variety of work samples, they go beyond what grades, numbers, and scores alone can show; they are able to examine the depth, the detail, and the range of their own learning" (Gregory et al., 2011, p. 15). This deeper grasp of metacognition helps students and teachers determine the next steps for learning. The components of the student-led conference lend structure to the conversation while responses to this type of conferencing provide indicators for acceptance and improvement.

FAVORABLE RESPONSES TOWARD STUDENT-LED CONFERENCING

Three research studies showcase student-led conferencing, providing support for this nontraditional format (Brodie, 2014; Hackmann et al., 1995; Lambert, 2016). In the first study, Hackmann et al. (1995) discuss the impact on conference attendance and format preferences. The faculty at a Midwestern middle school developed a model for SLC "to encourage students to accept responsibility for their academic success, to increase students' oral communication skills, self-confidence, and to increase guardian participation" (Hackmann et al., 1995, p. 4). Results from this study indicated that 93.1% of the guardians attended the conference, an increase from the 89% to 90% attendance data for traditional conferences. According to questionnaire results, 94% of the guardians preferred the student-led format, and 95% of the students preferred the student-led format. Teachers also indicated strong support for the student-led model.

In the second study, Brodie (2014) conducted a student-led conferencing pilot study at two middle schools in preparation for program changes within the school district. Data from this study revealed that 89% of the guardians preferred the student-led format for conferences. Also in Brodie's (2014) study, guardians could see evidence that their children were self-aware of their learning (81%), were well-prepared (84%), and were showing academic growth (84%). While teachers originally felt reluctant to relinquish their leading role in the conference, student-led conferencing outcomes supported an acceptance of this shift of responsibility (Brodie, 2014). Teachers noted that giving students a voice in the presentation of their work helped to personalize their educational experience.

In the third study (Lambert, 2016), indicated similar results of positive perceptions about the conferencing format. Students and guardians attended a student-led conference at the beginning of the year and a traditional conference near the end of the year. In the conference survey near the end of the year guardians, students, and teachers compared the two formats. The results indicated a preference for SLC over traditional conferences. There was no significant difference in the perceptions of guardians when compared to the perceptions of students; therefore, both groups demonstrated similar positive perceptions. Responses to the survey questions and statistical data that indicated similar positive perceptions from guardians and students provided support for the continued implementation of SLC.

All three studies showcase the positive responses to student-led conferencing from different viewpoints—students, guardians, and teachers. The data reveal consistently positive attitudes toward the impacts of conferencing when students take the lead. Along with positive responses toward SLC, many benefits exist for students, guardians, and teachers. Examining these benefits allows conversations about communication to continue.

BENEFITS FOR STUDENTS, GUARDIANS, AND TEACHERS

As noted above, the perception of the value of SLC is well-documented in educational research for students, guardians, and teachers. Specific benefits arise from the successful implementation of student-led conferencing. The positive impacts on accountability, academic outcomes, guardian engagement, and collaboration support the use of student-led conferencing in schools.

Accountability

By giving students a voice in the conferencing experience, students consistently reported increased "confidence and pride, and actually, some amount of surprise in their ability to explain their work, to set goals, and to express their attitudes about school and learning to their guardians and other significant adults" (Bailey & Guskey, 2001, pp. 9–10). This empowerment is capable of permeating other aspects of their day-to-day lives. Simply transforming the way students, guardians, and teachers engage in free, expressive conversations about academic progress has a positive impact on student accountability.

According to Kinney (2012), teachers became convinced that SLC helped transfer accountability to students. "Student-led conferencing is one effective assessment strategy that shifts the focus of accountability to the student" (Kinney, 2012, p. 55). Excluding the students from the conference fails to acknowledge their insight and input toward their own educational growth and behaviors (Tuinstra & Hiatt-Michael, 2004). Results from Buchino's (2011) online questionnaire following SLC implementation with middle-school students indicated that the guardians preferred the student-led conference to the traditional conference, students took responsibility for their own learning, and teachers felt prepared for the conferences.

Hackmann, Kenworthy, and Nibbelink (1995) explained that during traditional conferences teachers may find it difficult to discuss problem behaviors with the guardians, and teachers may experience negative responses from guardians. The traditional format provides little or no experience for students to practice their First Amendment rights of free speech at school. The power and importance of free speech could be better realized in an alternate conferencing format, such as student-led conferencing.

Academic Outcomes

Focusing on student involvement in formative-assessment practices and culminating in a summative student-led conference produces a positive impact on student achievement (Tuinstra & Hiatt-Michael, 2004, p. 65). As students build academic skills in schools on a daily basis, the desire to share their progress is realized in a student-led conferencing experience. Including the students in the conferencing conversation adds a valuable layer of communication about academic outcomes. Without this layer of student involvement, an important piece of the puzzle that represents student learning is missing (Clark, 2012).

Multiple aspects of formative assessment, such as academic feedback, rubrics, higher order questioning, peer assessment, and self-evaluative assessment, provide teachers and students the opportunity to collaborate in the learning process. Tuinstra and Hiatt-Michael (2004) reported that teachers agreed that students were more focused and that SLC had contributed to higher academic success. The SLC event allows students the free expression of their perceptions of academic pursuits.

Lambert's (2016) pilot study in one elementary school examined the impact of student-led conferencing on universal screening scores for one group of third-grade students. The students participated in collecting work evidence, practicing for their conference, and setting goals for their academic progress. The screening scores for all students improved over time regardless of participation in the actual student-led conference. Lambert's (2016) study indicated that benefits reside in the preparation process. "Since all of the students in the third-grade class participated in the preparation, practice, and formative instruction leading up to the SLC event, the expectations included an increase in universal screening scores for all of the students" (p. 81). Students were active in choosing the evidence that best represented their skill sets. This evidence was presented to parents during the conference and goals were established. Academic goals that are set by students, communicated to parents, and supported by teachers can be a guiding force behind student achievement.

Offering the opportunity for students to take the lead in the presentation of their own work evidence in the form of a student-led conference encourages ownership and responsibility for quality outcomes with the potential for academic success. "When students are engaged as active participants in their own learning progression they believe that they are capable learners who use goal setting strategies and independently regulate their efforts as they apprehend desired outcomes" (Clark, 2012, p. 242). One teacher's response reflected this change in mindset, "Listening to my kids talk to their parents [sic] with dignity and respect has completely changed my faith and belief in the ultimate goals of [SLC]" (Kinney, 2012, p. 57). According to Lambert (2016), three survey indicators approached significance, indicating a positive change in perceptions toward the guardian involvement, the reliability of the guardian commitment, the belief that guardians do a good job, and the belief that students can achieve goals.

Guardian Engagement

Offering conferencing options provides multiple opportunities for guardians to be involved in the conversations. Guardians could request the opportunity to meet with the teacher in a traditional format in addition to, or in place of, the student-led format; however, according to one middle-school study (Culver & Cousino, 2000), only 1–3% of guardians requested a traditional conference format. According to Culver and

Cousino (2000), SLC can be accomplished in 9 hours for about 100 students. Guardians reported that SLC had the advantage of a scheduled time; this accommodation alleviated wait time in an arena setting. The guardians also considered SLC to be more meaningful and informative since some students do not share academic information at home.

Culver and Cousino's (2000) research implied that guardians who saw their child's work evidence in the student-led conference were motivated to take more responsibility for interventions at home. Similar results were evident in Lambert's (2016) pilot study with one rural elementary school. A Mann-Whitney test indicated that the perceptions of the student-led conference regarding the question that the conference experience will help provide better support at home/school was greater for guardians ($M = 163.0$) than for students ($M = 138.0$; $U = 60.0$, $p = 0.28$). "Teachers need to learn to value the knowledge of parents [sic] and recognize the contributions that they can make to the children's success in school" (Shim, 2013, p. 7). Guardians experience the impact of their support at home when they participate in a conversation with their children at school about their academic progress. Tuinstra and Hiatt-Michael (2004) reported positive responses from guardians including (a) feelings of pride toward their child for leading a conference, (b) requests for the continuation of the SLC format, and (c) student academic success following participation in student-led conferencing.

Collaboration

Students develop the capacity to evaluate work products, self-manage assessment data, and lead discussions with others. "Students who believe that they are capable learners are ready to assess their own work, identify their current strengths and weaknesses and be productive and persistent in planning the next steps they need to take to make improvements" (Clark, 2012, p. 236). The collaborative work between students and teachers initiates the release of freedom of expression, empowering students to move forward with their learning. Collaborative inquiry lends itself to student involvement in assessment (Love, 2009). "Collaborative inquiry is the bridge that enables schools to connect the increasing amount of school data available to improve student learning" (Love, 2009). Establishing collaborative inquiry rests on the following tenets: "distribute leadership and capacity, build collaborative teams, use data frequently and in depth, focus on instructional improvement, nurture a collaborative culture based on commitment to equity and trust" (Love, 2009). This approach to using data focuses on the benefits and opportunities afforded to students, working in tandem with teachers and guardians, to improve their own academic achievement.

CHALLENGES OF SLC

This format, however, offers challenges for effective implementation in schools where the traditional format is favored and structural changes to common practices are treated with skepticism. The challenges of time, absent guardians, insufficient preparation, grade level/school size, and rural environments must be considered before student-led conferencing can be successfully implemented.

Time

According to McBride et al. (2002), the most significant barrier to guardian involvement is time. Traditional conferencing formats can heavily impact the amount of time the guardians must set aside to be at the school. Teachers and schools designate limited times to conduct conferences with guardians. Creating the necessary time to conduct a student-led conference can be challenging. Guardians may have busy after-school schedules, travel long distances to the school, work during scheduled conferencing hours, have limited options for personal transportation, or have negative relationships with schools. A variety of options for guardian attendance such as early morning, late evening, or in the home, could improve equity of access to more guardians.

While several SLC can occur simultaneously in the classroom, guardians may be uncomfortable with this use of their conference time. If guardians request a traditional conference in addition to the student-led conference, teachers may feel overwhelmed by the extra demands on their time. Preparing for SLC also takes time; however, according to Kinney (2012), schools that have invested the time and effort to make this shift from a traditional format to a student-led format have demonstrated improvements in attendance. Since implementing SLC to support their 4-year plan for tracking the progress of all students, an Oregon high school experienced a 5-year attendance average at the conferences of 97%, representing a 15% growth in attendance.

Absent Guardians

Guardians' attendance is crucial to a successful student-led conference. When guardians fail to attend the conference, the students are left with a portfolio, a prepared presentation and no audience. Some schools choose to create an all-hands-on-deck approach to SLC. They develop a list of volunteers or school employees to take the role of guardians for the students. The volunteers listen to the students present their portfolios, they look at their work samples, and they offer encouragement to the students for their willingness to advocate for themselves despite their absent guardians. These volunteers may be employees that see the students every day, such as cafeteria workers or custodial staff. Another option is to take the student-led conference to the guardians, offering a home visit. This level of support for students who are seeking to express their rights of self-advocacy and to make their case using the evidential portfolio is a powerful tool for practicing their First Amendment right of free speech.

Insufficient Preparation

The student-led conference requires planning and preparation. The students perform better with practice, a script, and a comfortable level of teacher support. There are many responsibilities involved in teaching from day to day in the classroom; therefore, teachers have limited time to allow for rehearsing a student-led conference. As students create their portfolio of academic evidence they may need guidance for that decision-making process. Choosing work samples should be intentional and selective. Taking time to decide whether to include exemplary work samples, samples that show growth, samples for specific subjects, assessment results, or behavioral reports can be a challenge. School leaders' understanding of SLC is crucial to effective implementation. Suggestions for school leaders, generated from the Tuinstra and Hiatt-Michael (2004) study, included a 10-step process to implement SLC. The process involved reading the informational literature about student-led conferencing, visiting schools already using student-led conferencing, consulting an educational expert in student-led conferencing, and teaching students to be responsible for their learning by setting goals and evaluating their work. With the support of school leaders, guardians, teachers, and students the SLC environment can be a powerful place for free expression.

Grade Level, School Size

Grade level and school size create differences that impact the implementation of successful SLC. Young students may need more practice, fewer work samples, and stronger teacher support to feel confident in their student-led conference. Large schools attempting to schedule SLC may face challenges of time and space. Conducting multiple conferences simultaneously, developing creative conferencing schedules, and enlisting comprehensive staff participation (counselors, coaches, librarians, etc.) are a few ways to address the logistically challenges of student-led conferencing.

LIMITS TO STUDENT-LED CONFERENCING RESEARCH

While current research supports the student-led conferencing format, implementation of SLC is limited (Minke & Anderson, 2003), hindering schools from embracing the nontraditional format of student-led conferencing. Also, research regarding guardian involvement in schools inconsistently represents a variety of school settings and environments. "Unlike the body of literature about urban parents [sic], few studies have explored the strengths, weaknesses, or concerns that might be unique to rural parents [sic]" (Graham & Underwood, 2012, p. 1233). It is likely that guardian involvement or partnership practices in rural schools may differ from other settings; however, too few studies have been conducted with research questions that investigate the unique and specific effects of the rural setting on family-school connections and outcomes (Semke & Sheridan, 2012).

Student-led conferencing also offers a strong strategy for serving students with disabilities and English language learners. These underrepresented student populations often react positively to the student-led conferencing format (Conderman, 2000; Shim, 2013). By examining the impact of student-led conferencing on rural students, students with disabilities, and English language learners, conversations shift toward transforming conferencing scenarios in schools and classrooms around the nation.

Rural Environments

The focus on rural environments offers another layer to the conversation. Over 7.1 million students attend rural schools in the United States, warranting a need for investigating the current phenomena of guardian-school relationships in rural schools. Nearly half of these students are from low-income families. More than one in four is a child of color, and one in nine has changed residence in the previous year (Showalter et al., 2014). Graduation rates demonstrate conflicting data regarding rural school graduates. "Rural high school graduation rates exceed the national average, even among rural low-income students. Nonetheless, rural students overall are significantly less likely to hold a college degree than students in metropolitan areas, 51% to 62% respectively" (Center for Public Education, 2018).

The rural learning environment is unique and complex, representing differences in family structure and economic status. According to the U.S. Census Bureau (2010), there are 41.7% single-guardian households in the southern region of the United States, making it the region with the largest percentage of single-guardian households in the entire United States. More than 20% of the nation's 2,000 poorest performing high schools are located in rural areas, and 3.4 million American students currently attend rural high schools (Alliance for Excellent Education, 2010). Rural schools require multiple things from educators who work in these environments, and those obligations differ from what might be required in urban settings.

Geographic isolation influences rural schools in many ways (Chalker, 2002; King, 2012; Semke & Sheridan, 2012). Students, guardians, and teachers face school challenges imposed by rural location which may impede their participation at the school. As mentioned earlier in this chapter, time is a significant factor for all guardians; however, academic research also reports the environmental differences between urban and rural areas which impact guardians' involvement at school. Long distances to the school, unavailable transportation, and conflicting work schedules are a few associated roadblocks to guardian engagement at rural schools (Semke & Sheridan, 2012).

Two specific studies emphasize the barriers to guardian support at rural schools. A qualitative study conducted by Graham and Underwood (2012) involving nine focus groups and five interviews to examine rural guardians' access of support services revealed several barriers to accessing services. While urban locations present similar barriers, the following barriers strongly influenced rural areas in the Graham and Underwood (2012) study: receiving information with limited rural electronic services, scheduling convenient times for single-guardian families to attend school events, and expecting transportation to rural schools after school hours. Weiss and Correa (1996) reported from a panel of school administrators and teachers in rural Florida demonstrating barriers confronting teachers, such as isolation and poverty of students, lack of guardian involvement in schools, insufficient numbers of professional staff, and limited educational programs and funding. Considering the impact of geographic barriers to guardian involvement is important for successful student-led conferencing. Free expression in schools for *all* students should hold high value in all learning environments.

Students With Disabilities

Conderman et al. (2000) discussed three important reasons for the implementation of SLC in inclusion settings involving students with disabilities who receive instruction guided by an instructional education plan. Traditional conferences generally exclude students with disabilities, focus mainly on the teacher's perspective of progress and goals, and usually communicate only norm-referenced assessment results. In contrast, SLC offer work-sample portfolios that showcase strengths while providing a platform for free speech, encouraging students with disabilities to self-advocate.

English Language Learners

In a study conducted by Shim (2013), three themes emerged as obstacles affecting guardian-teacher interactions for English language learners (ELL): teachers' judgments toward ELL students, lack of influence on the teacher's decisions, and fear of speaking up. Shim (2013) suggests efforts in "facilitating ELL parent [sic]-teacher communication[s] that are open and collaborative which in turn will benefit ELL students' educational, social, and emotional growth" (p. 7). With school settings and diverse populations in mind, school leaders are then able to consider alternatives to the traditional model of conferencing. Student-led conferencing offers one alternative model. Developing intentional structural components for the conferencing event helps build an environment that is primed for positive interactions with English language learners and their parents.

CONCLUSION

If school leaders want to empower students with their First Amendment rights of free expression, they should take a closer look at communication in schools. Supporting student leadership in schools requires a reexamination of the communication methods between students, guardians, and teachers. Students are seeking more autonomy in their involvement in educational conversations, guardians deserve more consideration for their time and influence, and schools must examine more authentic ways of encouraging freedom of expression. This chapter described the background of conferencing methods, building a case for a closer examination of the student-led format. The student-led model is perceived as the preferred method of conferencing, including rural students, students with disabilities, and English language learners. Traditional academic conferences, which are not designed to include students as leaders, usually exclude students from the meetings. The teachers and guardians discuss the student's academic progress, share grades, talk about behavior and possibly discuss improvement strategies without the involvement of the student.

In contrast to the traditional format, a student-led format transfers the rights and responsibilities of the discussion to the students. The components of the SLC include practice, self-evaluation, guardian participation, goal setting, and portfolios. The students lead the conference, sometimes following a script, usually guided by previous practice and coaching from the teacher. The teacher facilitates the conversation by being available during the conferencing sessions to offer support to the students. The students share evidence of their learning in the form of assessments, writing projects, math tasks, etc. during the conference. Students take pride in their work, demonstrate communication skills, and practice advocating for a defense of their work products.

Favorable responses toward the SLC format were demonstrated with three showcase studies—Hackmann et al. (1995); Brodie (2014); and Lambert (2016). These studies highlighted the impact of using the SLC format. Evidence indicated stronger preferences for the SLC format over traditional guardian-teacher format, improved academic outcomes, and increased guardian participation in conferencing events.

The benefits of the SLC format were expressed through accountability, academic outcomes, guardian engagement, and collaboration. By offering students a voice in the conversation, the potential is presented for impacting student achievement and commitment. Students self-evaluate, set goals, and monitor their own progress. Democratic practices are developed and encouraged as teachers relinquish the control of sole communicator in the guardians-school arena. The students are placed in the driver's seat, guided by people who are invested in their success. Challenges exist in the limits of time, absent guardians, preparation, grade level/school size, and the type of environments, specifically rural settings. These benefits and challenges are to be weighed carefully by school leaders as they seek alternate forms of communication with educational stakeholders.

Not only does a student-led conference provide a culminating event to formative practices conducted in the school setting, but it also provides the catalyst for refinement and adjustment to ongoing student learning. By sharing the assessment process with students using their work as evidence and allowing them to lead guardians through the process of self-evaluation carried out by the students, an effective cooperative bond develops between students, guardians, and teachers with the ultimate goals of positively impacting student achievement, improving guardian-school relationships, and supporting students' rights to a quality education and free expression of their academic progress.

AUTHOR NOTE

Correspondence concerning this chapter should be addressed to Cheryl Lambert, Eriksson College of Education, Austin Peay State University, Clarksville, Tennessee, 37044. Contact: lambertc@apsu.edu

REFERENCES

114th Congress. (2015). Every Student Succeeds Act. Pub. L. No. 114-95. https://www.gpo.gov/fdsys/pkg/BILLS-114s1177enr/pdf/BILLS-114s1177enr.pdf

Alliance for Excellent Education. (2010). *Current challenges and opportunities in preparing rural high school students for success in college and career: What federal policymakers need to know.* Alliance for Excellent Education.

Bailey, J., Jr., & Guskey, T. (2001). *Implementing student-led conferences.* Corwin.

Bayez, J. (2013). An intermediate school transition to electronic portfolios [Lecture notes]. http://scholarspace.manoa.hawaii.edu/handle/10125/27136/

Black, P., & Wiliam, D. (1998). Inside the black box: Raising standards through classroom assessment. *Phi Delta Kappan, 80*(2), 139–144, 146–148.

Brodie, B. (2014). Student-led conferences. *Principal Leadership, 15*(1), 34–37.

Buchino, M. (2011). Student-led conferences give junior high students insights into their academic strengths and challenges. *Momentum, 42*(4), 54–56.

Center for Public Education (2018). *Out of the loop: At a glance.* http://www.centerforpubliceducation.org/Main-Menu/Public-education/Out-of-the-Loop-At-a-Glance

Chalker, D. (2002). *Leadership for rural schools.* Scarecrow Press.

Chatel, R. (2003). The power and potential of electronic literacy assessment: E-portfolios and more. *New England Reading Association Journal, 39*(1), 1–7.

Clark, I. (2012). Formative assessment: Assessment is for self-regulated learning. *Educational Psychology Review, 24*(2), 205–249.

Conderman, G., Ikan, P., & Hatcher, R. (2000). Student-led conferences in inclusive settings, *Intervention in School and Clinic, 36*(1), 22–26.

Culver, L., & Cousino, G. (2000). Building a partnership. *Schools in the Middle, 9*(5), 12–15.

Duffy, J., & McDonald, J. (2015). *Teaching and learning with technology* (5th ed.) Pearson.

Dweck, C. (2006). *Mindset: The new psychology of success.* Random House.

Fuge, D. (2018). *Student-led conferences by first-grade students: Parent perspectives* (Doctoral dissertation). https://search.proquest.com/openview/13749e693bcf6be1d9a14fac4536c806/1?pq-origsite=gscholar&cbl=18750&diss=y

Graham, K., & Underwood, K. (2012). The reality of rurality: Rural parents' experiences of early years services. *Health & Place, 18*(8), 1231–1239.

Gregory, K., Cameron, C., & Davies, A. (2011). *Knowing what counts: Conferencing and reporting* (2nd ed.). Solution Tree.

Hackmann, D., Kenworthy, J., & Nibbelink, S. (1998). Student empowerment through student-led conferences. *Middle School Journal, 30*(1), 35–39. https://doi.org/10.1080/00940771.1998.11494561

Hattie, J. (2012). *Visible learning for teachers: Maximizing impact on learning*. Routledge.

Hiatt-Michael, D. (Ed.). (2001). Home-school communication. In *Promising practices for family involvement in schools* (pp. 39–57). Information Age.

King, S. (2012). Increasing college-going rate, parent involvement, and community participation in rural communities. *The Rural Educator, 33*(2), 20–26.

Kinney, P. (2012). Student-led conferences support learning. *Principal Leadership, 13*(3), 55–57.

Lambert, C. (2015). An analysis of the impact of the initial implementation of student-led conferences with third-grade students in one elementary school. *Tennessee Educational Leadership, 42*(2), 14–19.

Lambert, C. (2016). *An analysis of the initial implementation of student-led conferences in a rural elementary school with third-grade reading students* (Doctoral dissertation). https://umwa.memphis.edu/etd/

Love, N. (2009). *Using data to improve learning for all: A collaborative inquiry approach*. Corwin.

McBride, B., Bea, J., & Wright, M. (2002). An examination of family-school partnership initiatives in rural prekindergarten programs. *Early Education and Development, 13*(1), 107–127.

Semke, C., & Sheridan, S. (2012). Family-school connections in rural educational settings: A systematic review of the empirical literature. *School Community Journal, 22*(1), 21–48.

Shim, J. (2013). Involving the parents of English language learners in a rural area: Focus on the dynamics of teacher-parent interactions. *Rural Educator, 34*(3), 18–26.

Showalter, D., Klein, R., Johnson, J., & Hartman, S. (June, 2017). *Why rural matters (2015-2016): Understanding the changing landscape* (Report of the Rural School and Community Trust). https://www.ruraledu.org/user_uploads/file/WRM-2015-16.pdf

Stiggins, R., Arter, J., Chappuis, J., & Chappuis, S. (2006). *Classroom assessment for student learning: Doing it right, using it well*. Pearson.

Tuinstra, C., & Hiatt-Michael, D. (2004). Student-led parent conferences in middle schools. *School Community Journal, 14*(1), 59–80.

U.S. Census Bureau. (2010). *2010 census urban and rural classification and urban area criteria*. https://www.census.gov/programs-surveys/geography/guidance/geo-areas/urban-rural/2010-urban-rural.html

Weiss, K., & Correa, V. (1996). Challenges and strategies for early childhood special education services in Florida's rural schools: A DELPHI study. *Journal of Research in Rural Education, 12*(1), 33–43.

APPENDIX A

Directions to students:

1. Introduce your guardians to your teacher.
2. Tell your guardians that you will be showing them your school work.
3. Look at the Table of Contents.
4. Read aloud your "Dear Guardian" letter.
5. Show your work following the order of the table of contents.
   (a) What was your score?
   (b) What did you learn from this work?
   (c) What is your self-reflection about your work? "Self-reflection" is how you feel about the quality of your work and why.
6. Share your progress report.
7. Read the two goals you have set.
8. Write the third goal with your guardians.
9. Ask your guardians to read the homework letter.
10. Say "thank you," to your guardians.

Directions to teachers:

1. Provide logistical support for the conference.
2. Circulate around the conference area, making himself/herself available to offer explanation about conference procedures.
3. Be available to answer questions about how students set goals and chose sample work.
4. Answer guardians' questions about students' strengths and areas to improve.
5. Offer positive feedback about student academic performance and the SLC.
6. Assist students and guardians to identify the next steps in learning.
7. Review goals and the connection between goals and learning when needed.
8. When needed, offer specific suggestions to guardians as to how they may help students achieve their goals.
9. Consult with the student and guardians as they set a date when they will meet to discuss the progress made in addressing goals and improving learning.

10. When appropriate, offer to meet with the guardians privately to discuss the student's progress toward meeting academic and non-academic goals.

Directions to guardians:

1. Provide encouragement, praise, and reinforcement.
2. Assist the student in identifying strengths and learning goals.
3. Work with the student and teacher to identify the next steps for learning.
4. Agree upon a date to meet with the student and teacher for the purpose of discussing the progress made in addressing goals and improving learning (Lambert, 2016).

APPENDIX B

Student goals for success:

- My strengths are:
- I need to work on:
- My first goal is:
    - To reach this goal, I will:
- My second goal is:
    - To reach this goal, I will:
- My third goal is:
    - To reach this goal, I will:
- People who can help me attain these goals are:
- The distractions that might get in the way of me reaching these goals are:
- I agree to work hard and try my best to achieve my goals (Student Signature).
- I agree to support my child as he/she tries to achieve these goals (Guardian signature).
- I agree to support my student as he/she tries to achieve these goals (Teacher Signature) (Lambert, 2016).

CHAPTER 5

STUDENT AND TEACHER PERCEPTIONS OF DEMOCRATIC CLASSROOM ORGANIZATION, MANAGEMENT, AND INSTRUCTION

Jeffrey D. Nokes
Brigham Young University

Some have argued that authoritarian classrooms do little to prepare students to participate in a democracy. As a result, some teachers have introduced democratic elements into their classes. In democratic classes, students help make and enforce rules, give input on curriculum, and help identify and solve problems. This chapter reports the reactions of a first-year teacher and her students to her inclusion of democratic elements in her class. She describes her nervousness in doing so, as well as the positive outcomes she observed. Students, likewise, describe how their involvement in classroom management and their input on curricular decisions impacted their experiences in the class.

At the Schoolhouse Gate: Stakeholder Perceptions of First Amendment Rights and Responsibilities in U.S. Public Schools, pp. 99–116
www.infoagepub.com
Copyright © 2022 by Information Age Publishing
All rights of reproduction in any form reserved.

The 21st century has featured an increasing emphasis on creating democratic classrooms both in the United States (Barton & Levstik, 2004; Hess & McAvoy, 2015) and internationally (Akar, 2016; Deucher, 2009; Thornberg & Elvstrand, 2012). Such classrooms are seen as a vital factor in preparing young people for active civic engagement. Many teacher education programs urge prospective teachers to prepare to include democratic elements in their classroom management systems and to give students a larger role in curricular decisions and in solving problems (Sentürk & Oyman, 2014). However, because democratic classrooms restructure traditional power hierarchies, there appears to be a great deal more democratic talk than democratic action in schools (Thornberg & Elvstrand, 2012), particularly secondary schools (Deuchar, 2009). And because this instructional approach has been uncommon in the past, many prospective teachers may have had little personal experience observing democratic instruction. Ideas that sound exciting when studied in university classrooms might prove difficult to implement without that experience. In this chapter, I explore the experiences of first-year teacher Chiara and her seventh-grade students as she integrated some democratic elements into her classroom management system and as students contributed to curricular decisions.

LITERATURE ON DEMOCRATIC CLASSROOMS

The preparation of a civically minded population was one of the original purposes of public education in the United States (Barber, 1997). Theorists and educational researchers suggest that public schools in general and social studies classrooms in particular should prepare young people to work for the common good (Barton & Levstik, 2004; Thornberg & Elvstrand, 2012) and to answer the question, "how should we live together?" (Hess & McAvoy, 2015, p. 77). Researchers and educational philosophers have proposed that the preparation needed for participation in a democracy is best done in democratic rather than autocratic schools and classrooms (Goodlad et al., 2004; Hess & McAvoy, 2015). For example, Akar (2016) found that in many civics classrooms in Lebanon, undemocratic methods, such as dogmatic textbooks and a focus on memorization, left little room for discussion and proved to be a substantial barrier to active citizenship. To summarize an immense body of research, students cannot learn how to be engaged citizens of a democracy while attending authoritarian classes.

Much has been written about the characteristics of democratic instruction. Democratic classrooms include ample opportunities for student involvement in decision-making and problem-solving (Deuchar, 2009;

Sentürk & Oyman, 2014); collaborating with the teacher to establish rules and consequences (Hunt & Hunt, 2005; Kesici, 2008; Turabik & Gün, 2016); leveling complaints and forming indictments (Kovacs, 2009); acting civilly toward others, even those they disagree with (Hess & McAvoy, 2015); exploring current classroom, local, national, and international issues (Deuchar, 2009); exercising their freedom of speech during civil discourse without fear or anxiety (Hess & McAvoy, 2015; Sentürk & Oyman, 2014); resolving conflicts (Thornberg & Elvstrand, 2012); developing knowledge about governance processes (Parker, 2004); constructing rather than merely consuming knowledge (Daher & Saifi, 2018); and selecting learning and assessment experiences (Hunt & Hunt, 2005).

Teachers have found a number of practical ways to integrate these features of democratic classrooms into their instruction. One of the most popular, used to promote collaborative problem solving, is the class meeting (Thornberg, 2010). The original intent of class meetings was to allow students and the teacher to collaboratively and deliberatively resolve problems. Class meetings could provide students with a venue for raising complaints and making suggestions, then working together to make things better. However, in his investigation of class meetings, Thornberg (2010) discovered that teachers often set the agenda for class meetings, suppressed students' creativity, and focused discussions on how to get students to follow their rules. Such manipulation of class meetings created a cynical view of democracy among students. Thornberg and Elvstrand (2012) argue that democratic classrooms cannot be established merely through activities or conventions but must become a way of being and interacting in class, based upon relationships of equality and fairness within the classroom and school community.

Much has been theorized about the positive outcomes of democratic instruction, though little has been done to investigate the long-term impact of these classrooms. Some researchers have proposed that democratic schools and classrooms are places where young people learn what it means to be a public—to be citizens (Hess & McAvoy, 2015), learn about their rights and roles in governance (Parker, 2004), build richer critical thinking skills (Turabik & Gün, 2016), and begin to develop and solidify their national and civic identity (Barton & Levstik, 2004). In spite of these valuable long-range outcomes, teachers—especially new teachers—may be more interested in short-term results, such as maintaining order in the classroom and building their reputation as a teacher. So while the potential benefits of democratic instruction are promising for the future, teachers are sometimes leery about creating democratic settings for fear of appearing indecisive or disorganized (Hunt & Hunt, 2005; Nokes et al., 2011) or of feeling uncertainty about stepping into an unfamiliar role (Hess & McAvoy, 2015). As such, it is no surprise that these concerns might become a higher priority than any potential long-term promise of democratic instruction's benefits (Hess & McAvoy, 2015).

Numerous other barriers may prevent teachers or students from engaging in democratic classrooms. For instance, the practice of suppressing student voices, so common in traditional classroom settings, may inhibit students' participation even when they have the chance to influence class governance. Students accustomed to a subordinate role may be reticent to assume an equal station with their teacher and peers. Further, teachers' hopes and needs for student compliance may discourage them from giving students a more active role in classroom management (Thornberg & Elvstrand, 2012).

STUDY QUESTIONS AND PROCEDURES

As with most action research projects, we approached the school year with questions specific to Chiara's setting: Are the claimed benefits of democratic instruction realized when an inexperienced teacher introduces modest democratic reforms within her specific teaching context? What would the short-term impacts be on classroom management, a central concern of Chiara's? Because the context is such an important part of action research, I describe it in some detail.

Participants, Context, and Action Research Plan

Chiara was a student in a course entitled Methods of Teaching Social Studies, a class that I taught for prospective teachers. Students in the class read materials on democratic classrooms and discussed methods for implementing democratic instruction. The notion of a democratic classroom appealed to most of the students in the methods class, and Chiara was particularly excited about the idea. She approached me after class and informed me that rather than student teaching in an experienced teacher's classroom she would be teaching as an intern the following school year. (Interns have full responsibility for their own classes, with a teaching colleague at the school serving as a mentor). She asked if I would like to conduct research in her classroom related to the democratic teaching methodologies she intended to experiment with. We decided to conduct an action research project in which she would experiment with democratic instruction in some of her classes and observe whether those students engaged differently than students in her more traditional classes.

As the school year approached, I observed the challenges associated with a new teacher implementing democratic teaching methods. Chiara and I considered creating a problem-based curriculum that involved community leaders, but the thought of having a constant flow of visitors in her class overwhelmed her. She favored a more traditional scope and sequence with more modest experimentation. We both understood that the internship was Chiara's keystone field experience and would play a large role in whether she would be hired as a history teacher in the future. She was wary of attempting an unfamiliar teaching approach that might create an unsuccessful experience and ruin her chance for employment. Eventually we scaled back our plans for research. We decided that she would start the school year in a traditional way to get a semester of teaching experience. Then, when her classes changed at the semester, we would randomly choose one of her classes and she would introduce into that class a few modest democratic elements, teaching her other classes as she had done during the first semester.

Unlike many student teachers and interns, Chiara had an unusually strong classroom presence. She was not nervous about confronting misbehavior. She posted rules on her classroom wall and followed through with both positive and negative consequences with energy and precision. She was assertive and unafraid to demand appropriate behavior. She maintained an efficient and businesslike environment. This is not to say that she was unpleasant with the students. Her personality was warm and friendly. She planned engaging and interesting activities. Most of the students were happy to be in her class, enjoyed the learning activities, and followed the rules while they were there.

As the start of the second semester approached, I wondered whether Chiara would be able to establish any elements of a democratic classroom. There was very little that was democratic about her teacher instincts. She made and posted the rules without students' input. She made all of the curricular decisions on her own. She determined the consequences for good and bad behavior. She enforced the rules herself and solved problems as they arose. I expected that it would be a challenge for her to turn over some of these responsibilities to students in her democratic class. Still, she planned to follow through with the scaled-back research project we had devised. The day before the new semester began, we drew out of a hat her eighth-period class for the study. Eighth period was the final 48-minute class of each day. Chiara's teaching colleague looked over her class rolls with her and commented that there were many unruly students in that class. Chiara, fearing that she might lose control of that class, again considered scrapping the research project, but decided to move forward.

Chiara taught at a school located on the suburban-rural frontier in the intermountain West of the United States. Approximately 900 seventh- through ninth-grade students attended the school. Some students were bussed up to 20 miles to school from their rural homes, and others lived in the suburban neighborhood of about 18,000 where the school was located. The majority of students were white (84.1%) with many Latinx students (14%) and a small number of Pacific Islanders and other minorities. Thirty-two percent of students at the school received free or reduced-price lunch. The 12- and 13-year-old seventh graders in Chiara's eighth-period class mirrored the limited diversity of the school. They studied Utah history and government.

I was a regular participant observer in Chiara's class, attending her seventh- and eighth-period classes frequently during the second semester of the school year. Chiara and her students became accustomed to my presence and associated freely with me. Chiara made a particular effort to invite me to class when she intended to do something she considered democratic. Chiara and I spoke frequently about her students, course content, concerns, successes, and ideas for instruction that might make her eighth-period class more democratic.

Chiara's Democratic Classroom Design

Democratic instruction was not natural for Chiara, and she continued to use more traditional, authoritative methods in her classes outside of eighth period. However, she found several ways to make her eighth-period class more democratic. In addition to the traditional curricular materials, she ordered a classroom set of two daily newspapers, one politically conservative and the other politically liberal, for eighth period. Students were taught strategies for reading the newspaper, such as using the index to find items of interest, and for identifying the biases of article authors. Using models in the newspapers, students were assigned to write letters to the editor on topics of their choice. Some students mailed their letter, though none of the letters were published in the newspaper. Students were assigned to read newspaper articles on a few occasions, though Chiara never made the newspapers a major part of the course curriculum.

Additionally, students in eighth period participated in the creation, adaptation, and enforcement of classroom rules. On the first day of the semester, Chiara proposed several rules to her eighth-period class. Then, unlike in her other classes, she invited the students to make appropriate adaptations to her rules. Students felt that most of the rules were fair, but they proposed a change to the tardy policy, requesting that they not be marked late until 30 seconds after the bell rang to start class. Through negotiation among themselves and with Chiara, tardiness was eventually defined as being out of their seats 10 seconds after the bell rang to begin class, a policy that Chiara enforced on the second day of class and the students enforced thereafter as described below.

A few weeks into the semester, Chiara noticed that students had written on some of the desks. Against her instincts but with my prodding, she conducted a class meeting during which she sought solutions for this problem from her eighth-period class. The students energetically considered using an adjacent office as a sort of jail cell for perpetrators. They debated other possible penalties before arriving at what they viewed as an appropriate consequence—anyone caught writing on the desks would have to clean desks during lunch or before or after school. This was the same consequence that Chiara had imposed on her earlier classes without their input.

One of the most highly anticipated activities of Chiara's eighth-period class was a weekly mock trial, during which students were tried by their peers for minor classroom infractions, such as littering. Through this "environmental court," held the last part of class on most Fridays, students enforced classroom policies by serving as jurors, lawyers, witnesses, plaintiffs, and defendants, learning about the judicial system in the process. Another highly anticipated activity was student congress, four sessions of which were held during the semester. Chiara encouraged students to present bills or resolutions related to class governance. Students wrote resolutions that would permit soft drinks and treats in class, eliminate the seating chart, and reform other class rules. Through surprisingly rigorous debate, students tempered their own rules, determining in the end that they would be able to choose one assigned seat for the last 2 weeks of the school year and that they would be allowed to bring water bottles and nondisruptive snacks to class as long as they were careful not to spill.

One other event that proved to be particularly memorable occurred when a student proposed that the class create a time capsule that would be opened 5 years later during their senior year. Students debated the merit of this activity, in the end resolving that it would be a good way to study current popular culture. Chiara agreed and set aside class time for them to build their time capsule. Students wrote letters to their future selves, and many brought artifacts to be placed inside. Chiara did not commit a great deal of time to the construction of the time capsule, to environmental court (about 15 minutes each week), student congress (four classes during the 90-day semester), or class meetings (part of three class sessions), though she frequently had class discussions in eighth period, just as she did in her other classes. These modest elements of democratic instruction allowed Chiara to teach a traditional curriculum while granting eighth-period students a larger role in managing the class and selecting some activities.

Data Collection and Analysis

During my observations of Chiara's classes I kept field notes, recording Chiara and the students' behaviors and my personal reflections that included praise, suggestions, and other musings. I shared my field notes with Chiara throughout the semester and we used them to reflect on effective instructional practices. The theme of democratic methods was central to my field notes and to our discussions, though our conversations included other aspects of teaching as well. The field notes, then, served not as a data source but as a reflective tool, enriching our discussions about classroom events. My participation in class, including my field notes, helped me understand Chiara's and students' references to learning activities talked about during the interviews and focus groups described below.

Data sources included semistructured interviews with Chiara, student focus groups, and interviews with individual students. A colleague of mine and I conducted two semistructured interviews of Chiara, one early in the semester and the other at the end of the school year. Interviews were audio recorded and transcribed and went through a process of open coding (Strauss & Corbin, 1990). We independently coded a portion of the same transcript, then met and discussed the patterns we observed, creating a common language for the codes. We then coded the remainder of the interview and again met to refine our coding scheme. Using this final scheme, we independently coded the second interview, achieving an 84.7% agreement on codes. Through discussion those discrepancies were resolved to our satisfaction. The analysis revealed several themes in Chiara's reaction to her attempts to create a democratic classroom. These themes were then presented to Chiara as a "member check," and she validated the findings.

In addition to the interviews of Chiara, most of the students in her eighth-period class provided data on their perceptions of her instruction. Near the end of the school year, two colleagues of mine and I conducted semistructured interviews of nine students. Twelve other students participated in two focus groups of six students each. In all, 21 of the 32 students in the class were interviewed either alone or as part of a focus group. Plans to interview the remaining students never materialized as end-of-the-year school activities took priority over our research. Interviews and focus groups were recorded and transcribed and went through a process of open coding (Strauss and Corbin, 1990), during which my colleague and I created a coding system through an iterative process of independent and collaborative coding, similar to that used to code Chiara's transcripts. Students' names that appear in this chapter are pseudonyms.

FINDINGS

The coding of the interviews and focus groups revealed patterns in Chiara's and students' reactions to democratic class organization, management, and instruction. I present the findings drawn from the interviews of Chiara first, followed by those drawn from student interviews and focus groups.

Chiara's Reflections on Her Democratic Class

Interviews with Chiara showed a) the challenge she faced in sharing control with students, b) the way her inexperience interfered with democratic methods, and c) her perception of students' responses to democratic instruction.

The Challenge of Sharing Control. Chiara had a difficult time with balancing democratic and assertive classroom management strategies. She explained that at times "my teacher's mind was [saying], 'you need to come down hard and strict, set the rules so when someone goes off you have to reign them in,' but that was the exact opposite of what we were trying to do [in the democratic class]." Chiara experienced particular discomfort when she got to know her eighth-period class, which had been chosen at random to experiment with democratic pedagogy. She recalled,

> I don't know if it's just because it's eighth period, or it's the end of the day, but they definitely seemed much more rowdy. They were definitely much stronger personalities ... so it was kind of scary to think "this is the class I'm going to try to give more freedom to? This is the class that I'm going to indirectly better control by not controlling them?" That was definitely a scary idea.

Chiara elaborated on these tensions, stating, "I was juggling how much leeway do I give these kids and how much do I say, 'Okay, this is how we're doing it.'"

Inexperience. Chiara worried whether including democratic elements in the class would be effective, particularly in light of her status as a first-year teacher. For instance, when integrating the student congress and the environmental court she wondered, "How is this going to end up? ... Is this going to be a success or is it just going to flop?" She attributed her anxiety to her inexperience. At the end of the semester, she explained, "It's scary to try something new [democratic teaching] when you're already trying something new [teaching]."

When things went awry in a lesson, she blamed, in part, her "lack of teaching experience." In hindsight, she suggested, "looking back now, I see [creating a democratic classroom] is much more complicated and refined than I thought. I probably wouldn't volunteer to do [the study] now because I would feel unqualified as a new teacher to take that on. I think good incorporation of the democratic classroom needs a highly skilled educator." As she looked to her future classrooms she expressed the intention to include some democratic activities, having seen their success, though she doubted the ability of most first-year teachers to incorporate sweeping democratic reforms.

Students' Responses to Democratic Instruction. With the passage of time and the implementation of various democratic activities, Chiara observed a change in her eighth-period class. She reported that the students became more involved in instructional activities that included discussion or student input. She explained that the students in her last class were "coming more out of their shells and wanted to participate more and do more things and get more involved and didn't just sit quietly and wait for me to tell them what we're going to do next." They came to "love" expressing their views about controversial issues. Chiara contrasted the eighth-period class with the other classes she taught. While conducting discussions in her other classes "it was like pulling teeth to get someone to answer, but with eighth period I generally would have to stop them so that we could get on to the next part of class." She claimed that eighth-period students' eagerness to participate improved many class activities.

Additionally, as time went by, eighth period relied less on Chiara for classroom management. She observed that students in the eighth-period class became more self-directed. She reported that the management of eighth period required the expenditure of "less energy." Chiara mused, "I can't explain why, but they somehow became more manageable the second term—more so than [other classes]. She added, "They really were a well-behaved class, which I never [expected], because I felt [at first] that I [might have] to be more of a taskmaster just because they were more of a loud, dynamic class, but the exact opposite ended up happening." She continued, "Midway there was definitely, you could tell there was a shift. That energy became more channeled, and especially when, by giving them freedom, by saying you don't have to be in your seat when the bell rings, you have 10 seconds, students took it upon themselves to be the disciplinarians." In comparison, Chiara reported that some of her other classes "got harder to manage at the end [of the school year]."

Further, Chiara reported that her relationship with the students in her eighth-period class was enhanced, as well as their relationships with each other. Students came to know each other better, and Chiara learned more about her students and became more connected to them. She contrasted her relationship with students in other classes with eighth-period students, explaining, "I'm sure there [are] kids in seventh period that I could've gotten to know better had they been in eighth, but I just feel like I didn't really allow them to open up. I just never got to know them like that." Improved relationships translated into improved feelings toward the eighth-period class as a whole. "By the end of the year, I found myself just looking forward to eighth period more. I enjoyed that class. It was more fun." Chiara attributed at least part of the differences between eighth period and her other classes to the nature of a democratic classroom. She hypothesized that

> where we went with eighth period helped to channel their energy. They got into the democratic classroom. They really got into the idea of having the student court, having the opportunity to debate and to discuss. They loved that, and so I felt like the different things that we did do with them ... to encourage democratic classroom helped channel that energy that they had and focus it.

In summary, discussions, debates, congresses, and court hearings as well as other democratic practices allowed Chiara to get to know her students better. Moreover, time devoted to developing rules and consequences together with students gave them a sense of ownership and responsibility, which led to increased self-management in her view.

Students' Reactions to the Democratic Class

Unlike Chiara, who expressed mixed feelings about democratic instruction, the students were universally positive in their reaction. Coding of their interviews and focus group transcripts revealed four patterns: (a) they found Chiara to be strict but nice, (b) they thought that having input on rules made them easier to follow, (c) they enjoyed democratic activities, and (d) some recognized the long-term benefits of such activities to prepare them for civic engagement.

Strict but Nice. All nine students who were interviewed individually had difficulty describing Chiara's management style, though many described her with terms synonymous with "strict but nice." This difficulty students faced in articulating her management style may have been due in part to the manner through which rules were cocreated and coenforced. Without exception, students in the class appreciated the demeanor of their teacher, though students had a difficult time identifying precisely what she did that helped them behave appropriately.

Classroom management was not just a matter of keeping students quiet, however—a point that was surprising to some students. Lindsey explained: "[Other] teachers just yell at us ... until we're quiet and [Chiara] wants us to talk to her and talk to each other." Students described

Chiara as someone who cared about their learning and who inspired them to participate. Theresa described the class in the following way: "We like to learn, and we're really involved in what we do. We like to participate ... [Chiara] got us involved." In one focus group, when asked why Chiara was able to maintain control of the class with minor management interventions, Curtis replied simply, "She likes us." Amber summarized the feelings of many students when she explained, "[Chiara] puts her personality and energy into each of us."

It is important to note that none of the students either in focus groups or during interviews described Chiara as weak, disorganized, or unprepared, an image sometimes feared by teachers who give students a voice in the classroom (Nokes et al., 2011). Instead students perceived Chiara as strict but kind, often juxtaposing synonyms of these two words in the same sentence as Jake did: "She's more disciplined, more nicer."

Input on Rules. Eight of the interviewed students and both focus groups reported that having some input on the class rules made them seem more rational and fair, increased the likelihood that students would understand and follow them, and helped students recognize applications for the real world. Jake remembered the process used to create the rules:

> She had most of the basic rules—if you're tardy and all that stuff, but then she let us decide some better rules—change them a little bit. So now, instead of when the bell rings you're tardy, you can have 10 seconds after the bell rings before you're tardy.

Theresa explained the process used to revise rules through student congress:

> "We got a bill and we each had little groups and we each wrote a bill. One person ... chose a bill and we went up [in front of the class] and we had one side vote and the other side vote if they wanted it to be a law. And then, if it passed, [Chiara] would either veto it or she'd sign it and then it would be a law if she signed it."

Giving input on the rules made them seem more rational and fair to the students. For example, Riley rationalized the class policy associated with writing on the desks, which he helped create:

> "I don't see any other way that we could have been punished, because it's fair that if we draw on the desks, then we have to take it off, or if we throw something on the floor, then we have to pick everything up."

Eli agreed, I think they're fair, because we're going to be the ones that are following them, so we should get to pick them." Ryan explained, "She was nice enough to let us make [the rules]. We should be nice enough and give her enough respect to keep them.

Further, students appeared to accept a greater amount of responsibility for monitoring themselves. Ben commented,

> [Even though] we got to choose where we sit, we still have to be quiet. That rule didn't change, so we have to monitor ourselves on that one. And because we got to sit by our friends we still have to listen when [Chiara] is talking.

Katie stated it most simply, "We made them. We should keep them." Students began to view rules as something larger than a way to behave in class. Jake explained, "I think she wants us to know that if we set a goal that we want to do, we have to live up to it and follow it."

Democratic Activities. Democratic activities, particularly those that involved debate, controversy, and the "messiness" of democracy were highly engaging for students. When asked about student congress in one of the focus groups, the following dialogue ensued:

James: [Student congress] was pretty fun.
Rachel: I liked it just because it gave us a chance to give our own opinions.
James: And made the end of the day fly by. Like when we were doing something fun and all of a sudden time would fly by.
Sarah: That happens a lot in this class.
Rachel: Yeah. Same with the court. But the congress flew by.

In interviews and focus groups, students were vocal about the messiness of democracy, but many seemed to relish the process nonetheless. Kali recalled some of the class debates, stating, "some people disagree and other people agree and they just … I don't know, it kind of gets just wild and stuff." Often students would present questionable ideas that would then be considered by classmates. For instance, Ben remembered,

> We were having environmental court, and Caleb thought he was going to win, so he wanted to make a new rule that if you lost you had to go into the back room and that was jail, and you had to stay there for like a half hour after school, and everybody thought that was really funny. That would have been funny if that happened, because it'd be more like real court, because then you'd have to go to jail afterwards.

After a brief discussion, the class rejected the plan. Although individuals might make unrealistic proposals, the class as a whole could distinguish between good and bad ideas and what Chiara could and could not allow.

Additionally, many students appreciated the interaction that took place during the discussion of controversial issues. Ben commented, "You get other people's views and ideas. You get to hear what they basically think about it, and if they think something different, then you can get a debate about it." Other students also commented about the value of listening to others' opinions. Several made comments like Kyle's: "I think it was good to see and hear other people's views about things." Theresa summarized, "[Debate] teaches us to be fair and to listen to other people, so it's good learning skills."

The Long-Term Value. Although the majority of students did not articulate how democratic activities might help them in the long run, students in one focus group and four students in interviews did. Some of them suggested that the course fostered democratic dispositions in them that would carry over into the real world. When asked why Chiara had them debate resolutions and write letters to the editor, Liam observed, "because that happens in real life. She's teaching us that if we don't like something or if we don't agree with something that's going on, we can talk to somebody about it and see if it can be changed." Others discussed the disposition to sacrifice self-interest for the common good. Theresa explained, "sometimes you have to learn to just do things you don't want to do.... [The class] also teaches us a lot about working together and waiting our turn and participating."

Other students highlighted the skills of democracy that they developed in the course. Angie explained, "I think [this class] teaches you good skills for if you ever get a job because you need to learn to work with other people and you need to learn to cooperate with them and not worry only about yourself." Jake described the skills associated with communicating about controversial issues by explaining "[class debates] help us learn in real life how we're supposed to talk." There was a sense that by "talk," he meant communicating with others, including listening and allowing others a turn to speak. Amber struggled between the notion of sticking up for what she believed and allowing others to have their way. She explained,

> I think it's good sometimes to just lose yourself in a group and forget just your opinion and hear somebody else's.... Also, another life skill is sometimes when we're in court, we have to argue for what we want.... A lot of people say not to argue, but I think it's a good thing to learn, because you're never going to get anything just with the snap of your fingers in real life, and I think it's good to learn that sometimes you have to work for things that you want.

To summarize, without exception students appreciated Chiara's democratic management style. They recognized her assertive yet nonauthoritarian way of involving the class in management and decision making. They appreciated her responsiveness to their suggestions, such as their recommendation for a revised tardy policy and a time capsule. The majority of students found that rules were easier to understand and follow when they had some input on them. Students enjoyed the democratic activities through which they became involved in classroom management and had opportunities to discuss and debate. Finally, many students found the democratic activities to be a good preparation in the dispositions and skills needed for civic engagement.

IMPLICATIONS AND CONCLUSIONS

There are several implications for classroom practice from the findings of this study. First, even though only modest reforms were made within a more traditional curriculum, the perceptions of both Chiara and her students with respect to the effects of democratic teaching were overwhelmingly positive, particularly regarding students' input on rules and rule enforcement. Students' debates of rules and rule changes helped them see the rationality and importance of rules, something Thornberg and Elvstrand (2012) noted as lacking in undemocratic classrooms. Debating classroom policies helped them perceive rules from their teacher's perspective, which led to increased self-regulation. The process helped students to sense that their ideas and suggestions were valued (Hunt & Hunt, 2005). Chiara's initial fears about her inability to control the class by sharing governance with students were unfounded. The findings of this study contrast with those of Thornberg and Elvstrand (2012) who contended that students often doubted their own ability to make fair rules, instead trusting the teacher to make and enforce equitable policies. In contrast, students in this study appeared confident in their ability to assume an active role in classroom governance. Perhaps contextual factors, such as students' ages, can explain the differences between this research and earlier studies. An additional benefit of the democratic methods was the perception of improved learning. Researchers have suggested that students who are involved in curricular decisions learn content and critical thinking skills better (Deuchar, 2009; Turabik & Gün, 2016). The students in this study believed such was the case. The opposite has been reported in other settings, where undemocratic methods interfere with students' development of skills needed for civic engagement (Akar, 2016).

A second implication of this research is related to teachers' fears and uncertainty about democratic classroom design. Chiara approached the idea of establishing a democratic classroom with excitement at first, but with a great deal of trepidation as the realities of teaching set in. This research was delayed and the design modified as a result of her fear. She attributed some of her fear to her inexperience with teaching in general, and teaching in a democratic setting in particular. Hess and McAvoy (2015) suggest that such fear prevents even seasoned teachers from allowing students to discuss controversial topics. In addition, the messiness, uncertainty, and increased work load of including students in classroom governance overwhelmed Chiara, as has happened to other teachers (Hunt & Hunt, 2005). The implications for teacher preparation programs and for professional development are evident. Teachers (preservice and in-service) need opportunities to observe experienced teachers model democratic teaching approaches if they are to feel comfortable attempting such practices in their own classrooms. Mentors who have found an effective balance of assertiveness and openness to student input might serve as mentors. However, research suggests that such models might be difficult to find (Thornberg, 2010; Thornberg & Elvstrand, 2012).

A third implication is the need for further research on this topic. The classroom described in this study represented one particular context. Certainly, Chiara was not a typical new teacher, with a great deal more confidence and assertiveness than most. Nor was she a seasoned teacher, approaching classroom management with a tried and true system in place. Her background allowed her to experiment in ways that might have been difficult for most new teachers and for many experienced teachers. Further, the eighth-period students represented a unique mix of personalities and backgrounds. Chiara's blending of democratic and authoritative approaches created additional variables. Needless to say, the results of this study are not generalizable. I echo Thornberg and Elvstrand's (2012) call for more case studies on the implementation of democratic instructional practices in a variety of settings.

To conclude, this action research project shows that new teachers can maintain order in their classrooms through a combination of democratic and assertive management techniques. Teachers do not need to radically change traditional practices in order to experience positive effects. However, without prior experience observing democratic classrooms, it seems unlikely that new teachers will engage in such unfamiliar instructional approaches. I provided encouragement and support for Chiara throughout the semester. In addition, though I remain in agreement with Thornberg and Elvstrand's (2012) contention that democratic classrooms cannot be established merely through activities or conventions, the use of activities, such as student congress and class meetings, creates conditions that facilitate democratic interactions. For instance, it seems unlikely that a student would have suggested that the class create a time capsule if students had not previously given input on other policies. As new teachers enter classrooms, they might use structured democratic activities as a form of scaffolding for themselves until they have established a democratic way of being and interacting. This study also suggests that democratic classrooms may prepare students for civic engagement outside of the classroom, as many other researchers have suggested (Akar, 2016; Barton & Levstik, 2004; Hess & McAvoy, 2015; Thornberg & Elvstrand, 2012), though this hypothesis must be investigated by future research. The results of this study suggest that giving students input on rules and rule enforcement may be an effective classroom management strategy, even for beginning teachers, though further research, including longitudinal studies, is needed.

AUTHOR NOTE

Correspondence concerning this chapter should be addressed to Jeffery D. Nokes, History Department, Brigham Young University, Provo, Utah, 84602. Contact: jeff_nokes@byu.edu

REFERENCES

Akar, B. (2016). Learning active citizenship: Conflicts between students' conceptualisations of citizenship and classroom learning experiences in Lebanon. *British Journal of Sociology of Education, 37*(2), 288–312. https://doi.org/10.1080/01425692.2014.916603

Barber, B. R. (1997). Public schooling: Education for democracy. In J. I. Goodlad & T. J. McMannon (Eds.), *The public purpose of education and schooling* (pp. 21–32). Jossey-Bass.

Barton, K. C., & Levstik, L. S. (2004). *Teaching history for the common good*. Routledge.

Daher, W., & Saifi, A. G. (2018). Democratic practices in a constructivist science classroom. *International Journal of Science and Mathematics Education, 16*(2), 221–236.

Deuchar, R. (2009). Seen and heard, and then not heard: Scottish pupils' experience of democratic educational practice during the transition from primary to secondary school. *Oxford Review of Education, 35*(1), 23–40. https://doi.org/10.1080/03054980802018871

Goodlad, J. I., Mantle-Bromley, C., & Goodlad, S. J. (2004). *Education for everyone: Agenda for education in a democracy*. Jossey-Bass.

Hess, D. E. & McAvoy, P. (2015). *The political classroom: Evidence and ethics in democratic education*. Routledge.

Hunt, T. J., & Hunt, B. (2005). New voices: Students are ready for democracy—If the teachers can handle it. *English Journal, 94*(5), 103–107. https://doi.org/10.2307/30047363

Kesici, Ş. (2008). Teachers' opinions about building a democratic classroom. *Journal of Instructional Psychology, 35*(2), 192–203.

Kovacs, P. (2009). Education for democracy: It is not an issue of dare; It is an issue of can. *Teacher Education Quarterly, 36*(1), 9–23.

Nokes, J. D., Egan, M. W., & Casebolt, C. (2011, December). *"It's scary to try something new when you're already trying something new:" Helping a novice teacher build a democratic social studies classroom* [Paper presentation]. National Council for the Social Studies/College and University Faculty Assembly, Washington, DC.

Parker, W. C. (2004). Diversity, globalization, and democratic education: Curriculum possibilities. In J. A. Banks (Ed.), *Diversity and citizenship education: Global perspectives* (pp. 433–458). Jossey-Bass.

Sentürk, I., & Oyman, N. (2014). Democratic classroom management in higher education: A qualitative study. *Educational Sciences: Theory and Practice, 14*(3), 940–945.

Strauss, A., & Corbin, J. (1990). *Basics of qualitative research: Grounded theory procedures and techniques*. SAGE.

Thornberg, R. (2010). School democratic meetings: Pupil control discourse in disguise. *Teaching and Teacher Education, 26*(4), 924–932. https://doi.org/10.1016/j.tate.2009.10.033

Thornberg, R., & Elvstrand, H. (2012). Children's experiences of democracy, participation, and trust in school. *International Journal of Educational Research, 53*, 44–54. https://doi.org/10.1016/j.ijer.2011.12.010

Turabik, T., & Gün, F. (2016). The relationship between teachers' democratic classroom management attitudes and students' critical thinking dispositions. *Journal of Education and Training Studies, 4*(12), 45–57. https://doi.org/10.11114/jets.v4i12.190

CHAPTER 6

FIRST AMENDMENT RIGHTS AND SPEECH

Views From Students on News and Social Media in Schools

Sarah J. Kaka
Ohio Wesleyan University

This qualitative case study was an analysis of a First Amendment study database that examines student views of technology and expression. High school students provided their perspectives on free press and expression as they relate to social media. It sought to explore the perceptions of high school students about First Amendment freedoms of speech and press, and their views of these rights as they relate to social media and their uses of it. The study found that students no longer get their news from traditional news sources, limitations of students' press rights do exist, students believed that their peers' speech should be limited on social media, and that administrators censor access to digital information.

Social media has outpaced print sources as the main source of information in the United States. Thirty-six percent of Americans aged 18–29 get their news and information from social media, followed by 27% that get

At the Schoolhouse Gate: Stakeholder Perceptions of First Amendment Rights and Responsibilities in U.S. Public Schools, pp. 117–135
www.infoagepub.com
Copyright © 2022 by Information Age Publishing
All rights of reproduction in any form reserved.

their news from news websites (Shearer, 2018). Television is still the most popular source of news for older Americans, with 65% of those aged 50–64 and 81% of those age 65+ citing television more than any other source for their news (Shearer, 2018). Echoing those findings, a *Project Information Literacy* study discovered that 72% of young college students get their daily news from social media (Head et al., 2018).

The rate at which people can now access news on social media cannot be matched by traditional, in-print newspapers or television news programs, so it is no surprise that people are utilizing social media to keep tabs on what is going on in the world. Couple this with a 2019 Pew Research Center study that found access to technology has informed more people and given them a political voice, but also found that people are easier to manipulate due to the ease of spreading false information through the press and social media (Smith et al., 2019). The combination of the findings of these two studies is somewhat troubling when one considers that 63% of high school students learn about current events and news through press on the internet (Shearer, 2018), but that people who read news on the internet are easy to manipulate (Smith et al., 2019).

Historically, print media has been *the press*, and the press is how we have come to collectively define journalists and media outlets (newspapers, magazines, radio, television, and the internet). The courts have defined the press as anything that is published (Freedom Forum Institute, n.d.). Now, however, social media platforms such as Facebook, Twitter, and Instagram can also be lumped into that collective group, since they are published online. In fact, some believe that social media platforms are the only truly free press that is left in America (Cramer, 2014). In our current state of press and social media use, one cannot help but wonder whether or not our First Amendment rights are still being upheld, especially within the confines of public school walls.

Currently, there are no studies in the literature that focus on high school students' perceptions of the use of social media with regard to students' First Amendment rights, so this study is much needed and fills a gaping hole in the literature. High school students provide a unique perspective on First Amendment freedom of speech and press rights, and since they are the ones at the heart of this debate, their voices are essential to the literature. They are the future of news and journalism in America. Therefore, in order to explore the perceptions of students, a qualitative case study was conducted that sought to answer the following research questions:

- What are the perceptions of high school students about First Amendment freedoms of speech and press?

- What are their views of these rights as they relate to social media and their uses of it?

This case study is an analysis of data from a First Amendment study database (Patterson & Chandler, 2022) that examines student views of social media, freedom of press, and freedom of speech as related to their lives. In small focus groups, 127 Midwestern high school students representing six school districts and eight classrooms provided their perspectives on these topics. Findings include a dearth of traditional news sources in schools and a proliferation of emerging issues with regard to freedom of speech and social media rights.

LITERATURE REVIEW

Freedom of the press in schools is somewhat different from that of press outside of schools. Thanks to the U.S. Supreme Court's ruling in *Hazelwood School District v. Kuhlmeier* (1988), school administrators can limit student speech in school-sponsored newspapers and other school related activities as long as the censorship decisions are based on legitimate pedagogical concerns. While this in itself is a fair ruling, the implications of it are still seen in schools today, with the long-lasting "Hazelwood effect" (Paxton & Dickson, 2000). The Journalism Education Association's Scholastic Press Rights Commission believes that school administrators are leveraging this ruling to utilize their right of prior review, which "occurs when anyone not on the publication/media staff requires that he or she be allowed to read, view or approve student material before distribution, airing or publication" (Bowen, 2010, para. 1). This has led to students publishing less controversial content in school newspapers for fear of censorship or retribution (Bowen, 2019). According to LoMonte, (2015), "K–12 school administrators have become unapologetically heavy-handed in retaliating for speech that may provoke controversy or reflect unfavorably on the school's image" (para. 6).

High school newspapers are suffering due not only to content limitations. As far back as 2007, schools were seeing newspaper elective classes abandoned in favor of more time and resources being spent on core courses, in part due to the implementation of No Child Left Behind (Wojciki, 2007). No Child Left Behind led to a redirection of class time and money away from electives toward literacy and math. While many advocates of school journalism insist that school newspapers support literacy and critical thinking, it can have a large overhead cost with computers, publishing software, and printing costs (LoMonte, 2015). Waning interest in print journalism has also led to fewer and fewer high school newspapers in existence today (Kartik-Narayan, 2018; Ortiz, 2015).

Freedom of speech rights for students in school have their roots in the *Tinker v. Des Moines* (1969) case, which set the precedent that teachers and students do not shed their First Amendment rights when they walk onto school grounds. This was based on the Supreme Court's ruling that the school district could not ban students from wearing black armbands to protest the Vietnam War.

But do those rights extend to social media use? More recently, students and schools are concerning themselves with freedom of speech when it comes to what is posted on social media. In *Burge v. Colton School District* (2015), a federal district court judge ruled that a student couldn't be suspended for posting negative comments about his teacher on social media. Burge's Oregon middle school had done just that, after he made derogatory and violent posts on Facebook about a teacher. The judge ruled that because the posts were made on a personal computer off campus and during out-of-school hours, the school did not have the authority to punish him (Keierleber, 2015).

In *R.L. v. Central York School District* (2016), U.S. district court judges ruled that a student's First Amendment freedom of speech rights were not violated when he was suspended for posting a bomb threat on social media. In this case, the district canceled school for the day, which passed the *substantial disruption* threshold set by *Tinker v. Des Moines* in 1969 (LoMonte, 2016). In *Shen v. Albany Unified School District* (2018), a federal judge ruled that out-of-school postings on social media could be punishable in school and considered in-school speech, because the social media posts were by students and for students with the intention of disrupting school. The student had created an Instagram account that targeted minority students and staff members by posting inflammatory content on the site (Walsh, 2017).

In general, a student's right to free speech on social media use outside of school is protected under the First Amendment, unless it does one of these: it obstructs a school's ability to deliver an education to the students, impedes on the processes of the school, interferes with school safety and the safety of students, or infringes on the rights of faculty or other students (Abud, 2018). However, the National Coalition Against Censorship (2019) has detailed fifteen different instances of students getting in-school consequences for something that was posted on social media out of school. Examples include students being removed from a sports team for tweeting something offensive about the state's athletic association (Arguello, 2016), being suspended for retweeting gossip (Klein, 2014), and being suspended for being a whistle-blower about other students who had posted a racially charged video (Widman, 2016).

THEORETICAL FRAMEWORK

This case study utilizes the uses and gratifications theory to ground the research (Blumler & McQuail, 1969). This theory allows researchers to begin to understand the ways in which people seek out press and media sources, why they choose the media they do, and how they interact with press and media (McQuail, 2005). This study seeks to ascertain the ways in which students are accessing their news through different types of media, so it is a fitting lens through which to view the data. It provides us with a framework for understanding why students choose the media that they do over other forms of press (Flanagin & Metzger, 2001). Bucy et al. (2007) purport that media are a vital source of need gratification and that the paths to fulfillment of those needs are chosen by the audience. The *audience* in this study are the high school students, and they are choosing which media source to approach based on their own specific needs and reasons.

Whiting and Williams (2013) identified ten uses of and gratifications from social media, including social interaction, information seeking, passing time, entertainment, relaxation, communicatory utility, convenience utility, expression of opinion, information sharing, and surveillance/knowledge about others. The uses of interest in this study are information seeking, information sharing, and expression of opinion. The researcher seeks to better determine the ways in which media are used to gratify the needs of high school students regarding how they are going to get their news, how information is being shared with and among them, and whether or not they believe they can openly express their opinion in the media both in and out of school.

METHODS

To explore the students' views regarding free press and speech as they relate to school newspapers and social media, a qualitative case study was conducted of 127 Midwestern high school students from six school districts. The benefit of conducting a case study is that it allows the researcher to explore specific cases within a real-life setting to gain insight into participants' experiences through analysis of interviews, observations, and related documents (Creswell & Poth, 2017; Patton, 2015). The themes and patterns that emerge from data collection and analysis allow the researcher to make generalizations about the case as well as lessons learned from the study (Yin, 2018).

Participants and Data Collection

The data came from an established database (Patterson & Chandler, 2021) that included transcriptions of 36 focus groups comprised of three to six students each. The six participating Midwestern high schools were chosen through convenience sampling. Out of the 127 students who participated, 73 of 127 (57%) were from suburban schools, 33 of 127 (26%) were from rural schools, and 21/127 (17%) were from urban schools. The large majority of participants were high school juniors and seniors who either had taken or were currently enrolled in American government. Eleven of the urban students were sophomores, who were not yet in American Government, but who were enrolled in Advancement Via Individual Determination (https://www.avid.org/), key components of which are to promote critical thinking and inquiry.

All students in the study volunteered to participate, provided pseudonyms, and consented to be audiotaped. Focus groups were conducted during the school day, with the exception of one conducted after school, and lasted 40–50 minutes. Each focus group began with student completion of a demographic survey on iPads, followed by a brief card sort activity to review human rights and First Amendment rights in particular. All focus group conversations were recorded and then transcribed.

Data Analysis

Both inductive and deductive data analysis were performed (Yin, 2018), and the data were coded in cycles (Miles et al., 2014). Prior to coding, the researcher reviewed focus group data and noted initial patterns. During the first cycle of inductive coding, *in vivo* codes, which use the participants' own language as labels for sections of data, and evaluative codes, based on their expressed thoughts regarding freedom of the press in news and social media, were created from the data. In addition, the researcher memoed throughout coding steps, taking notes on emerging themes and patterns (Miles et al., 2014). During the second cycle of coding, deductive analysis occurred as codes and patterns were compared with the Uses and Gratifications Theory to identify the ways in which media is used to gratify the needs of students and their ability to express their needs openly via social media, both in and out of school (Yin, 2018). During the third cycle of coding, the results of the first two cycles were compared, and final themes and patterns were identified through further review and memoing.

FINDINGS

There were four main themes that emerged from analysis of the focus group data: students no longer get their news from traditional news sources, limitations of students' press rights do exist, students believed that their peers' free speech should be limited on social media, and students did perceive that administrators censored their access to digital information. These themes echoed through the six different school districts, across all demographic factors.

Theme 1: Students No Longer Get Their News From Traditional News Sources

For the students in the focus groups, the predominant source of news, both school and otherwise, was social media based. Anna said,

> social media has definitely become a very big thing in today's world, and it's like everybody always says stop and think before you say, but it's a really big thing now. Like, you could say one wrong word, and it's everywhere by the morning.

All focus groups indicated that Twitter is where they get their news. Leila said that she feels "like whatever information, like actual new information you need, you can get from Twitter." When asked how they know what's going on in school, students' answers aligned. Jake said, "pretty much for me it's Twitter, our school's social media;" Elizabeth had a similar answer, and said, "so you learn about the school on Twitter;" Kathleen explained, "a lot of school organizations use social media in place of any kind of [newspaper]." Others reported getting their nonschool news from a "news app that I have on my phone," said Steven, or from "watching CNN Student News in class sometimes," Aaron said.

Students also reported that their school districts and administrators had Twitter accounts that showcased district goings-on. Rae said, "The administration all has social media. There's [Home Town] School District accounts that are like always talking about what's happening." Twitter was a main source of district news for students, although the news that was being shared via Twitter was not always newsworthy, according to some, as it was more about sports or upcoming events. Jake said, "they send out updates for sports and whatnot and their times and locations and anything going on if there's any play or whatever it may be." Sydney, like the few other students who don't use Twitter, hears about events and school happenings, "like word of mouth kind of thing."

One challenge that students noted was the proliferation of false information. Jacob discussed his concerns about the media and freedom of speech and believed that "sometimes [the media] likes to abuse their power and for false reasons and false accusations." Similarly, Andy believed that when students use social media as their sole news source, students have the potential to be more exposed to false information. He said,

> I think with all the fake media and not just on Donald Trump but obviously more Facebook posts like that where people share false things … and then it's like people have this information that's not correct and I feel like it's important for the teachers to talk about that stuff with us so that we have the correct information.

The majority of students that participated in the focus groups reported that their school had no school newspaper. In fact, only students at two of the schools shared that they still had one. According to the students, lack of popularity in school journalism led to the abandonment of most programs. Some students described how they did have a school newspaper at one point, but it died off due to lack of student interest, and many didn't have the inclination to bring it back as they believed it was outdated. Bob said, "it's more of there's a lack of student interest than it is the school trying to oppress anything."

When asked whether they thought they needed a real school newspaper, Blue commented, "No, because everybody uses technology nowadays." James said, "There would really be no point in printing a newspaper.… I mean I don't think anyone would really read it in our school. [We read the] press on Twitter or something." Lucy said, "We don't have a specific newspaper, but I feel like everyone spreads whatever they want to share on Facebook, Instagram, Snapchat." One group of students said that they did have a paper in previous years, but "it was sort of discontinued, it wasn't super popular … only four people signed up to do it," according to Leila.

The two schools that did still have a school newspaper had students in the focus groups who were very supportive of the student-run press, even though opinions were mixed regarding the usefulness of the papers. Kaiden remarked that at his school, the paper was strong, and had elements that allowed for student free speech:

> like letters to the editor, like students can really like present any opinion or belief that they want, and people working on the newspaper, like they have all sorts of different types of stories. Even I think there were stories like critical of like administration for like certain issues that were going on.

Contrary to that, at the other high school with a newspaper, students felt that the newspaper was not worthwhile and only contained school-event news. Jimmy said that "They don't write about serious stuff in the news.... They don't do anything with politics or news." Jami concurred, and said, "They only write about things that are involved in the school.... There's no current events."

Theme 2: Limitations of Students' Press Rights Exist

Some of students' First Amendment rights are limited when they walk in the doors of the school, but those limitations often expand beyond the school walls. Clementine believed that, in general, "we give up some of our rights when we enter the school." While many students understood that, it was not always something of which they were supportive. Echoing Andy's thoughts about fake media (Theme 1), Jack was concerned about limiting students' free press rights. He believed, "if you don't have freedom of the press [in school], then you're gonna be fed false information, and then you can't protest the right stuff, or you're not thinking for yourself, necessarily."

However, Leila thought that the school should have a say in what students shared in the press. She said,

> I think [post what you want] as long as, like, because younger kids in our school district could be looking at it ... but I think it would just have to stay appropriate for the younger kids as well.

When asked if they should be allowed to post whatever they wanted about the school or district on Twitter, most students believed that their rights to free speech were limited, as there are consequences inside of school for posts that take place outside of school. Seth said, "you have the freedom of speech to criticize [the school]." Asia agreed to an extent, with a caveat. She said they can post what they want on social media, "if you're not hurting [the school] or saying anything negative." Jimmy thought that, "[Administrators] can't control how you feel really toward anything unless it's through the school, like our newspaper is, or journalism, then I can understand [censorship], but [not] if it's outside of school and has nothing to do with them," which gets to the heart of free school press—should schools censor what students publish in school press, or exercise their right to prior review?

Students at a variety of schools provided examples of their peers posting negative information about their schools on social media, which then led to in-school consequences, such as detention, in-school suspension, or even removal from a sports team. Bryan stated,

> You have to be careful in social media, if you're, like if we're talking [negatively] about the stuff in the school, because I know there have been kids who have gotten in trouble for it. It's a lot more censored than [it used to be].

Students had mixed answers to whether or not they could exercise their freedom of the press by writing about controversial issues in their school paper (if their school had a paper), or if they should have been able to exercise their freedom (if their school did not have a paper). Jimmy said, "You can't just publish anything here, 'cause … if something's offensive to the school or views the school in a bad way, then they wouldn't let them publish it, I think." Jami said, "I feel like it's definitely free, but it's up to your discretion to be responsible with it, because even though you have free press, everyone can see it, where if you post something on Instagram … even though you have freedom, you can't abuse it or it's going to come back in negative ways." Jabroth believed that students at his school "feel it's right to only talk about safe stuff [in the newspaper] and not take it to an extreme."

Lucy expressed a broader view of free press in school newspapers, stating,

> It's kind of like the right of American citizens to talk about controversial topics. I mean, again, to an extent you can't specifically say this person is like–yeah you can't go into like specifics, like a specific person like targeting or bullying, but I, that's your right to talk about controversial opinion. It's your right to believe in your opinion, and speak your opinion, and … try to convince people.

Theme 3: Peers' Free Speech Should Be Limited on Social Media

Most students agree with Lucy's point, though, that students should not post offensive or bullying content online. The majority of students agreed with the opinion that they should not post things online that abuse First Amendment rights, or are inappropriate for an online audience. They were especially concerned about students posting things harmful to others or supportive of bullying, or things for which subjects of posts did not give consent. Kaiden said, "if it's like threatening harm or inciting violence, or any type of that, then those students shouldn't be posting." Jami agreed, saying, "If it's just a bad opinion [about the school], it's fine. But if it gets into borderline threatening or anything, that's where it becomes an issue," and intervention by the school would then be necessary. Anastasia concurred, stating,

> I think there's like—there's a boundary for what you can and can't post. Like if it's like ... like verbally hurting somebody where like you're physically threatening them, then I think that shouldn't be allowed or like it's promoting something that could like possibly harm someone. But if it's like in good nature, then it should be okay.

Students believe that using social media to bully or hurt someone was a misuse of their First Amendment freedoms. Tyler said,

> I feel like if you're down on someone or bullying them on social media and just like harming them, making them feel bad, I think that should be censored. But if there's something you don't like about the school, and you tweet it, I don't think they should make you take it down or something.

Ryan agreed, stating,

> If you have a video of someone goofing off and they just don't want you to post it because they don't want people to see what they're doing, that you should respect that but again, if someone's bullying or being racist or whatever and they don't know that you have the video, you should definitely be allowed to post it.

Bernice appreciated some of the safeguards that Twitter and Facebook have in place to prevent this kind of behavior. She said,

> you can report posts if they're hateful. So you can get them taken off if they're bashing a certain person or they're just offensive in general, because they try to keep it positive on Twitter.... They do have restrictions on what you can and can't post, which I think is cool."

Ruth, along with many other students, strongly believed that things should not be posted on social media without other people's consent:

> If it's not harming anybody else, but it's their opinion, then yes, they can post it. So, if they wanna post something about the government or about Trump or about the walkout, for example, then they can do that, but if it's gonna hurt another student physically or emotionally, then no.

In addition to students' inappropriate use of social media, some students were concerned about schools and what the students consider a misuse of power, since they can be punished for posting items on social media outside of school hours that result in in-school consequences and can lead to students feeling a lack of privacy from school authorities. Steven said,

> Yeah, they've gotten some people in trouble before for things they've tweeted, or pictures they've found on the internet, which I think like the pictures they find of just kids posting stuff, like at parties or something, I don't think they [school personnel] should have the right to get them in trouble for like their party on their own time, and I don't know, they're partaking [in] these activities off the school grounds. No school supervision or anything, and I just think that's their own business.

Kathleen agreed with this sentiment, stating,

> I don't think [the school] should be allowed to see what we post off of school. I think if we tweet something on our own time, why should they care like if we're not tweeting in the school or about the school, why do they get to get us in trouble for that?

Garrett echoed this thought as well, saying that he believes school administrators, "shouldn't interfere with our private lives unless we choose to give them that avenue ... as far as private lives go, I don't think they should have any say in it at all."

Theme 4: Perceptions That Administrators Censor Access to Digital Information

One area of interest that students noted was the control of access to websites while at school and the district's blocking and perceived censorship of information that students can obtain. Students from most schools indicated that there was a Wi-Fi filter at their school. Bernice said, "If you use the school Wi-Fi, you can't access some things." Alex's school has similar filters in place, and she added that her school has rules in place about going around the filter. She said, "Well, we're technically not supposed to get off the Wi-Fi. That's a rule. We're not supposed to but everyone does." Mack said her school's Wi-Fi is also blocked, and that

> Technically, at school you're not allowed to get on Snapchat, or Instagram, or Facebook. It's blocked. Technically, if you use your data instead of your Wi-Fi, then you can get on it anyways. The school's trying to limit that stuff, but it's not very effective.

Sierra echoed that and added that at her school she was "pretty convinced that the school has a data block, which basically just means your data's slowed down." Thomas believes there is a reason for this. He said,

> They insist that even when you're on your phone, [you] use the school's Wi-Fi. Don't use your own data, because then you can have access to sites, and they can track what sites you use [on the school's network].

Kylie is not bothered by this, though, as she understands the district's need to do this to maintain a positive instructional environment. She said,

> They have Wi-Fi, but yeah, they have it blocked–you can't really get on anything.... If we got to be able to get on Wi-Fi and get on every social media, I think people would abuse it. Some kids would get on things that aren't appropriate for school, and I feel like they would be on their phones a lot more. Like, if we were on the computers and you could get on Instagram or Facebook, I feel like people would be, like, more to get on that than do their work on the computer.

Garrett agreed with her. He said,

> I understand they have to maintain their own liability protection if we're doing stuff on their Wi-Fi, and by extension, I guess on school property. I think they should have a little bit of say on that, if only for preserving the school for the other students around you.

Not everyone shares this perspective, though. When discussing the blocking of access to specific sites, Steven echoed Thomas's sentiments about administrators blocking sites, and said that he feels "like the administration here likes to keep us in the dark."

DISCUSSION

This study yielded noteworthy results with regard to the research questions:

- What are the perceptions of high school students about First Amendment freedoms of speech and press rights?
- What are their views of these rights as they relate to social media and their uses of it?

Regarding their perceptions about First Amendment freedoms of speech and press rights, the students believed that they do have the right to exercise their freedom of speech and freedom of the press, but that there are limitations to those rights within school settings and sharing of information about schools, especially when one considers social media as a form of press. As the four main thematic findings showed, students no longer get their news from traditional news sources, limitations of students' press rights do exist, students believed that their peers' free speech should be limited on social media, and students did perceive that administrators censored their access to digital information.

Also noteworthy were the findings on school newspapers and the dearth of them. There is a substantial lack of traditional school newspapers sources as reported by the students. Of the six schools represented in this study, only students from two schools claimed to have a school paper still in use. Of those two, students at only one school believed that they had a truly free press where the administration would willingly allow students to publish what they wanted about controversial topics. The students from the other school felt that they would not be able to and that their administration would fall in line with the *Hazelwood School District v. Kuhlmeier* (1988) ruling that administrators could exercise prior review and restraint of school-sponsored newspapers. One interesting finding was that in schools that had no newspaper, students did not indicate a desire to have one—there was a strong lack of interest in reviving dead papers or starting up new ones. Students felt that a school newspaper was antiquated and outdated, since online news sources and social media were more up-to-date and of-the-moment than a newspaper could ever be.

Since most students are not learning about new—school or otherwise—from school newspapers, they turn to other sources to fill the void. Some students cited parent newsletters or in-school daily announcements as sources of school news, but the vast majority of students described their use of social media as their main news source for school, local, and national news. Twitter was most often cited as the place where they learned about what was happening in the world around them, both in and out of school. Both students and school districts are posting news and information on Twitter. This brings up the validity and reliability of the information to which they are being exposed to in this era of false information in the media. Some students did discuss this issue, and indicated the need to proceed with caution when seeking out information via social media.

Students also believed that their freedom of the press and freedom of speech rights were somewhat limited as a result of being in school, both due to limitations of their press rights and access to websites on the school district's Wi-Fi. Due to school rules and policies in school handbooks, they did not feel as if they could be as forthcoming with their thoughts in school media as they would like. They acknowledged that this was for their own safety and seemed to understand the liability schools have if something negative were to happen on the school's Wi-Fi, such as cyberbullying or threats of violence.

Students also felt that their rights to free speech were limited, as there could be consequences inside of school for social media posts that take place outside of school. They did not feel as if they could criticize teachers or the school without being asked to take the posts down. Students did not think this should be the case, though, and felt as if they should be able to post what they wanted to without fear of retribution from the school. Some students did not feel as if schools would allow them to publish about controversial issues either in real or hypothetical school newspapers. Others did believe that it would be acceptable to write about controversial issues, such as immigration or gun violence, but this would need to be done responsibly and from an objective point of view.

One positive finding from this study is that students believe that people should not be using social media to post inciting, hurtful, or harmful videos, pictures, or content unless they obtain the consent of those involved. They believe that using social media to bully is problematic, and many cited examples of students being hurt by this.

When examining the uses and gratifications theoretical framework (Blumler & McQuail, 1969), the uses of interest in this study were information seeking, information sharing, and expression of opinion. Each of these uses was unpacked throughout the study. The researcher sought to better determine where high school students are going to get their news, how information is being shared with and among them, and whether or not they are expressing their opinion in the media. These findings as discussed allowed the researcher to determine that students' information seeking gratifications were filled mainly through social media, and not through traditional media routes, such as newspapers, as inquired about in the uses and gratifications framework; they went to Twitter to find out what was happening in and out of schools. Additionally, information was mainly shared publicly among high school students on social media platforms such as Twitter, Instagram, and Snapchat, but not as much on Facebook. Students in this study believed that Facebook was a platform for an older generation. As a result, schools were also sharing information with students through Twitter. Student needs to express their opinions through social media or school newspapers were not fully gratified, as they felt that school rules limited their rights to truly post what they wanted to for fear of in-school consequences or censorship.

TOPICS FOR FUTURE STUDY

The results of this study bring to light some questions that are challenging to answer, and further research needs to be done to better understand the answers to them and the implications of those answers. A few of those questions are the following:

- If there are no longer school newspapers, are we raising an entire generation that doesn't understand the importance of responsible journalism?
- Is this lack of high school support assisting in the death of traditional newspapers out in the "real world"?
- In addition, one can't help but wonder if the litigious nature of society is leading to a generation of students that are shielded from controversy.
- Are schools so afraid of opening themselves up to a lawsuit that they block websites and prevent students from openly accessing what is on the internet today? How, then, are students supposed to learn to become digitally literate and recognize the false information that some students discussed? These internet filters fail to give students the opportunity to delve into the issues that plague our society today, especially those that are fraught with controversy (Johnson, 2003). Should schools remove the filters and blocks and instead focus more on teaching students responsible internet usage?

CONCLUSION

If students believe that their opinions on current issues are not being allowed a forum in today's public school newspapers due to a limitation of students' free speech and press rights, how will students learn to think critically about matters of importance in the world around them? It is the role of the social studies teacher to teach students the importance of utilizing their first amendment rights and of being civically engaged and informed, so that they can make educated opinions and not just post and share inflammatory content on social media. Even though this may be difficult and potentially uncomfortable for administrators and teachers and may open them up to criticism, it is important to create citizens who understand bias, perspective, and the differences among people's perspectives. It is for citizens to be able to argue their viewpoint in a civil, respectful manner, even through social media use.

This does not mean that we should direct students to a specific stance. It does mean, however, that there are certain freedoms under the First Amendment to which all people are entitled. Positions that undermine these core values should not be silenced, but also should not be upheld as equally acceptable or just. While this work can be challenging, we uphold the responsibility of our profession when we teach students to exercise their First Amendment rights, including freedom of the press and freedom of speech.

AUTHOR NOTE

Correspondence concerning this article should be addressed to Sarah Kaka, College of Education, Ohio Wesleyan University, Delaware, OH 43015. Contact: sjkaka@owu.edu

REFERENCES

Abud, G., Jr. (2018, March 19). Can schools discipline students for social media use outside of school? *Education Week*. https://blogs.edweek.org/teachers/teacher_leader_voices/2018/03/can_students_be_disciplined_fo.html

Arguello, R. (2016, January 8). Tweet about WIAA earns suspension for athlete. *Post Crescent*. https://www.postcrescent.com/story/sports/2016/01/08/prep-athlete-suspended-tweet/78525606/

Blumler, J. G., & McQuail, D. (1969). *Television in politics: Its uses and influence*. Chicago: University of Chicago Press. https://doi.org/10.1177/000271626938600174

Bowen, J. (2010, April 15). JEA board defines prior review. *Journalism Education Association*. http://jeasprc.org/jea-board-defines-prior-review/

Bowen, J. (2019, May 3). Prior review imposes ineffective educational limits on learning, citizenship. *Journalism Education Association*. http://jeasprc.org/prior-review-imposes-ineffective-educational-limits-on-learning-citizenship/

Bucy, E. P., Gantz, W., & Wang, Z. (2007). Media technology and the 24-hour news cycle. In C. A. Lin & D. J. Atkin (Eds.) *Communication technology and social change: Theory and implications* (pp. 143–163). Erlbaum.

Burge v. Colton School District 53, 100 F, Supp.3d 1057 (2015).

Cramer, T. (2014). Is social media the only truly free press? *EContent, 37*(8), 4. http://www.econtentmag.com/Articles/Column/T.0/Is-Social-Media-the-Only-Truly-Free-Press-99671.htm

Creswell, J. W., & Poth, C. N. (2017). *Qualitative inquiry and research design: Choosing among five approaches* (4th ed.). SAGE.

Flanagin, A. J., & Metzger, M. J. (2001). Internet use in the contemporary media environment. *Human Communication Research, 27*(1), 153–181.

Freedom Forum Institute. (n.d.). Who is "the press"? *Freedom Forum Institute FAQs*. https://www.freedomforuminstitute.org/about/faq/who-is-the-press/

Hazelwood School District v. Kuhlmeier, 484 U.S. 260 (1987), 79 F.2d 1368 (1988).

Head, A. J., Wihbey, J., Metaxas, P. T., MacMillan, M., & Cohen, D. (2018). *How students engage with news: Five takeaways for educators, journalists, and librarians.*

Project Information Literacy Research Institute. http://www.projectinfolit.org/uploads/2/7/5/4/27541717/newsreport.pdf

Johnson, D. (2003). Freedom and filters. *Library Media Connection, 21*(5), 110.

Kartik-Narayan, A. (2018, March 21). Don't stop the press. *Southside Weekly*. https://southsideweekly.com/dont-stop-presses-student-newspapers-south-side/

Keierleber, M. (2015, May 7). *Oregon student wins free-speech lawsuit against school*. Student Press Law Center. https://splc.org/2015/05/oregon-student-wins-free-speech-lawsuit-against-school-overturning-discipline-for-critical-facebook-posts/

Klein, R. (2014, March 18). 20 high schoolers suspended for retweeting gossip. *Huffington Post*. https://www.huffpost.com/entry/mckay-high-school-retweets_n_4981878?guccounter=1

LoMonte, F. D. (2015, February 17). Don't silence young (female) journalists. *Education Week, 34*(21), 24–25.

LoMonte, F. (2016, May 12). Pennsylvania court extends school's disciplinary reach into student's off-campus Facebook joke. *Student Press Law Center*. https://splc.org/2016/05/pennsylvania-student-facebook-discipline-upheld/

McQuail, D. (2005). *McQuail's mass communication theory* (5th ed). SAGE.

Miles, M. B., Huberman, A. M., & Saldaña, J. (2014). *Qualitative data analysis: A methods sourcebook* (3rd ed.). SAGE.

National Coalition Against Censorship. (2019). *Watch what you tweet: Schools, censorship, and social media*. National Coalition Against Censorship. https://ncac.org/watch-what-you-tweet-schools-censorship-and-social-media

Ortiz, V. (2015, April 13). Lack of money, interest forcing many high school newspapers to close. *Chicago Tribune*. https://www.chicagotribune.com/news/ct-high-school-newspapers-dying-met-20150409-story.html

Patterson, N., & Chandler, P. (Eds.). (2021). *At the schoolhouse gate: Stakeholder perceptions of First Amendment rights and responsibilities*. Information Age.

Patton, M. Q. (2015). *Qualitative research and evaluation methods* (4th ed.). SAGE.

Paxton, M., & Dickson, T. (2000). State free expression laws and scholastic press censorship. *Journalism & Mass Communication Educator, 55*(2), 50–59. https://doi.org./10.1177/107769580005500206

R.L. v. Central York School District, 183 F.Supp.3d 625 (2016).

Shearer, E. (2018, December 10). *Social media outpaces print newspapers in the U.S. as a news source*. Pew Research Center. https://www.pewresearch.org/fact-tank/2018/12/10/social-media-outpaces-print-newspapers-in-the-u-s-as-a-news-source/

Shen v. Albany Unified School District, 3:17-cv-02478-JD (lead case) (N.D. Cal. Aug. 24, 2018).

Smith, A., Silver, L., Johnson, C., Taylor, K., & Jiang, J. (2019). *Publics in emerging economies worry social media sow division, even as they offer new changes for political engagement*. Pew Research Center. https://www.pewinternet.org/wp-content/uploads/sites/9/2019/05/Pew-Research-Center_Technology-and-Politics-in-Emerging-Economies-Report_2019-05-13.pdf

Tinker v. Des Moines Independent School District No. 21, 258 F.Supp. 971 (1966), 383 F.2d 988 (8th Cir.1967), 393 U.S. 503 (1969).

Walsh, M. (2017, December 1). Judge backs discipline of students who posted or 'liked' online racial taunts. *Education Week.* http://blogs.edweek.org/edweek/school_law/2017/12/judge_backs_discipline_of_stud.html

Whiting, A., & Williams, D. L. (2013). Why people use social media: A uses and gratifications approach. *Qualitative Market Research, 16*(4), 362–369. https://doi.org/10.1108/QMR-06-2013-0041

Widman, A. (2016, April 13). Racially charged video leads to discipline for 3 Pickerington central students. *Columbus Dispatch.* https://www.dispatch.com/content/stories/local/2016/04/12/pickerington-racism.html

Wojcicki, E. (2007, April 6). The slow death of high school journalism. *Huffington Post.* https://www.huffpost.com/entry/the-slow-death-of-high-sc_b_45158

Yin, R. K. (2018). *Case study research and applications: Design and methods* (6th ed.). SAGE.

PART III

CHOICES TO ACT

CHAPTER 7

"I WALK FOR ..."

Teacher Activism in Action

Kristy A. Brugar
University of Oklahoma

Dalton C. Savage
Edmond Memorial High School

In the spring of 2018, teachers across the country voiced their concerns with the state of public education. Notably, there were teacher walkouts in West Virginia, Kentucky, Arizona, and in our home state of Oklahoma. The purpose of this chapter is to describe the experiences of 4 secondary school social studies teachers as they navigated their roles of teacher, citizen, public employee, and community member during the Oklahoma teacher walkout. In this portraiture research, we interviewed 2 early career teachers (3 years of teaching), a middle career teacher (more than 20 years teaching experience), and a veteran teacher (more than 40 years of teaching experience). We share the ways in which these teachers were actively involved in their immediate communities and the overall movement.

As the day began April 2, 2018, a crowd gathered in front of and around the Oklahoma capitol building with the understanding that the formal program, including speeches, would begin at 10 A.M. As 10 A.M.

At the Schoolhouse Gate: Stakeholder Perceptions of First Amendment Rights and Responsibilities in U.S. Public Schools, pp. 139–
www.infoagepub.com
Copyright © 2022 by Information Age Publishing
All rights of reproduction in any form reserved.

approached, an announcement was made to the crowd that an elementary-aged boy, Brandon (all names of private citizens and teachers interviewed are pseudonyms), had been separated from his mother. His mother needed help finding him so the two could be reunited. Brandon's mother made her way to the podium where she called out to her son, panic rising in her voice, choking back tears. Recognizing the panic, a teacher who was standing near the podium took the microphone and addressed the crowd. She asked the thousands of people standing in front of the Oklahoma State Capitol building to simply sit down. If we all sat down, except for Brandon, he would easily be seen among the sea of people and reunited with his mother. Within a minute, thousands of people sat down so this one little boy could be seen. He was quickly reunited with his mother.

This swift and altruistic act by thousands exemplified the willingness of teachers and community members involved in the Oklahoma teacher walkout to do what was necessary for their students. This chapter focuses on the experiences of four teachers among the thousands involved in this collective action. Our research question is, "What were the experiences of social studies teachers who participated in the walkout?" Our purpose for this chapter is to share stories of four secondary social studies teachers as they navigated their roles of teacher, citizen, public employee, community member, and leader, while they spoke and assembled for public education during this event.

EXPERIENCES OF TEACHERS AND TEACHER ACTIVISM

In 1985, Giroux wrote about teachers as transformative intellectuals. In that work, he advocated that teachers play a key role in reforming education and the work of teachers. Through organizing and defending schools, teachers act as responsible citizens. Teacher activism is broadly defined as those pushing against the status quo and addressing issues of educational reform and social justice. Teacher voice and action are not always involved in development and implementation of educational policies (Ingersoll, 2006; Taylor & Bogotch, 1994). Quinn and Carl (2015) found, however, that when teachers organized, they were able to facilitate change. Notable from their study was the assertion that teacher agency was built when opportunities to inform classroom instruction, educational structures, and awareness of the collective power were evident.

There has been a long-standing interest in teacher agency and activism. Picower (2012) studied teacher activists' practices across place and their years of service. She identified common commitments among her participants including, *reconciling the vision*, *moving toward liberation*, and *standing up to oppression* (p. 564). Reconciling the vision referred to acknowledging that education was both liberating and oppressive. With this acknowledgment, teachers could move toward liberation by enacting classroom practices that aided students to better understand inequality and to identify ways they could take action for change. Teachers enacting the third commitment could then stand up to oppression by engaging in ongoing and collective actions (p. 564).

Krutka et al. (2018) explored teacher activism in online spaces, particularly the Facebook site for the walkout and the #OklaEd network. They identified eight lessons learned as they examined these spaces: teacher networks can offer support; teacher participation can disrupt narratives; teacher networks can amplify mobilization; teacher networks can encourage flexibility; leadership is critical, but must be representative; online activities are not enough; legislative change is ongoing; misinformation or distraction tactics not evident ... yet (pp. 384–389).

Research done by Swalwell and Schweber (2016) explored the experiences of seven secondary social studies teachers who participated in protests in Wisconsin. They described their findings in four categories: time period in teachers' lives, a deepening political awareness and activism, teaching, and the silencing of voices (p. 290). The researchers described the impact these protest experiences had on the lives of these teachers, including lasting significance and deepening of their political awareness and levels of activism. They also noted changes in the choices these teachers made about social studies content and pedagogy during this time. These choices included recognition of the need for balanced presentation of content, the importance of including controversial events, and the disclosure of their own political beliefs and activities. Finally, Swalwell and Schweber (2016) found that teachers silenced themselves in subsequent years.

These studies show that teacher activism is not new, that it has been effective in the past, and that while protests of various types can impact societal change, they also change the protesters themselves. With ideas of teacher activism and activities in mind, our research question is, "What were the impacts on these teachers of their experiences with the walkout?"

METHOD

This chapter is an opportunity to share experiences of four teachers during the walkout. We draw from aspects of portraiture (Lawrence-Lightfoot & Hoffman Davis, 1997). Lawrence-Lightfoot and Hoffman Davis describe portraiture as an "intentionally generous and eclectic process that begins by searching for what is good and healthy and assumes that the expression of goodness will always be laced with imperfections" (p. 9). The researchers, or portraitists, are "active in selecting the themes that will be used to tell the story, strategic in deciding in points of focus and emphasis, and creative in defining the sequence and rhythm of the narrative" (p. 12).

As part of understanding the stories of our teacher participants, it was important for each of us to memo about our own experiences during the walkout (Birks et al., 2008). These memos and recollections helped us contextualize the stories and experiences that were shared as we created each portrait. These portraits were framed around the teacher's experiences both prior to and during the Oklahoma teacher walkout. This background information on the participants helped us identify three themes: the activities in which they participated, their experiences with community and community support, and the attention brought to public education.

Context

In 2018, there was unprecedented activism by teachers across the country, notably teacher walkouts or strikes in West Virginia, Kentucky, Arizona, and in our home state of Oklahoma. Oklahoma ranks among the lowest in reference to teacher pay, while it ranks as one of the highest states for cuts to public education (Maiden & Ballard, 2017). In the 2018 state of the state address, Governor Mary Fallin called for the Republican super majority and the limited Democrat caucus in the state legislature to address school funding and give teachers a much-deserved teacher pay raise—an average of $6,100. As the 2018 legislative session progressed, votes in support of school funding and teacher pay raises fell short, far less than the 75% majority needed to raise taxes in the state of Oklahoma.

In late March 2018, on the eve of the walkout, media outlets and state leadership communicated differing messages and motivations for this work *stoppage*. State officials had stated teachers were going to walk out on their students. Further, Governor Mary Fallin told CBS News, "Teachers want more," referring to teachers wanting more than a proposed average $6,100 raise. She went on to compare the state's teachers to spoiled teenagers saying, "It's like kind of having a teenage kid that wants a better car" (Villafranca, 2018). This statement became great fodder and ignited a fervor, as thousands of teachers moved from educating students in classrooms to educating their students, and the greater public, from the grounds of the capitol. This statement positioned teachers to defend their actions to walk out.

In 2018, the education situation in Oklahoma was challenging, to say the least. Overall, Oklahoma lead the nation in cutting public school funding since 2008. Teacher salaries were among the lowest in the nation. There was (and continues to be) a shortage of teachers to fill open positions. This has lead to ever-increasing numbers of alternatively or emergency certified teachers working in classrooms across the state. In additions, class sizes had increased and classroom resources (e.g., textbooks) have not been updated or replenished.

On April 2, 2018, teachers did just that. From across the state of Oklahoma, teachers walked out of their classrooms and headed to the capitol in Oklahoma City. More than 25,000 teachers were joined by students, parents, and other community members, all advocating for improved funding for Oklahoma public schools, classrooms, and students. A mantra commonly heard and seen on signs teachers carried was "I Walk For ...". Teachers completed this statement by simply stating, "my students," "new textbooks," or "better funding."

The walkout—not a strike, as Oklahoma is a "right-to-work state" (70 Oklahoma Statute, Section 509.8)—lasted 10 days to, arguably, mixed results. In right-to-work states like Oklahoma, employees are entitled to work without joining a union. Therefore, in Oklahoma, teacher union membership varies from community to community. The state boasts two teachers' unions: Oklahoma Education Association and Oklahoma City (American Federation of Teachers) and one nonunion teacher organization (Professional Oklahoma Educators). Within each of the teachers' unions, there are individual community unions that community members create.

Participants

Four Oklahoma teachers participated in this study: Dalton (coauthor) and Jenna, two early career teachers; Owen, a middle career teacher; and Carl, a veteran teacher. Beyond those of the authors, all names of people and schools are pseudonyms. Each teacher was selected based on having had a professional relationship with one of the authors and a known involvement during the walkout. For example, Carl had served as a mentor teacher for preservice teachers in Kristy's university class. He was also active on social media and shared information, including pictures of his involvement, before, during, and after the walkout. Each teacher represented a different community (suburban and rural) and had varying years of teaching experience ranging from 2 years to 44 years (see Table 7.1). Our participants were all actively involved in the walkout and described themselves as deeply invested in education in Oklahoma.

Table 7.1

Teacher Participants

Participant	*Years of Service*	*Community Type*	*School*
Carl	44	Rural	Southtown Middle School
Dalton	2	Rural	Westtown Middle School
Jenna	3	Suburban	University High School
Owen	22	Suburban	Northtown High School

Rationale

In this study, we (Kristy and Dalton—the authors and researchers), describe and explain the experiences of four secondary social studies teachers (Dalton and three others) as they navigated the walkout in April 2018. We designed a semistructured interview protocol that was informed by Lave and Wenger's communities of practice (1989). We paid attention to the way(s) in which individuals acted and interacted within communities around common interests.

Our interview protocol (see Appendix) consisted of five broad questions about their professional lives in general, as well as their experiences during the walkout. We conducted individual interviews lasting from 45 minutes to over two hours. We conducted Carl's interview together. Dalton interviewed Owen, and Kristy interviewed Jenna and Dalton. The interviews were conducted and transcribed approximately six months after the walkout. Also, the interviews took place about one month before fall elections, including a gubernatorial race during which education was a "hot topic," and memories and reminders of the walkout were at the forefront of conversations. Case in point, Dalton, Jenna, and Carl reposted photographs and messages on social media about their experiences.

Teachers' Stories

In our conversations with these three teachers and in discussions of Dalton's experiences, each expressed great passion for public education and funding for public education. In addition, each teacher spoke about activities associated with the walkout, their interactions with the community, and community actions that supported and furthered attention for public education and educational funding.

In the following sections, we share four portraits (two of early career teachers, one insider and one outsider; one middle career teacher; and one veteran teacher) in which we describe these teachers and their experiences during the walkout. Each story opens with some background information on the participants and is further organized around evidence of the three emergent themes from the interviews: the activities in which they participated, their experiences with community and community support, and the attention brought to public education. Each of our teachers participated in a variety of activities, experienced community and community support, and noted the attention brought to public education. We begin by presenting a vignette of the early career teachers, Dalton and Jenna, before moving onto the midcareer teacher, Owen, and ending with Carl, the veteran.

Dalton: "Insider" at the Walkout

At the time of the walkout and this study, both Dalton and Jenna were pretenure faculty in their districts. This identifier is significant, as they acted and participated in the walkout without the job security and connections to the school and community of our more veteran participants.

Dalton is from a small farming and manufacturing community in southern Oklahoma. Dalton was born in Texas, but has lived his entire life, including his PK–20 school years in the Sooner State. As a self-described "Okie," Dalton chose to become a teacher to help improve education in his state. As an undergraduate, while attending the University of Oklahoma, Dalton completed an internship at the state capitol and was interested in politics beyond his coursework. In addition, he completed his teacher internship in the Oklahoma City metro area and began his first teaching job in a rural community outside of Oklahoma City.

During the walkout, Dalton was in his second year of teaching, which by almost all measures made him a novice teacher. During his short tenure as a teacher, Dalton often discussed his feelings of great concern over school funding and teacher pay. As teachers were walking out and rallying in West Virginia about a month before the Oklahoma teachers walked out, Dalton and his Oklahoma colleagues began to have discussions of whether this type of work stoppage would be effective in getting the legislature to earnestly address the needs for Oklahoma public schools.

Dalton was seen by his peers and colleagues as an expert community member, rather than a novice teacher. Through his experiences at the state capitol, he was able to navigate and to help his colleagues navigate within and through the Oklahoma legislature. Each day of the walkout, he met with his school colleagues and drove to the state capitol. While many stayed outside the building, Dalton and a few peers joined hundreds of teachers in the building. After navigating the security lines and legislative agenda, Dalton helped his colleagues identify talking points and key legislators to speak with about motions on the floor.

During that time, Dalton observed that three distinct groups of teachers emerged. First were the *visible* teachers who helped with logistics. This group set up tents and provided food and beverages. From 7:30 a.m. to 3:00 p.m., these teachers rallied around the capitol with their signs and made their presence known, both visibly and vocally. Next, there was a group of teachers who became *insiders*. This group met with legislators, sat in on committee meetings and legislative sessions for the House and Senate, and stayed long hours to advocate for change in Oklahoma public education. Dalton most identified with this group, as he helped his colleagues maneuver through the capitol while setting up key meetings with legislative stakeholders. Finally, a third group that emerged was the *armchair advocates*. The armchair advocates made social media pushes and were outspoken with family and friends about the work stoppage but rarely, if ever, made the 20-mile trip to the state capitol.

Jenna: "Outsider" to the Oklahoma Walkout

At the time of the walkout, Jenna was in her third year of teaching, an assignment that included teaching U.S. government classes. Due to her brief tenure as a teacher, her story is a bit shorter. Originally from Illinois, she attended the University of Oklahoma and did her teaching internship at the school at which she currently teaches. She made the conscious decision to teach in Oklahoma (she interviewed in neighboring states) and, specifically at University High School. As an undergraduate teacher education student, Jenna expressed interest in being involved in her school community through a variety of activities from developing relationships with colleagues and students to sponsoring clubs and coaching sports. She quickly became involved at University High School and was an active participant in the walkout. At the time of the walkout, Jenna had not yet earned tenure in her school district, so her involvement may have been seen as professionally risky. However, when she was asked about this, she simply stated, "It's not just us, it's for future generations as well."

As a third-year teacher, Jenna was cognizant of and attentive to the actions of her more experienced colleagues, including individuals from her home department and school as well as fellow university alumni/Oklahoma public school teachers. Regardless of her novice status, Jenna spent every day at the capitol, earning her place in the "Outsider" category by spending almost all her time outside the capitol building. For the most part, she described "walking around the capitol building" and spending time with colleagues at the University High School "home base" (a tented area where faculty and community members could check in with one another, get refreshments, and review actions and events transpiring within the capitol building). These experiences were note-worthy for Jenna, as she was able to further identify as a member of her school community and an Oklahoma teacher—meaning a teacher who participated in the walkout. Jenna, as well as our other participants, identified participating in the walkout as a defining experience in their professional lives (Swalwell & Schweber, 2016).

Owen: Experiencing the Community

At the time of the walkout, Owen was in his 22nd year of teaching. He was primarily responsible for Advanced Placement U.S. and comparative government classes. In addition, he served as the social studies department chair at Northtown High School, where he spent the majority of his teaching career. He took a visible leadership role before, during, and after the walkout. Further, he navigated among several different communities of stakeholders, including administration, teachers, teachers' unions, and citizens involved in this grassroots movement. Owen described each of these as key stakeholders in the walkout. However, it was his view that they "failed to effectively communicate between one another—they needed help."

Owen and thousands of other teachers across Oklahoma had experienced years of budget cuts. In Owen's estimation, the walkout was a long time coming. "If we did not do something, nothing would happen." He described the district as unorganized and thought "it would take a strong grassroots effort to bring about real change in our state." A grassroots movement for funding changes in Owen's school started weeks before the walkout. Then, in late March, an 8th grade social studies teacher took the first step, via social media, to substantively mobilize teachers and community members across the state to speak up collectively about public school funding.

All of our participants mentioned the role of social media as part of the walkout. However, this was particularly important for Owen. He used his years of teaching and leadership experiences to lead the social media movement for his school district. Owen designed a website and multiple social media platforms (Twitter, Facebook, GroupMe, and Remind) for teachers, administrators, parents, community members, and students. Each platform served a unique purpose. Twitter was used as a roadmap for how his school district was going to navigate the capitol and its grounds. Facebook was used in multiple ways to communicate with teachers, administrators, parents, community members, and students. GroupMe and Remind were used to keep teachers "in the know" of what was happening on the ground at the capitol.

As mentioned earlier, the walkout was an opportunity to educate the community at-large and students. One of many note-worthy experiences was classes that were held by teachers on the grounds of the state capitol. Teachers from Northtown High School, including Owen, led this effort by creating a "Classroom at the Capitol." Owen and his colleagues felt class must go on for students. Each day of the walkout, teachers from Northtown High held classes in various subjects on the capitol lawn. This sent a powerful message to state legislators and the community writ large that simply because school was closed, it did not mean learning had stopped.

It is important to remember that the walkout involved and impacted individuals beyond classroom teachers. From businesses to individuals, supplies were donated to teachers, staff, parents, and the rest of the education community in order to advocate for students at the state capitol. For Owen, the food and drink donations were overwhelming. His school had so many donations that they "adopted" other schools with fewer donations by sharing their own community's offerings. This showed the power of *teachers helping teachers*, and more generally, an Oklahomans helping Oklahomans mentality that was seen throughout the walkout.

Carl: Bringing Attention to Public Education

Without question, Carl was a veteran teacher in every sense. At the time of the walkout, he had spent 44 years teaching in Southtown, a small, rural school district. The impact of public school funding had been felt in Carl's school district, which had moved away from the traditional 5-day school week to a 4-day school week. Four-day school weeks are becoming increasingly more popular across Oklahoma, particularly in rural areas, as a way to save money on electricity, transportation, and staff costs. The 4-day school week was enacted in Carl's district in order to help save money and offset money lost from a decrease in funding over the past decade.

Carl was an elder statesman who was an active and visible teacher leader. His enthusiasm for learning and teaching in his community and the state of Oklahoma was contagious. Even in the briefest conversation with Carl, one would become acutely aware of the importance to him: community and community involvement, as well as professionalism and professional development of teachers. Throughout his career, he participated in state and national professional development experiences multiple times each year. Further, he noted presenting over 500 workshops across the state of Oklahoma during his career. As an extension of his work in his classroom and with teachers, he spent time at the state capitol each spring break visiting with various congresspeople and advocating for social studies education. In other words, one would be hard-pressed to find a social studies teacher in Oklahoma who did not know Carl and/or whom Carl did not know. "People got me involved. I see it as part of being professional, and it's fun." Carl was devoted to his community, and his community was devoted to him. Carl's community footprint could be seen throughout Southtown, as he was responsible for helping grow and expand the city through various projects throughout his time both as the local mayor and veteran teacher.

Carl spoke extensively about various education stakeholders' motivations to be involved in the walkout, starting with his own.

> When I was a young teacher, I helped to organize our association [local teachers' union].... People were shocked. This was small town Oklahoma. I was President the first year we negotiated a contract.... Negotiations and contracts were a whole new world.... It was intimidating at that time. Administrators didn't really like that it was threatening, but it worked. It made gigantic differences."

The motivations of teachers in Carl's school varied, but at the end of the day, they wanted a better educational experience for their students. Yes, the money associated with the teacher pay raise was great, but it did not do enough to help students and fund schools across Oklahoma's rural and urban districts. This may have been the first teacher walkout for some teachers in Carl's school, but it was his second one. He was around for HB 1017 (Education Reform Act of 1990 which funded education initiatives [maximum class sizes, minimum teacher salaries, alternative teacher certification, funding equity, early childhood programs, school consolidation, new statewide curriculum standards, and statewide testing] through increased taxes). Carl felt if change were to be made "people had to do something." And he knew he could help garner his community's support. He said, "It helps if you have credibility." When Carl went to the school board he had taught half of them, and the other half, he had taught their kids (Carl's description). He believes, "When schools were losing programs, year after year, people were compelled to react/respond."

Carl taught at least three generations of students in his small community. His students had taken what they learned in his class and used those skills to serve in various leadership capacities across Oklahoma. For example, one of Carl's students was an Oklahoma state representative representing a neighboring community. While at the walkout, Carl met with his former student on the fifth floor of the state capitol building to "catch up and discuss ways to help improve Oklahoma's education system."

Carl's community rallied around its teachers. Parents saw opportunities that were no longer had available for their children. When schools were losing programs year after year, people were compelled to respond. Restaurants sent food, and community leaders paid for buses to transport teachers to and from the capitol during the walkout.

The walkout left Carl quite excited. He shared, "It created a whole lotta interest in the upcoming election [fall 2018]." Education was put to the forefront of voters and citizens' minds. Several people in Carl's school wanted to know more about the Constitution and civic education. They sought him out before and after school to ask questions. In years past when Carl tried to do things regarding civic education, people were not interested. Following the walkout, he felt, "All of a sudden, following the teacher walkout, people were willing to register to vote.... It was a teaching moment." Although not everything that was asked of the legislature for education funding was authorized in the end, Carl claimed that sometimes you just have to "face the reality.... You have to have idealism and belief, but you need to be realistic too." Oklahoma certainly got attention—national attention—and the conversation regarding education in Oklahoma continued past the walkout and into the fall elections. The phrase, "We Will Remember in November," became the rallying call for those who supported the goals of the walkout. Education was at the forefront during Oklahoma's 2018 midterm elections. Educators, support professionals, administrators, and public school advocates from across the state filed to run for various statewide and local offices. When the deadline came, 112 public education advocates had filed to run in Oklahoma's 2018 elections (Park, 2018). As the elections approached, teachers from across the state began actively campaigning to continue the work left from the walkout.

CONCLUSION

Carl, Owen, Jenna, and Dalton expressed a passion for public education and funding for public education. As we explored these social studies teachers' experiences with the walkout, we heard them speak about the activities, the community and community support, and attention for public education and educational funding brought forth by the walkout. Similar to Swalwell and Schweber (2016), these were defining experiences in the professional lives of these teachers.

Those experiences during walkout have been felt beyond those 10 school days in April 2018. In November 2018, state elections were an extension of the walkout activities in reference to community involvement and attention to public education. The Oklahoma Education Association announced that an additional 16 pro-public education candidates won their elections. In addition, Governor-elect Kevin Stitt's victory speech included emphasis on the need to continue to address public education in the state.

Education in Oklahoma was not fully funded, but the teacher pay raise and school funding bill (House Bill 1010XX, 2018) was 95% funded for the first year. Teachers and education advocates were able to facilitate change and pressure the conservative legislature to raise taxes to improve schools across the state (Quinn & Carl, 2015). Approximately $550 million in new revenue was being put toward education in the state. These were victories for Oklahoma students and teachers. And although the walkout ended, the intense pressure to fund Oklahoma schools has remained (Krutka et al., 2018). Schools across Oklahoma continued to send delegations to the state capitol to keep the needs and interests Oklahoma's children at the forefront of legislators' minds. Carl, Dalton, Jenna, and Owen are four examples of dedicated classroom teachers who actively advocate for education as critical to the future of Oklahoma and the entire nation. The fight continues to fully fund Oklahoma public schools as well as public schools across the nation.

AUTHOR NOTE

Correspondence concerning this article should be addressed to Kristy A. Brugar, College of Education, University of Oklahoma, Norman, Oklahoma, 73019. Contact: kristy.a.brugar@ou.edu

REFERENCES

Birks, M., Chapman, Y., & Francis, K. (2008). Memoing in qualitative research: Probing data and processes. *Journal of Research in Nursing, 13*(1), 68–75. https://doi.org/10.1177/1744987107081254

Education Reform Act of 1990, House Bill 1017, 44th Legislature (1993).

Giroux, H. (1985). Teachers as transformative intellectuals. *Social Education, 49*, 376–377.

House Bill 1010XX, 56th Legislature, Second Extraordinary Session. (2018).

Ingersoll, R. (2006). *Who controls teachers' work? Power and accountability in America's schools.* Harvard University Press.

Krutka, D. G., Asino, T. I., & Haselwood, S. (2018). Editorial: Eight lessons on networked teacher activism from #OklaEd and the #OklaEdWalkout. *Contemporary Issues in Technology and Teacher Education, 18*(2), 379–391. https://www.learntechlib.org/primary/p/183635/

Lave, J., & Wenger, E. (1991). *Situated learning: Legitimate peripheral participation.* Cambridge University Press.

Lawrence-Lightfoot, S., & Hoffmann Davis, J. (1997). *The art and science of portraiture.* Jossey-Bass.

Maiden, J., & Ballard, S.C. (2017). State of the states: Oklahoma. *Journal of Education Finance, 42*(3), 317–319.

Park, M. (2018, June 27). More than 100 Oklahoma teachers are running for office. Dozens advanced in primaries last night. *CNN.* https://www.cnn.com/2018/06/27/health/oklahoma-teachers-primary-political-office/index.html

Picower, B. (2012) Teacher activism: Enacting a vision for social justice. *Equity & Excellence in Education, 45,* 561–574. https://doi.org/10.1080/10665684.2012.717848

Oklahoma Statutes, 70 Section 509.8 (2014).

Quinn, R., & Carl, N.M. (2015, May). Teacher activist organizations and the development of professional agency. *Teachers and Teaching, 21*(6), 745–758, https://doi.org/10.1080/13540602.2015.1044331

Swalwell, K., & Schweber, S. (2016). Teaching through turmoil: Social studies teachers and local controversial current events. *Theory & Research in Social Education, 44*(3), 283–315. https://doi.org/10.1080/00933104.2016.1201447

Taylor, D. L., & Bogotch, I. E. (1994). School-level effects of teachers' participation in decision making. *Educational Evaluation and Policy Analysis, 16*(3). https://doi.org/10.3102/01623737016003302

Villafranca, O. (2018, April 3). Oklahoma teachers fight for increased funding: "We're doing this for our kids." *CBS News.* https://www.cbsnews.com/news/oklahoma-teachers-fight-for-increased-funding-were-doing-this-for-our-kids/

APPENDIX: SEMISTRUCTURED INTERVIEW PROTOCOL

- Tell me a bit about your teaching/teaching experience.
- How would you describe the role of colleagues in your professional life?
- As you think back to last spring, how do you remember or think about the teacher walkout?
- We know that teachers did many different things during the 2-week walkout. What
- were some of the things you did?
- Is there anything else you would like to share about the walkout?

CHAPTER 8

DEFENDING ACADEMIC FREEDOM

Advice for Teachers

Michael D. Simpson
National Education Association

Over 40 years ago, the U.S. Supreme Court famously observed:

> The classroom is peculiarly the "marketplace of ideas." The Nation's future depends upon leaders trained through wide exposure to that robust exchange of ideas which discovers truth "out of a multitude of tongues, [rather] than through any kind of authoritative selection."[1]

That sentiment is particularly appropriate for social studies and history teachers, who should be free to expose students to controversial ideas and to teach critical thinking skills. But are you free? Do you have the constitutional right—call it academic freedom—to teach what you want and to discuss controversial issues in the classroom? The short answer is "no." Indeed, after a 2006 Supreme Court decision, it's pretty clear that teachers can be required to read from a script written by their employer. Happily, in practice, most school boards don't try to exercise that degree of

At the Schoolhouse Gate: Stakeholder Perceptions of First Amendment Rights and Responsibilities in U.S. Public Schools, pp. 153–163
www.infoagepub.com
Copyright © 2022 by Information Age Publishing
All rights of reproduction in any form reserved.

control. And there are actions teachers can take to keep it that way. But first, an abbreviated history of academic freedom in the courts.

Simply put, the question boils down to "who decides?" Who decides what is taught in K–12 classrooms? Obviously, there are three groups of stakeholders who have a strong interest in exercising that authority: teachers, parents, and school boards. But ultimately, who has the legal right to make the call, to decide what will be taught and what will not be taught? The U.S. Supreme Court has referred to "academic freedom" in 36 cases dating back to 1952, but it has never squarely answered the question,[2] and for the last four decades, the lower federal courts have struggled with the issue, often reaching confusing and inconsistent results.

TEACHERS' RIGHTS

In the heady days of the 60s and 70s, a number of federal courts recognized expansive free speech rights for high school teachers in the classroom. In one early case, for example, the First Circuit Court of Appeals ruled in 1969 that a high school English teacher couldn't be fired for distributing to students an article containing the word "motherf*****" and discussing it in class.[3] Two years later, a Massachusetts federal court reached the same conclusion regarding a high school teacher's use of the word "f***" with students.[4] In one of the cases involving a high school history teacher, a federal appeals court held that a Texas school board violated the First Amendment rights of Janet Cooper by firing her for using a controversial role-playing technique to teach about the post-Civil War Reconstruction period.[5]

In what may be the zenith of teacher academic freedom cases—and the coda as well—a federal court in Texas ruled in 1979 that a high school teacher was unconstitutionally fired for distributing surveys to students that dealt with such controversial topics as sexual intercourse, euthanasia, mind-altering drugs, and artificial reproductive methods. The court wrote, "[A] teacher has a constitutional right protected by the First Amendment to engage in a teaching method of his or her own choosing, even though the subject matter may be controversial or sensitive."[6]

While that may be rousing language and music to any teacher's ears, it is—as lawyers say—no longer good law. Since 1980, the law has evolved, or rather devolved, to the point where it is fair to say that K–12 teachers have no constitutional right to decide what to teach or how to teach it. As we will see, teachers don't even have the right to express their personal views in the classroom. In the last 30 years, there have been more than 100 court decisions involving a claim of "academic freedom," and with the exception of a few outlier cases, the teachers have always lost.[7] Here's a representative sampling:

- Peggy Boring was a high school drama teacher from North Carolina who was demoted for selecting a controversial play for her students to perform. The play—*Independence*—included a lesbian character and her sister who was pregnant and unwed. Boring sued, and the federal appeals court ruled in 1998 that the play was a part of the curriculum, and Boring had no right under the First Amendment to select controversial plays.[8] "A public high school teacher," the court said, has no "First Amendment right to participate in the makeup of the school curriculum."
- Cissy Lacks was a 23-year veteran English teacher in suburban St. Louis when she was fired in 1995 for allowing her students to use "street language," including profanity, in the plays they wrote and performed in her creative writing class. A federal district court in 1996 held that the school board violated her right to academic freedom and awarded her $826,000 in damages and reinstatement. The Eighth Circuit Court of Appeals reversed, holding that the First Amendment did not protect her "student-centered teaching method," a technique that allows students initially to express themselves in creative works without censorship, despite testimony that this method was an effective means of getting reticent students to write.[9]
- Colorado teacher Al Wilder was fired midyear after a 25-year career for showing a controversial R-rated movie to his logic and debate class of 17- and 18-year-olds without getting his principal's prior approval as required by the "controversial materials" school policy. In rejecting his academic freedom claim, the Colorado Supreme Court held, "It cannot be left to individual teachers to teach what they please." A teacher, the court added, "has no First Amendment right to use nonapproved controversial learning resources in his classroom without following the District's [controversial materials] policy."[10]
- Texas high school history teacher Timothy Kirkland was nonrenewed in retaliation for recommending books for outside reading that were not on the school district's approved reading list, including works by Orwell, Hemingway, and Kafka. The Fifth Circuit found no First Amendment violation, observing, "Although the concept of academic freedom has been recognized in our jurisprudence, the doctrine has never conferred upon teachers the control of public school curricula."[11]

- Other courts have reached the same conclusion.[12]

Most of the old cases won by teachers relied on the Supreme Court's 1969 *Tinker* decision, the celebrated student armband case where the Court notably held, "It can hardly be argued that either students or teachers shed their constitutional rights to freedom of speech or expression at the schoolhouse gate."[13] How quaint those words sound now and how outdated they seem these days when the "schoolhouse gate" has been replaced by the schoolhouse metal detector.

Sadly, to the extent that *Tinker* once could be read as supporting the right of academic freedom for teachers, it was implicitly overturned by the Supreme Court's 2006 decision in *Garcetti v. Ceballos*,[14] a devastating case on a 5–4 vote. *Garcetti* held that, when a public employee speaks in the course of performing their job duties, the First Amendment affords no constitutional protection whatsoever; the First Amendment simply does not apply. That is so, the Court reasoned, because such "speech" doesn't belong to the employee; rather, the speech belongs to the employer. They who pay the piper call the tune, and the employee is nothing more than a pitch-person for the boss's product. The government employer has hired its employees to deliver the employer's message, and the employer can lawfully tell its employees what to say (and what not to say).

One post-*Garcetti* case really drives this point home. Deborah Mayer was a middle school teacher in Monroe County, Indiana. While discussing current events with her class as she did every Friday, the subject of the Iraq War came up. One of her students asked whether she supported the war. She answered briefly that she did not. Some parents heard about her antiwar statement and complained to her principal, and Ms. Mayer was nonrenewed at the end of the school year.

She sued, and the Seventh Circuit Court of Appeals accepted as true her allegation that the real reason for her nonrenewal was her brief antiwar statement in the classroom. Applying *Garcetti,* however, the court squarely held that, because Mayer was speaking in her role as a teacher, the First Amendment did not apply. In clarion language that sends shivers down the spine of those who believe that the classroom should be a "marketplace of ideas," the court said:

> The school system does not "regulate" teachers' speech as much as it hires that speech. Expression is a teacher's stock in trade, the commodity she sells to her employer in exchange for a salary. [The First Amendment] does not entitle primary and secondary teachers, when conducting the education of captive audiences..., to advocate viewpoints that depart from the curriculum.... [School children] ought not be subject to teachers' idiosyncratic perspectives.[15]

Game, set, match. Judges can't write more clearly than that. The U.S. Supreme Court refused to review the decision. While the *Mayer* case is not the only post-*Garcetti* decision refusing to grant any First Amendment protection to teacher classroom speech, it certainly is the last nail in the academic freedom coffin, at least until there is an ideological change on the Supreme Court.[16]

There is one important caveat: the fact that a teacher's classroom speech is not protected under the First Amendment does not mean that it is a proper basis for discipline or discharge. Teachers who have tenure (continuing contract status), or who work under a collective bargaining agreement that gives them job protection can't be fired except for "just cause." Generally, that means that the teacher has to engage in serious misconduct to justify dismissal, and a casual comment in the classroom hardly rises to that level. Indeed, if Deborah Mayer had been tenured (she was not), then it is likely that an arbitrator or labor board would have overturned her dismissal. At the same time, however, a tenured teacher who ignores a specific directive about classroom instruction—an order not to teach Romeo and Juliet, for example, because of its mature themes—risks a charge of insubordination. As we have seen, even a tenured teacher has no right to ignore such a directive.

PARENTAL RIGHTS

So, if teachers don't have the right to decide what is taught in K–12 classrooms, do parents? That's an easy one; the answer is "no." The 1980s and 90s witnessed an explosion in so-called "parental rights" litigation through which parents sought to wrest control of curricular content from school officials. It was, by all accounts, an unmitigated failure. These lawsuits generally advocated three legal theories: First, relying on two Supreme Court decisions from the 1920s,[17] parents asserted that they had a constitutional right to control the "education and upbringing" of their children, including the right to decide what ideas they are exposed to in school. Taking a page from the playbook of the disestablishmentarians, who had successfully challenged religious practices in public schools, Christian conservatives also argued that certain textbooks and curricular content promoted the "religion" of "secular humanism" and thus ran afoul of the First Amendment's requirement of church/state separation. Finally, they claimed that exposing their children to information and points of view that conflicted with their sincerely held religious beliefs violated their First Amendment right to the Free Exercise of their religion. Recognizing the chaos that would ensue if each parent were able to insist on a "designer curriculum" for their child, the courts have soundly rejected these creative arguments. Here is a sampling of some of the "parental rights" cases:

- Parents can't force a school district to stop using *The Learning Tree*[18] or the *Impressions Reading Series*[19] as a part of the curriculum, even though the books allegedly "indoctrinated children" in values directly opposed to their Christian beliefs.
- Parents don't have the right to have their children excused from a mandatory health education course[20] or diversity training devoted to issues of sexual orientation and gender harassment,[21] despite the claim that such instruction directly conflicts with their strongly held religious beliefs.
- Parents can't sue school districts for exposing their children to mandatory AIDS education[22] or for surveying students on matters relating to sex,[23] even though such instruction impinged on their religious values regarding chastity and morality.
- Parents can't force a school district to stop using certain textbooks because they advance the "religion" of secular humanism and ignore the existence, history and contributions of Christianity; the Establishment Clause does not require "equal time for religion" in school textbooks.[24]
- Minority parents don't have the right to force a school district to stop assigning *The Adventures of Huckleberry Finn* as mandatory reading despite the fact that the book is rife with insulting and racially derogatory terms.[25]
- Christian parents don't have the right to have their children excused from classroom instruction they find religiously repugnant, specifically, the reading to a second grade class of the book *King and King*, the story of two princes who meet, fall in love, and get married.[26]
- Christian parents who have religious objections to a school's curriculum don't have the right to force the school district to pay for sending their children to a private religious school.[27]

A state legislature can't prohibit public schools from teaching the theory of evolution.[28]

The courts are unanimous, and the message is clear: parents don't have a constitutional right to determine what is taught in the classroom or even to have their children excused from instruction they find objectionable. By process of elimination, that means that school boards ultimately have the power to decide what is taught in K–12 classrooms.

Chief Justice Warren Burger has cogently explained the uniquely democratic nature of decision-making in public education: "Local control of education involves democracy in a microcosm.... If the parents disagree with the educational decisions of the school board, they can take steps to remove the board members from office."[29] This sentiment was echoed by Seventh Circuit Chief Judge Frank Easterbrook in the Mayer case discussed earlier. In ruling that teachers have no First Amendment rights in the classroom, he wrote that the power to decide what is taught "should be reposed in someone the people can vote out of office, rather than tenured teachers."[30]

THE LESSON HERE

In light of this harsh reality, how can you challenge your students with stimulating (and controversial) material and still keep your job? There are a number of actions you can take to insure that your classroom remains a marketplace of ideas.

First, ask your local bargaining representative to negotiate protection for "academic freedom" into your collective bargaining agreement (CBA). Teachers have the right to bargain in just over 30 states, and this issue certainly should be brought to the table. Arbitrators—who typically interpret and enforce CBAs—are much more sympathetic to teachers' claims of academic freedom than state and federal courts. Indeed, NEA affiliates in Hawaii and Delaware, for example, have won important arbitration decisions upholding academic freedom. In both cases, the arbitrator relied on pertinent clauses in CBAs to strike down school district policies prohibiting teachers from showing R-rated movies in class.[31] Model contract language recommended by NEA is set forth in the side bar.

Second, through your association representatives, you should urge the school board to adopt a comprehensive, written policy for handling parental complaints about the content of classroom instruction and efforts to censor textbooks or library books. The policy should require that any complaint be made in writing and should empower a committee with a majority of teachers to decide whether the challenged work is pedagogically sound. There are a number of online resources available to assist in devising such a policy.[32]

Third, be sure you fully comply with any school policy regarding the use of "controversial" materials in the classroom. Several courts have held that teachers can't be scape-goated for teaching from the approved curriculum when controversial content causes parental protests.[33] As the *Wilder* court held, failure to obey even a vague or ambiguous policy can lead to termination. If the policy requires prior approval, be able to explain and defend the educational suitability of the controversial material or technique. If the administrator decides to squelch your creativity, challenge the decision through any available appeal, such as a grievance or hearing before the school board, and mobilize collegial and community support.

Fourth, even though it may smack of self-censorship, you will be less likely to get into trouble if you steer clear of materials containing extensive profanity or sexually explicit language. These sorts of materials simply raise a red flag. A creative educator should be able to teach controversial and challenging ideas without utilizing language that some may find offensive. Finally, heed Justice Burger's advice and become politically active. If you suffer under a repressive school board, then vote 'em out of office.

Forty years ago, a more progressive Supreme Court held in *Tinker*:

In our system, state-operated schools may not be enclaves of totalitarianism. School officials do not possess absolute authority over their students. In our system, students may not be regarded as closed-circuit recipients of only that which the State chooses to communicate. They may not be confined to the expression of those sentiments that are officially approved.[34]

Thankfully, even though the courts have refused to recognize or respect the vital role that teachers play in maintaining the classroom as a marketplace of ideas, teachers and their professional associations still have alternative means to achieve that end. As the High Court has recognized, the stakes are exceedingly high:

No one should underestimate the vital role in a democracy that is played by those who guide and train our youth. To impose any strait jacket upon the intellectual leaders in our colleges and universities would imperil the future of our Nation. Teachers and students must always remain free to inquire, to study and to evaluate, to gain new maturity and understanding; otherwise, our civilization will stagnate and die.[35]

AUTHOR NOTE

This manuscript was first published in 2010 in a special issue of *Social Education*. It is being reprinted here with minor revisions and permission of the editor. Correspondence concerning this chapter should be addressed to Nancy C. Patterson, Bowling Green State University, Bowling Green, Ohio, 43402. Contact: ncpatte@bgsu.edu.

NOTES

1. *Keyeshian v. Board of Regents,* 385 U.S. 589, 603 (1967).
2. Indeed, in two of its decisions involving challenges to university affirmative action student admission programs, the Court has characterized "academic freedom" as a right that inheres in the institution itself, rather than any individuals. Regents of University of California v. Bakke, 438 U.S. 265, 312 (1970) ("Academic freedom, though not a specifically enumerated constitutional right, long has been viewed as a special concern of the First Amendment. The freedom of a university to make its own judgments as to education includes the selection of its student body." Grutter v. Bollinger, 539 U.S. 306, 329 (2003) (same)).
3. *Keefe v. Geanakos,* 418 F.2d 359 (1st Cir. 1969).
4. *Mailloux v. Kiley,* 323 F.Supp. 1387 (D. Mass.) aff'd, 448 F.2d 1242 (1st Cir. 1971).
5. *Kingsville Indep. School Dist. v. Cooper,* 611 F.2d 1109 (5th Cir. 1980) (Cooper was awarded $15,000 in damages, more than double her annual salary of $7,020).
6. *Dean v. Timpson Independent School District,* 486 F.Supp. 302, 307 (E.D. Tex. 1979).
7. In several cases decided prior to *Garcetti v. Ceballos,* the Sixth Circuit Court of Appeals recognized First Amendment protection for in-class and curricular speech by high school teachers, *Cockrel v. Shelby County School Dist.,* 270 F.3d 1036 (6th Cir. 2001); *Evans-Marshall v. Board of Educ. of Tipp City Exempted Village School Dist.,* 428 F.3d 223 (6th Cir. 2005). On October 21, 2010, however, the Sixth Circuit overturned this line of cases and, relying on *Garcetti,* specifically held that high school teachers enjoy no First Amendment protection for in-class, curricular speech. *Evans-Marshall v. Board of Educ. of Tipp City Exempted Village School Dist.,* 2010 WL 41 7286 (6th Cir. 2010).
8. *Boring v. Buncombe County Bd. of Education,* 136 F.3d 364 (4th Cir.) (en banc), cert. denied, 525 U.S. 813 (1998)
9. *Lacks v. Ferguson Reorganized School Dist.* R-2, 147 F.3d 718, rehearing denied, 154 F.3d 904 (8th Cir. 1998) cert. denied, 526 U.S. 1012 (1999).
10. *Board of Education of Jefferson County School Dist. R-1 v. Wilder,* 960 P.2d 695 (Colo. 1998). The court's decision prompted a stinging dissent by Justice Gregory J. Hobbs, Jr. (a former sixth-grade teacher) who expounded on the abiding value of academic freedom: "When we strip teachers of their professional judgment, we forfeit the educational vitality we prize. When we quell controversy for the sake of congeniality, we deprive democracy of its mentors."
11. *Kirkland v. Northside Indep. Sch. Dist.,* 890 F.2d 794, 800 (5th Cir.1989).
12. E.g., *Edwards v. California University of Pennsylvania,* 156 F.3d 488, 491 (3rd Cir. 1998) (opinion by Judge, now Justice, Samuel Alito: "we conclude that a public university professor does not have a First Amendment right to decide what will be taught in the classroom"; *California Teachers Association v. Davis,* 271 F.3d 1141 (9th Cir. 2001) (rejecting First Amendment chal-

lenge to California's Proposition 227, which requires teachers to teach non-English speaking students only in English); *Loeffelman v. Board Of Educ. of Crystal City School Dist.,* 134 S.W.3d 637 (Mo.App. E.D. 2004) (teacher has no First Amendment right to make comments in class opposing interracial relationships); *LeVake v. Indep. School Dist. No. 656,* 625 N.W.2d 502 (Minn. App. 2001) (high school biology teacher has no First Amendment right to teach criticisms of the theory of evolution contrary to the approved curriculum); *Calef v. Budden,* 361 F.Supp.2d 493 (D.S.C. 2005) (math teacher's acts of wearing anti-war button, calling the president "stupid" and an "idiot," and expressing harsh criticism of American military policy was not protected under the First Amendment).

13. *Tinker v. Des Moines Independent School District,* 393 U.S. 503, 510-11 (1969).
14. 547 U.S. 410 (2006)
15. *Mayer v. Monroe County Community School Corp.,* 474 F.3d 477, 479-80 (7th Cir.), cert. denied, 128 S. Ct. 160 (2007).
16. In each of the following recent cases, the court held that the school employee was speaking pursuant to their official duties and therefore had no First Amendment protection: *Veggian v. Camden Bd. of Educ.,* 600 F.Supp.2d 615 (D.N.J. 2009) (school employee's report of an alleged grade fixing scheme); *Omokehinde v. Detroit Bd. of Educ.,* 563 F.Supp.2d 717 (E.D.Mich. 2008) (school employee's internal protests to her supervisor regarding district's alleged misuse of Title I parental involvement funds and selection of outside vendors); *Carone v. Mascolo,* 573 F.Supp.2d 575 (D.Conn. 2008) (high school teacher's complaint to her supervisor about missing textbooks); *Woodlock v. Orange Ulster B.O.C.E.S.,* 281 Fed.Appx. 66, 2008 WL 2415726 (2nd Cir. 2008) (special education counselor's repeated complaints to school administration about the violent and threatening behavior of a special ed student); *Porr v. Daman,* 299 Fed.Appx. 84, 2008 WL 4831426 (2nd Cir. 2008) (teacher's comments about fire safety issues at the school). To be sure, there is dicta in *Garcetti,* suggesting that the Supreme Court at some point in the future may extend constitutional protection to "classroom instruction" and "academic scholarship," at least for higher education faculty. Indeed, a decision by a federal district court in Ohio (which is part of the Sixth Circuit) held that, *Garcetti* notwithstanding, a medical school professor's classroom instruction is entitled to First Amendment protection. *Kerr v. Hurd,* 694 F.Supp.2d 817 (S.D.Ohio 2010).
17. *Meyer v. Nebraska,* 262 U.S. 390 (1923) (striking down state law banning the teaching of foreign languages on the ground that such a law violates parents' right "to control the education of their [children]"); *Pierce v. Society of Sisters,* 268 U.S. 510 (1925) (recognizing a constitutional right of parents to send their children to private school)
18. *Grove v. Mead School Dist.* No. 354, 753 F.2d 1528 (9th Cir. 1985).
19. *Fleischfresser v. Directors of School Dist.* 200, 15 F.3d 680 (7th Cir. 1994).
20. *Leebaert v. Harrington,* 332 F.3d 134 (2d Cir. 2003) (The court declared, "If all parents had a fundamental constitutional right to dictate individually what the schools teach their children, the schools would be forced to cater

a curriculum for each student whose parents had genuine moral disagreements with the school's choice of subject matter.")

21. *Morrison ex rel. Morrison v. Board of Educ. of Boyd County, Kentucky,* 419 F.Supp.2d 937 (E.D.Ky. 2006).
22. *Brown v. Hot, Sexy and Safer Productions, Inc.,* 68 F.3d 525 (1st Cir. 1995).
23. *Fields v. Palmdale School Dist.,* 427 F.3d 1197 (9th Cir. 2005).
24. *Smith v. Board of School Commissioners of Mobile County,* 827 F.2d 684 (11th Cir. 1987).
25. *Monteiro v. Tempe Union High School Dist.,* 158 F.3d 1022 (9th Cir.1998).
26. *Parker v. Hurley,* 514 F.3d 87 (1st Cir.) cert. denied, 129 S.Ct. 56 (2008).
27. *Mozertv. Hawkins County Bd. of Ed.,* 827 F.2d 1058 (6th Cir. 1987).
28. *Epperson v. State of Ark.,* 393 U.S. 97 (1968)
29. *Board of Education v. Pico,* 457 U.S. 853, 891 (1982) (dissenting).
30. *Mayer v. Monroe County Community School Corp.,* 474 F.3d 477, 480 (7th Cir.), cert. denied, 128 S. Ct. 160 (2007).
31. *Department of Educ. and Hawaii State Teachers Association,* 66 LA 1221 (Tsukiyama, arb. 1976); *Board of Education and Capital Educators Association,* Case Number 1439 00812 90A (Tener, arb. 1989).
32. The American Library Association has free resources online for dealing with library book censorship at www.ala.org, including an article by Barbara Jones entitled, "Libraries, Access, and Intellectual Freedom: Developing Policies for Public and Academic Libraries" (1999). People for the American Way has developed a timeline of the evolution of creationism in schools. It is available at https://www.pfaw.org/report/timeline-how-creationism-has-evolved. *The Publishing Research Quarterly* (Vol. 5, Number 2/June, 1989) has published an article entitled "Coping with Textbook Controversies: From Policy Development to Implementation." It is available for purchase from Springer New York at www.springerlink.com.
33. *Stachura v. Truszkowski,* 763 F.2d 211 (6th Cir. 1985), rev'd on other grounds sub nom., *Memphis Community School Dist. v. Stachura,* 477 U.S. 299 (1986) (teacher cannot be punished because of parental protests over his teaching about human reproduction, where he utilized only approved textbook and films); *Cockrel v. Shelby County School Dist.,* 270 F.3d 1036 (6th Cir. 2001) (where school officials gave prior approval for outside speaker (on the uses for industrial hemp), they cannot use ensuing public outcry as basis for firing teacher).
34. *Tinker v. Des Moines Independent School District,* 393 U.S. 503, 511 (1969).
35. *Sweezy v. State of New Hampshire,* 354 U.S. 234, 250 (1957).

CHAPTER 9

THEY SPEAK FOR THEMSELVES

Students Name the Phenomenon of Civic Education and Freedom of Speech

Donna P. Phillips
District of Columbia Public Schools

In this phenomenological study, the author investigates the lived experience of democratic civic education for middle school students focusing on the civic education pedagogy, including the We the People simulated congressional hearing program from the Center for Civic Education, which created the conditions for students' expression of their First Amendment right of free speech. The students' experiences of free speech are isolated and examined to understand how teachers of civic education can most profoundly foster this type of dispositional learning. The themes most related to their experience of First Amendment freedom of speech that emerged include opportunities to have conversations, finding freedom within structure, and experiencing a transfer of authority as essential to their experience of civic education.

Civic education, whenever and however undertaken, prepares people of a country, especially the young, to carry out their roles as citizens. Researchers believe that some education practices can increase and improve the

At the Schoolhouse Gate: Stakeholder Perceptions of First Amendment Rights and Responsibilities in U.S. Public Schools, pp. 165–194
www.infoagepub.com
Copyright © 2022 by Information Age Publishing
All rights of reproduction in any form reserved.

quality and quantity of lifetime civic participation (Dalton, 2006; Frantzich, 2005; Levine, 2007). Empirical evidence that civic education is effective in conveying civic dispositions and skills is less robust than is evidence for civic knowledge. Students who have taken a civics course are more likely to self-report that they possess more civic skills than those who have not taken a class (Comber, 2005). Developing students' core civic orientations, a crucial step in instilling dispositions and skills, however, is more challenging than conveying content. Also, it may take time for the influence of a civics class to become relevant to students who are not of voting age. Nevertheless, a strong civics curriculum can move the needle in the direction of greater civic-mindedness.

In examining how civic education can influence development of student civic dispositions, especially those that support students' full expression of free speech, we recognize that not all civic education is the same. In this phenomenological study, the author investigates the lived experience of democratic civic education for middle school students who experienced a specific form of civic education.

This study is grounded in a civic education program offered by the Center for Civic Education—the We the People: The Citizen and the Constitution (WTP) Simulated Congressional Hearing (SCH) program. Students' participation in this program created the conditions for expression of their First Amendment right of free speech described here. The students' experiences of free speech are isolated and examined to understand how teachers of civic education can most profoundly foster this type of dispositional learning. The insights from this study may inform curriculum theorists and developers, school leaders, policymakers, and social studies teachers. What is the nature of and essential to students' experience of free speech in their civic education? What do the daily experiences of students in social studies classrooms have to do with their experience of civic education and free speech? What is the role of the teacher and the school in supporting students' free speech?

REVIEW OF LITERATURE

A preponderance of the research conducted on civic education curricula and programs seeks to discover how much civic knowledge students remember from their social studies courses, how many college students vote, and how active they are in politics and in their communities after graduation (Niemi & Junn, 1998; Patrick, 2002; Soule, 2004; Torney-Purta, 2002). This information is important and, indeed, has its place in civic education research. What these studies fail to capture, however, is the lived experiences of students as they engage in civic education.

A Tradition of Civic Education Research

There is much more to civic education than what we can see. We can see the results of a civic education when we witness citizens voting, attending town meetings, demonstrating, recycling, showing tolerance for others, and engaging in other civically engaged behaviors. Indeed, much of civic education research has focused on these areas. A review of much of civic education research shows what students know and how their knowledge might translate into civic skills. Far less research focuses on how students' civic dispositions are formed. As the following review indicates, there is a strong connection between knowledge and dispositions, but also a need for more research on dispositions themselves.

Behavioral Correlations. Walter C. Parker's (2003) book, *Teaching Democracy: Unity and Diversity in Public Life*, centers around three essential questions: What is citizenship? What does it mean in a multicultural, diverse society? How can we teach to foster deliberation and "nonidiotic" education? In his book, he draws on statistics about civic education, such as the correlations between citizenship outcomes and years of formal education. For example, "knowledge of principles of democracy" was shown to have a moderate positive correlation with increase in years spent in school. Similarly, there is a positive correlation between the citizenship outcome of participation in difficult political activities and its dimension of political engagement. This type of research is important for teachers and curriculum designers, as it has implications for civic education lesson design. As well, it helps to elucidate the connections between education and civic behavior. What it misses, however, is the experience of the actual students in civic education. For example, what are the lived experiences of students participating in deliberation?

Civic Knowledge. In another example, the Center for Civic Education published research on the effects of their programs on civic engagement and participation by young adults (Quigley, 1999). Comparing the results of the WTP as measured against other known civic engagement metrics such as the American Freshman: National Norms and National Assessment of Educational Progress, Quigley's report demonstrated, for example, that an all-time low of 13.7% of college freshmen at that time claimed to discuss politics frequently compared to a 29.9% high in 1968 (Quigley, 1999). Quigley also reported the results from the National Assessment of Educational Progress Report Card in Civics from 1990, showing that only 28% of eighth graders knew that Congress makes laws.

Similarly, Quigley (1999) cited 1997 research from the National Constitution Center that showed 90% of students agreed that the Constitution was important to them, but less than 40% of them could name all three branches of government, and over 50% of them did not know how many senators we have. Once again, teachers can take from the research what students at different ages may or may not know about civic education and citizenship and make decisions regarding curricular content accordingly. This research, however, still does not tap the actual experiences of the students being tested for their knowledge, and so this essential next step is still needed.

From Knowledge to Dispositions. Most relevant to this study is research that came afterwards. The James Madison Legacy Project (JMLP) is an initiative of the Center for Civic Education, a nonprofit corporation focused on improving the quality of civics education. The JMLP project aims to expand the availability and effectiveness of civics instruction in elementary and secondary schools by providing professional development to teachers of high-need students. This professional development is designed to improve teachers' civics content knowledge and develop their pedagogic skills to enhance students' achievement in attaining state standards in civics and government.

The JMLP professional development covers six content units aligned with the WTP textbook that encompass standard civics topics related to the founding, the U.S. Constitution, and the Bill of Rights, the institutions of government, and citizen engagement. The course content was organized around six units noted below:

1. What are the philosophical and historical foundations of the American political system?
2. How did the framers create the Constitution?
3. How has the Constitution been changed to further the ideals contained in the Declaration of Independence?
4. How have the values and principles embodied in the Constitution shaped American institutions and practices?
5. What rights does the Bill of Rights protect?
6. What challenges might face American constitutional democracy in the 21st century?

As part of the training, teachers in JMLP were required to either observe veteran WTP teachers conducting simulated congressional hearings, conduct their own class or school-level hearings, or participate in district-level hearings. Research was conducted to evaluate the effectiveness of the JMLP in imparting civic knowledge, dispositions, and skills to students via professional development for their teachers (Owen, 2018). The students' civic knowledge, dispositions, and skills were measured using a pretest-posttest design. Teachers and students took a pretest before they began their civics class and a posttest when they had completed the course.

Civic Knowledge. Students were tested on their knowledge of core concepts related to units of the curriculum. From this study, the researcher was able to isolate one item on the knowledge test requiring students to identify freedom of speech as a First Amendment right. Thirty-nine percent of JMLP middle school students answered this question correctly on the pretest and 61% on the posttest, representing a 22-percentage point improvement on this item after taking the WTP class.

In accounting for civic dispositions and skills, data from the pretest and posttest for the variables related to keeping informed and following government and politics demonstrate that the JMLP students' civic dispositions increased after taking the WTP class. Furthermore, to explore the connection between knowledge of the First Amendment and civic dispositions and skills, a contingency table analysis was performed. The findings lent support to the notion that the greater the core knowledge of the Constitution and American government, the more likely students were to develop civic dispositions and skills. Middle and high school students who answered the First Amendment item correctly were more likely to say that they were informed about government and politics, followed politics on social media, and felt that it was important for people to turn out to vote (Owen, 2018).

Civic Dispositions and Skills. Civic knowledge has been demonstrated to be a precursor to developing civic dispositions and skills (Delli Carpini, 1999). Civic dispositions are the public and private traits essential to the maintenance and improvement of constitutional democracy (Branson, 1998). Dispositions provide a foundation for individuals' active embrace of the norms of good citizenship. They encompass peoples' motivations to be civically engaged (Torney-Purta, 2002). The Campaign for the Civic Mission of Schools (Gould et al., 2011) defines civic dispositions as a concern for others' rights and welfare, fairness, reasonable levels of trust, and a sense of public duty.

These and other studies that involve civic dispositions are important to the field of civic education, because they raise awareness of the need for a different type of teaching and learning if civic education is to make a difference in the behaviors and dispositions of our young citizens. The JMLP study in particular is important, in that it quantitatively supports similar changes in student civic dispositions and expression of First Amendment freedoms that the author observed in her students.

Action Civics

Other recent research in civic education has focused on action civics, studying programs such as *Project Soapbox* (Andolina & Conklin, 2019). *Project Soapbox,* an action civics curriculum that involves a public speaking competition and allows students to

> choose a community issue of importance to them around which they will develop a speech … outline and write rough drafts of their own speeches … [and] deliver their speeches to a classroom of peers along with outside adult judges from the community. (p. 10)

In researching the effects of the Project Soapbox curriculum implementation, Andolina and Conklin (2019) administered presurveys to assess the classroom climate and noted many students reported their teachers created an environment that "supported student voice" and "allowed them to respectfully disagree with each other and their teachers, and express their own opinions" (p. 19).

The structure of student learning in Project Soapbox is similar in many ways to how students prepare for the WTP SCH, and so these findings have great resonance with the notion that collaborative, responsive class structures that allow for student voice are an integral part of students forming civic dispositions and expressing First Amendment rights. As stated by Andolina and Conklin (2019), "Indeed, part of what appears to be powerful about Project Soapbox is that the curriculum puts students in the position to hear, learn from, and connect with one another" (p. 29). Thus, as we turn to the methodology and outcomes of this study, we keep in mind the experience of the individual as reported by the individual, and how students' own voices in the classroom and in conversation with each other help them name the experience of civic education and free speech.

METHOD

There is no doubt a place and use for the above-mentioned research. In a democratic republic such as ours, learning how many young people vote and what programs may influence their future behaviors is important, but it is not the full picture. One needs to ponder the question of what it means to be *in* civic education. This is the job of the phenomenologist. As van Manen (2003) states, "Phenomenology is a philosophy of the personal, the individual" (p. 7). From here, one may come to understand how one's being in the world is shaped by one's experience in civic education. Thus, this study seeks to capture the lived experiences of students in civic education in order to discover the essence of such an experience to inform pedagogy, curriculum, and policy.

Understanding Lived Experience

The term *lived experience* may at first seem redundant, indeed even tautological. As Burch (1990) asks, "What might an experience be if it were not 'lived'?" (p. 132). He reminds us, however, that the term lived experience is not derived from English, and therefore one must understand its German etymological roots to appreciate how "lived experience" in phenomenology is different from Dewey's notion of experience. Derived from the German word, *er-lebnis*, lived experienced is that which "unfolds and endures from life by virtue of life itself" (Burch, 1990, p. 133). To examine lived experience, one seeks the essence of an experience, or as explained by Burch (1990), "The term suggests that this lived character consists not simply in what is felt or undergone by sentient beings in the passage of time but of what from this passing sentience is meaningfully singled out and preserved" (p. 133). Further, in contrast to other uses of experience in human science research, lived experience differentiates itself, in that the meaning does not lie in the experience itself, but rather in the reflection upon the experience after it has taken place.

This study explores the "textual reflection on the lived experience and practical actions of" students in civic education (van Manen, 2003, p. 4). As such, it draws on van Manen's model for hermeneutic phenomenological inquiry, a methodology that allows one not only to see the phenomenon, but to know it as well. According to van Manen (2003), phenomenology "describes how one orients to lived experiences" (p. 4). Hermeneutics, on the other hand, "describes how one interprets the 'texts' of life" (p. 4).

Investigating Experience as We Live it. As van Manen (2003) explains, "The lifeworld, the world of lived experience, is both the source and the object of phenomenological research" (p. 53). As such, the collection of "data" in this research is unique. In investigating the phenomenon, the author collected "data" in the form of recorded and transcribed conversations with students, observations of them in her classroom, and discussions, as well as their written texts and reflections. All of this is considered "data," but in phenomenology it is referred to as "text." In that all recollections, recordings, and transcriptions are transformations of the lived experience, we strive to "find access to life's living dimensions while realizing that the meanings we bring to the surface from the depths of life's oceans have already lost the natural quiver of their undisturbed existence" (van Manen, 2003, p. 54).

Turning to the Lived Language. An integral part of hermeneutic phenomenological research is the investigation of the lived language of the phenomenon. Thus, to get to the roots of the phenomenon, the etymological renderings of the lived language of civic education are explored. For example, the name for the course in which civic education resides—*social studies*—gives the discipline more depth once its roots are explored. Similarly, idiomatic phrases such as *having a voice* also reveal more about the essence of civic education. Researchers need to be open to the lived language of the students as they reveal the phenomenon in their own language. What words and phrases do they use to describe their experiences? Where do they find meaning in our country's foundational documents? Opening to this type of questioning is also in line with the goals of civic education in that in order to encourage critical, informed, democratic participation, citizens need to question societal norms, conventions, and assumptions normally taken for granted.

Background and Participants

The author, an 11-year veteran teacher, undertook this hermeneutic phenomenological study and engaged 29 students in a mixed ability-level eighth-grade American history class in suburban Maryland for the full 2005–2006 school year. The WTP curriculum was implemented in the fourth quarter of the year. All 29 students chose pseudonyms for participation in this study. The school enrolled approximately 1,175 students in Grades 6 through 8. The students in the class included those with the gifted and talented designation, on level, as well as students with Individualized Education Plans (IEPs) and 504s. Seventeen students were boys, and 12 were girls. There were four Black students, two of whom were half Caucasian and one who was Ethiopian. There were five Asian students and one student of Latinx origin. Of the remaining 19 "White" students, one was Iranian, two were Indian, and one was born in Russia. Another had just moved from Germany after living on an American military base for the last several years. There were 20 students coded as "gifted" in social studies. Of the remaining nine students coded as "on level" in social studies, two received special education services and two others received other academic support. The makeup of this class was typical of other social studies classes in the school, where students of different abilities were in class together instead of in separate tracks as they were in English and math. The class also typified the overall population of the community at the time of the research and was chosen as representative of the general school and community population.

Students in the Curriculum

The curriculum for eighth grade social studies took students on a journey through American History from right before the American Revolution, 1763, to the end of the Reconstruction era after the Civil War in 1877. The written curriculum was divided into four units, each one designed to last one full marking period. As an eighth-grade social studies team, there were several lessons that all teachers coordinated together for the benefit of the students. One of the lessons was the Mayflower Compact Simulation. The teachers used this as a way to introduce history pertinent to the development of American Democracy while allowing students to experience democracy for themselves as they crafted their own class compacts.

Another lesson added into the written curriculum was a tax simulation, during which students were charged ten cents per paper due to "budget cuts." Not paying would affect their grade. All the eighth-grade teachers conducted the simulation on the same day and encouraged students to play along for everyone's benefit, even after they found out it was not real. This led to a sit-in at lunch, a march around the school, several petitions, and a day where everyone in the eighth-grade wing knew what the students learned in social studies. While not directly researched in this study, the teachers' collaboration was an aspect of the students' lived experience of democratic civic education, as the whole-school effort shaped the environment in which the students experienced their free speech.

Between the written curriculum lessons and the teacher's own collaborative efforts, the year progressed with a mix of reading and writing lessons, games to learn about the Constitution, plays about the Constitutional Convention, a formal debate on the Federalist and Antifederalist arguments, close reads of the Reconstruction Amendments, and bimonthly current events, about which students read and wrote. Often, they were asked to connect them to the social studies principles for that unit or to essential questions, for example, "How do governments balance individual rights and the common good?" or "When, if ever, is war necessary?"

The most impactful pedagogical decision made was in implementing the WTP SCH. At this school, the SCH was a month-long process during which students formed small groups within each class. In their groups, they and became experts in one of six questions related to their study of American history, the Constitution, and the Bill of Rights, as described earlier in the JMLP study. These questions were:

- What were the founders' basic ideas about government?
- What shaped the founders' thinking about government?
- What happened at the Philadelphia Convention?
- How was the Constitution used to establish our government?
- How does the Constitution protect our basic rights?
- What are the responsibilities of citizens?

This was the fifth year of the WTP SCH implementation. Students engaged with their topic, first drawing from their own notes, assignments, assessments, and materials created during the year. They then wrote a 4-minute speech that they presented as expert testimony to a simulated congressional panel composed of state legislators, attorneys, judges, social studies teachers, administrators, college students, and other community members.

Students were given a weekly timeline of goals and deadlines. As the weeks progressed, the teachers' requirements become fewer as students took over the process themselves. Ultimately, students were responsible for completing their 4-minute expert testimony and preparing research for the follow-up questions by the SCH date.

To kick off the month-long process of preparing, practicing, and participating in the WTP SCH, students in each class voted for their captains, who then in a "secret" convention, choose their teams with the common good of the whole class in mind. Because the teacher turned over so much power to the students, once she gave out a few initial guidelines and facilitated student movement from one phase of preparation to the next, the students themselves took over the rest. They gave each other deadlines, feedback, peer pressure, criticism, encouragement, and validation. As will be explored subsequently, this culminating activity was a large part of the students' lived experience of civic education. Students then testified on their topic before the simulated congressional panel of community members in a day-long, schoolwide event.

Text (Data) Collection

The students participating in this study shared their lived experiences in civic education in several ways, including through individual and group conversations and reflective writing, over the course of a school year.

Written text from the students' work over the entire school year (September–June), as well as recorded and transcribed text from the students' class experiences and classroom observations from January through June, served as the basis for the text. The students were aware of all of these methods of data gathering and were aware of when they were engaging in them.

Students in Conversation. Twelve of the 29 student-participants engaged in individual conversations with the author as well as group or partner conversations with one another and the author and formed the core group of conversational partners. These conversations were tape-recorded and transcribed. The duration of these conversations varied from 30 minutes to an 75 minutes. Although such conversations are an essential aspect of the research in phenomenology, the questions for these conversations were not pre-scripted. There were, however, various prompts to get the conversations started, including:

- Describe some of your most powerful experiences in civic education from school.
- What is the meaning of civic education to you?
- Describe what it was like when you participated in the (simulation, discussion, debate, etc.)
- Tell me about a time when you used what you learned in civic education in the "real world."
- Describe a barrier you experienced in learning civic education.

From here, depending on the students' responses, there were follow-up oral questions to clarify their ideas and prompt them to keep their descriptions in narrative form rather than simply listing of experiences or explanations. Since a portion of the research focuses on the students' experiences in participating in the WTP SCH, an additional round of individual and partner conversations focused on that particular lived experience.

Students in Writing. As mentioned previously, all students participated in reflective writing as part of their regular instruction in civic education. In addition to this, some student participants were asked to engage in more extensive reflective writing about their experiences and learning in civic education. These students, while not self-selecting to be part of the core group of students, opted in for this additional reflective writing. Therefore, in addition to the core group of twelve students, several other students' voices were included through the use of their written reflections. Some reflective writing prompts included:

- Explain what you learned from (the recent lesson). What aspects of your learning were civic education? How did you feel, and what did you experience during this lesson?
- Share a time when you were an active citizen. How did you know what to do? What made your action that of citizenship? What was it like to do what you did?
- Describe a time when you spoke "True Words." What was the issue that caused you to speak? Why was this issue important to you? What was it like to speak in this way?

Students in Action. Finally, as a civic educator, the author had access to the actual classroom experiences of the students. One final element of text gathering was to tape-record specific classes, including formal class debates, informal class discussions, and the simulated congressional hearing. In listening to the recordings, the author addressed the following reflective questions:

- What was the "objective" for the class?
- What questions did the students ask?
- What questions did the teacher ask?
- What was the nature of the interactions between the teacher and students, and student and students?
- What did I hear, see or witness while the students were engaged in their learning?

These observations and recordings served to inform both the development of potential questions for students in individual, partner, and group conversations and the making of future pedagogic decisions. Students had opportunities to give feedback, written and oral, throughout the entire research process.

RESULTS: STUDENTS NAME THE PHENOMENON

The text produced from the conversations was used to uncover themes and essential elements of the lived experience of civic education. The themes were shared with students as they emerged throughout the year. Just as in the transcribed conversations, the text from the students' written reflections is another source from which themes for analysis were drawn. The themes were not the phenomenon itself, but rather entryways into understanding the phenomenon. As van Manen (2003) states, "Theme gives control and order to our research and writing" (p. 79).

Themes in phenomenological research are different from those in other situations, such as literary analysis. The phenomenological quality of a theme includes a "needfulness or desire to make sense" (van Manen, 2003, p. 88). A theme is the sense one tries to make of one's experiences as well as an openness to something. In isolating thematic statements, the phenomenological descriptions were approached in three different ways: (1) the holistic approach in which phrases were found that captured the fundamental meaning of the text as a whole, (2) the selective reading approach in which phrases and statements that strike as particularly revealing about the phenomenon were identified, and (3) the detailed reading approach in which each sentence or sentence cluster is questioned about the phenomenon being described.

As student text was examined and thematized, several prominent components of the lived experience of civic education emerged. The themes most closely related to their experience of First Amendment freedom of speech that emerged included having opportunities for conversations, finding freedom within structure, and experiencing a transfer of authority as essential to their experience of civic education.

Students in Conversation

In relation to First Amendment rights, students in this study most readily identified salient civic education experiences with the ability to have conversations. Students experienced civic education in the social studies as something that would help them join in on conversations, not only in the classroom, but also socially. Students in written reflection noted, "This [social studies] is useful, because if for example someone starts a conversation over a war and you are completely lost, it's kind of embarrassing, but if you know [something about it], you can continue the conversation (Sara). Alex B similarly stated, "To be a student in the [social studies] class is very interesting, because you can use the information in future to have conversations that actually are interesting and not stupid." Joy said,

> I will be able to do such things as go to history museums and understand what they are talking about by studying social studies. For example, if I were to get into a conversation about Pearl Harbor, I would be able to express how I feel about it.

Fletcher expressed the essence of social studies even further stating:

> To me social studies is mentally innovative. For example ... we learned about the churches. This summer my sister was talking with my grandpa.

> They were discussing politics and they started talking about the old church. At that point I understood the conversation so I could join in. This makes social studies mentally innovative because I had never had a discussion like that. Second, social studies means interaction, like the time when ... we had a project. For 2 weeks me and my partner discussed and questioned each other and expanded our knowledge.

As students of social studies, young citizens want to avoid embarrassment and "feeling stupid." How is their experience of civic education linked to their abilities outside of the classroom to understand what others are talking about and to participate meaningfully in social and civic dialogue? What does it mean to students to be able to "join in the conversation?"

Teachers may look at this understanding of social studies as a way to imagine their class environment. Curriculum as conversation seems to open many possibilities for both students and teachers. Curriculum *for* conversation gives it another turn as well. In a discipline where debates, discussions, and dialogue between and among students and teachers usually abound, it is an interesting turn to think of the curriculum as spurring conversation.

Related to conversation in social studies, some students also pinpoint another aspect of views on social studies, that is, the ability to express one's opinion. Kate states,

> This year I am looking forward to further expanding my knowledge in the subject and learning how to apply this to my life. I am also looking forward to having a chance to share my opinion with other students in class and during the simulated congressional hearing.

Ryan is aware that social studies is "a class where it is easy to have an opinion." Brandon hopes that he will "be able to speak out about something without making it up or just using info from the news."

Do students in other disciplines experience their education as one that will enable them to "speak out?" What does it mean for students to be able to "share" or "have" an opinion, and how is the experience of civic education related to this? What is basic to civic education in the social studies classroom that gives students this opportunity of voice and freedom of expression? Indeed, it seems that through structured discussion or natural conversation, students can feel that they have a voice, or that it is "easy to have an opinion." It is almost as if students expect to experience "falling into" conversation during social studies class.

Freedom Within Structure

In implementing the *WTP* program, the author identified several key aspects of democratic civic education as forces for change in shaping student civic dispositions. One of these forces for civic disposition change was the structure of the *WTP* program itself. In preparing for the hearings, students worked in collaborative research groups to write and edit speeches for their testimonies. As the students noted, it was this very structure that allowed them to develop a sense of their own independence, efficacy, and agency. For example, one student, Sam, describes how he experienced the balance of structure and independence in working in a collaborative group:

> You need enough freedom to write what you want to say and have or need the amount of time to, you know, get research together, type up what you want to say, and be able to answer questions. I noticed that we were able to do a lot on our own and a lot of research and thinking and writing on our own. I think that was a good thing, because it wasn't controlled. It was structured but just structured enough, so that we understood what we were doing, and we did it. Structure is always nice definitely, especially in classes like science and math where you know they get guidelines you have to follow. You don't really have choice. I think … classes like English and World Studies were pretty much like your opinion and your imagination. I think it's pretty much to have freedom. The more structurization [sic] you know, up to a point, is just strangling the imagination or creative process or … your opinion.

Sam's reflections point to a fine line between too much freedom and too much structure. He sees that too much structure could "strangle the imagination or creative process or … your opinion." Similarly, other students experienced collaborative working in teams on the SCH as time when the "teacher did not teach," or the teacher "let us go."

In other words, it was a shift in control—of authority and authorship—from the teacher to the students. The process of preparing for the hearings began in a very structured way with assignments, resources, grades and deadlines. As the weeks progressed, however, fewer and fewer points were assigned to the students' work. By the last 2 weeks of preparation, only about five out of 120 students asked about their grades for different assignments, and the captains (their peers) of each collaborative team had gained the authority to assign work and establish timetables for their teams. Likewise, students who were not team captains gained authorship over their own learning through their self-directed research and writing within their teams.

Transferring Authority

The experience of a transfer of authority from teacher to student is an essential aspect of civic education in that, as citizens, students are and will be expected to make thoughtful, informed, conscientious decisions: whom to vote for, whether to speak out against an injustice, when to make their voices heard, and when to remain silent. In authorizing their own process and learning in the educational setting within the social studies classroom, they are approximating this essential civic skill.

As citizens, American adults learn to exercise and regulate their own free speech in different social contexts, in the face of both authority and a spectrum of consequences. The same is true for students within their school buildings, but with the added authoritarian layer of the school, students may have little awareness of their constitutional free speech. A transfer of authority strips that authoritarian layer and affords students opportunities for judgment on, and exercise of, free speech within the classroom and school that are usually masked.

Students in Control. Students themselves recognized the value of this experience of transfer of authority. For example, as Amy reflected:

> This experience was incredible for so many reasons, mainly because it was different from any other social studies project. This project involved students taking over and leading our class and specific units. We had so much control over how well each did in the hearing, which is why it made it so special to us.

As Amy's reflection suggested, due to their opportunity to "take over," the students began to see a real connection between their own work and their ultimate performance in the hearing. Jamilla explained a similar experience with how the handing over of authority allowed her to experience control over her own learning.

> we, as the students, got to take control of the project, the whole project. It gives you a kind of responsibility with a bit of fun into the school year. I think the best part was that you knew that the students were in control.

Bernie concurred, stating,

> I learned a lot of things about myself and my teammates over the course of this month. I learned that it is not always easier to work in a group. I also learned that I am more of a leader than a follower. For me, I like to be in the driver's seat, to be in charge of the way things go. I did not know this about myself to [sic] now.

A Say, They Say. If students value such opportunities to learn from each other rather than directly from the teacher, what does this imply about the relationship between the teacher and the students in civic education and how they might best experience and fortify their free speech? The independence and control students experienced during the structure of their learning led them to experience their rights and freedoms in a more robust, agentic way. Students in democratic civic education were very quick to name democratic moments when they had a chance to vote or "had a say" in decision-making. Fletcher, for example, recounted an experience in civic education and claimed, "I felt like a citizen because we voted on stuff, like we got to vote on types of flags and it was really cool." In the anonymous surveys students completed after the SCH, many students stated they liked the way the captains were chosen: "[The voting] was like a democracy;" "It was like a true democracy and we voted;" and "Everyone had a fair vote."

In reflecting on the making of their class compact, many students also associated democracy with freedom of speech and "having a say." As Bernie stated, "The democratic part of making the compact is that everyone got a say in what went into it," and Brandon echoed, "I felt like our class had a say in something. I am glad we got to choose our own rules and sign on it if we agreed." Rohan agreed, stating, "The democratic part of this compact was that everyone had a say in making it, and everyone's opinion was listened to." Andrew named it most directly as free speech: "One aspect that was democratic was freedom of speech. We were allowed to say whatever we wanted and everyone else had to pay attention."

Students also were quick to point out when they felt like their voice was not heard.

> What I did not think was right was when the people up front would talk about one of the rules—freedom of speech, but still they denied a student's right of speech limiting it to three times only. What type of "government" would this class have if things like those happen? (Sara)

In civic education, the importance of allowing students to "have a say" cannot be overemphasized. It is only through the practice of using their voices and testing their beliefs and thoughts out on each other in the classroom environment that students will eventually come to embody the democratic principles they are exploring. When students can have a say, they become open to new possible ways of *being in the world*. Allowing students to have a say within the structure of the democratic classroom shows a teacher's respect for and support of their democratic intelligence. Students learn that democracy is giving reasons when we use authority. It is a constitutional moment, when students become aware of step into their authority as agents of democracy, to acknowledge this use of authority and the students' role in it.

Constitutional Moments. Students come into social studies classes expecting to learn about their rights and freedoms and other aspects of democracy. They experience democracy as times when they have had opportunities to have a say in decisions through voting, choosing rules, signing class compacts, and electing captains to lead them. Indeed, the *WTP* program allows for this type of empowering pedagogy, but the teachers themselves have to be able to deliver it.

Taking a Stand. As previously shown in Phillips (2014), a study drawn from the same research data, students were quick to name times when they could take a stand as salient experiences in civic education. This expression of their First Amendment right to free speech even took on a physical manifestation. One student explained how she connected her experience of standing up during the simulation with a real-life situation outside of the social studies class:

> It's kind of like when we did the simulation with the tax, you kind of saw how you could stand up for your rights and things like that, so when in one of my [other] classes, it's a student's right that you can stand up and a teacher can't say anything rude or offending about you. So, I stood up for that, and I thought that kind of goes with the simulation, because you learn how to stand up for yourself and what to do in those cases. (Jamilla) (as cited in Phillips 2014, p. 101)

In fact, not only does she name the opportunity to stand up for her views; she sees how this experience translates to continual free speech and expression as she navigates the inherent authoritarian structure of the school and classroom:

> One of the things that I learned from being in the system is that you should never allow the teacher or any authority/power push you down. Like if they say you do something that is wrong, you need to stand up. I think students don't realize authoritarian power until later. (Jamilla) (Ibid. p. 103)

This experience of standing up in the face of authority and injustice is the true essence of the lived experience of civic education. It is the embodiment of this action—whether in simulation or in authentic contexts—that allows students to form their First Amendment civic behaviors. Jamilla and other students also named the tension between experiencing their democratic rights within the authoritarian setting of the school. The navigation of this tension is also fundamental to forming civic dispositions. In framing the students' experiences of the tension between authoritarian settings and expression of democratic rights, the author describes how she seized on the opportunity to navigate this tension during the Mayflower simulation where students needed to create a class compact:

> As it came down to the end, I told the students the ship had almost reached land, and we had to finish the compact before we could disembark and begin our lives in the new world of 8th grade US history. In one class, however, the students and I had not yet reconciled our final compact with one another. The students questioned why the ship had to land, when we were not yet finished. I began to explain that we had a lot to learn and needed to get started. One student remarked that the compact was not really democratic, as I had the ultimate authority anyway. We discussed this openly as a class. Then, rather than try to bring closure to the issue and narrow the students' choices down to a vote, I allowed the conversation to continue, and continue it did, for 2 more weeks. We remained on the boat exploring the relationships between power, authority, and democracy, each day coming a little closer to landfall. We dwelled together in the tension. Some students reveled in it. Others were clearly uncomfortable. (Phillips, 2006)

It is essential for teachers to create the space and place for teacher and students to dwell together within that tension, and without, in order for students to capitalize on their democratic experiences in the classroom and in the school. The most fundamental of those experiences is the students' experience of using their voice and their free speech. Faced with similar tensions in the various societal structures, students can apply their lived experiences in other contexts, as Jamilla did by standing up to her brother and parents when faced with an unfair family situation.

Control, Command, and Corruption. Related to the transfer of authority, many students use the term "control" in describing how they experience their work with their classmates and independent of the teacher. Just as some students experience a sense of the students' control over the outcomes of their work together, other students experience a tension in trying to "control" their group members. For example, Jamilla, as a captain, relayed her struggle to lead her team during the SCH.

> I have changed, because I really see how hard it is to control people. You have to tell them you have power from the beginning or else they just won't listen to you and you won't be able to be in command of them.

Kelly, also a captain, found it challenging in this regard as well:

> The journey in the position of captain was filled with obstacles ranging from unwilling students to confusing communication. For example, scolding or forcing my teammates would not have successfully made my peers thoroughly finish their work since those of "lower" rank deserve to be treated equally and respectfully. Thus, as a leader, I controlled my friends' fate in

> many ways such as choosing teams and assigning roles and could easily have been "corrupted" by yelling at them or embarrassing them.

Claire had a similar revelation. After the SCH, she reflected:

> As I enter high school and society, I will remember that when acting as a leader, you are responsible for "controlling" your group. But it is also very essential to gain respect from your team members or whomever you are working with.

All three captains struggled with a changing sense of control in their role as captain of their team. Jamilla experienced a growing need for power in order to "be in command of" her team. Kelly learned that she "controlled [her] friends' fate" and, therefore, sought to wield her power carefully so as to show them respect. Claire recognized that while controlling her team she also had to "gain respect." Ironically, the students turned to a word evocative of "power-over" relationships—the very ones they describe they loathe. It is as if students take on the personae of the aggressors—those who have controlled them in the past—even while recognizing the lack of respect such power-over relationships have (Ellsworth, 1997). It may almost be inevitable, however, that students turn to this mode of being when given the chance, as they have been participants, even subjects, in the authoritarian structure of school and family.

CONCLUSIONS

What is the nature of and essential to students' experience of free speech in their civic education? What do the daily experiences of students in social studies classrooms have to do with their experience of civic education and free speech? What is the role of the teacher and the school in supporting students' free speech? The exploration of these questions has allowed for a deep understanding of the lived experience of free speech within democratic civic education for students. In their own words, students have experienced their civic education and, in particular, their First Amendment freedom of speech, in very distinct, yet universal ways. They have done so through the ability to have conversations, to muster the fortitude to have a say/take a stand, and to successfully experience a transfer of authority. The setting for all of these experiences was the classroom and school. The themes, and thus the understanding of the students' experiences of their free speech, have great implications for the role of the teacher and the school. Creating and supporting the conditions for free speech to thrive in the classroom and school setting begins with the teachers' orientations toward the curriculum, their students, and civic education. Civic education creates the conditions for exercise of free speech in a "simplified environment" that then can be transferred to real-world contexts. Next, the tension between the authoritarian nature of the school and the students' experiences of free speech requires not only attention but fortitude on the part of the students and teacher to navigate. Finally, students need the chance to name their own experiences for them to be experienced fully.

Conversation in a Simplified Environment

One of the primary purposes of schools in a democracy, according to Dewey (1916/2004) is, to "provide a simplified environment" (p. 16). The experience of civic education, then, is one of learning about the impact of one's actions on the larger society or community. As a simplified environment, schools allow students to interact with one another and create shared experiences. In the social studies classroom where the instruction is focused on history, culture, economics, geography and political systems, students "gain insight into what is more complicated" (Dewey, 1916/2004, p. 16) about being a citizen in a democracy. Furthermore, the teacher *as* civic education has a moral responsibility, as it is such teachers who, in turn, bring forth experiences of civic life and opportunities for free speech to their students in a "simplified environment." It is in the simplified environment of the social studies classroom where students have the opportunity to embody their civic knowledge and to name it as such.

The results of this study have uncovered, through the text of the student voices, the essential role and impact of student conversation in the classroom—fostering students' experience of and civic disposition toward free speech. The student text allows us to gain a deeper understanding of what Li (2002) claims to be the pedagogical import of true conversation in the classroom, that is, an opportunity to "let learn." Students named the times when conversations happened and how their exercise of their own voice in these serendipitous spaces allowed them to fortify their voices in other contexts outside the classroom.

The student text also revealed support for what Gadamer (1960/2003) noted as a "falling into" conversation. Students experienced optimal freedom of speech, not just in the structured, preplanned elements and activities of the classroom, but most saliently during the time when the teacher allowed for students' voices to find their own way toward understanding. Implications for this finding inform us about the need to ensure there is time and space in the mandated curriculum, so teachers can allow for this level of conversation, interaction, and student voice.

The social studies classroom is the ideal place for this conversation. While conservatives and liberals argue over the contested terrain of curriculum, what they are missing is that no matter what orientation the curriculum-as-plan has, the *teacher* has ultimate influence over the curriculum-as-lived. It is in the actual classrooms, when students voice conservative or liberal opinions on issues such as abortion, war, immigration, the environment, and presidential power, that teachers may *let learn* and allow students the space and time for conversation. A written curriculum is always written from one orientation or another. In the hands of the *teacher as civic education* the biases are made transparent so that the political nature of different issues is made available to students for conversation, and students do not have to choose one viewpoint over another. What civic education is and can do in the right hands is allow students the space and time to have these conversations. These are the same conversations the students in this study mentioned in their reflections at the beginning of the year that helped them participate in the larger society. These are the conversations that allowed them opportunities to approximate real-life situations. These are the same conversations from which teachers can learn from their students and make pedagogical decisions that are sensitive and responsive to the needs of the students themselves.

The WTP SCH is but one example of a lived curriculum that allows students to have these conversations and refine their exercise of free speech. Through their research and interaction with each other, students experienced the "civic glue" that will bind them to their society and to each other. The civic glue is their embodiment of students' democratic experiences in civic education and their experiences of lived relationships. They learned about issues and forming opinions. In the actual performance of the congressional hearing they had conversations with "real adults" about "real-life" issues. True civic education calls for more of these opportunities. Perhaps those enmeshed in the curriculum wars would fare better if their focus were not only on the *political* nature of the curriculum, but also on the *lived* nature of the curriculum. When students experienced interaction and approximations in the simplified environment and had to take and defend a viewpoint, they were transformed and were different people on the other side of that experience.

Thus, it is necessary in civic education for students to move beyond the games and simulations and be ready freely to make decisions between real possibilities. Approached another way, Dewey (1916/2004) emphasized the difference between activity and experience. To move the students' involvement in hands-on activities to true experience requires reflection. Thus, drawing on both Gadamer (1960/2003) and Dewey (1916/2004), play is essential in hands-on learning, as it affords students the chance to further imbed themselves in their culture and society. Free to take risks while at play, students make decisions in a simplified environment, allowing them to reaffirm their "being in the world." Giroux (1980) put it another way, stating: Students should be educated to display civic courage, i.e., the willingness to act *as if* they were living in a democratic society (p. 357).

In Tension With Authority

Noting and naming the tension between the authoritarian setting of the classroom and school, and the students' experience of democracy within it, one can draw conclusions about what it takes for students to truly embody their freedom of speech. Teachers, especially the teachers of civic education, must ask themselves: what kind of society do we want for ourselves and our children? This, in turn, should guide curricular choices and pedagogical decisions.

This research demonstrates how students yearn for interaction, conversation, and authority in their education. As pedagogues, we should want that same yearning for citizens. Citizens who urgently want to take part in society and be ethically and relationally attuned to the needs of others and their belonging in the community are the kind of citizens that Dewey and other progressives envisioned as the result of education for democratic citizenship. Thus, this research speaks to the need to transform the current "schooling" system in favor of one that first and foremost values and promotes experience above all else.

Indeed, it takes a leap of faith in human nature truly to allow for democratic civic education which in turn fosters authentic development and experience of free speech. Well-intentioned teachers, the author included, feign democracy by staging class votes on decisions, the outcome of which, either way, still meet the ends already determined by the teacher. The structure of schooling, despite student government associations, student members of the board of education, and the encouragement of professional learning communities, is still very much authoritarian. Within the relative freedom of the classroom, teachers and students in civic education dwell within the tension that learning civic education in an authoritarian setting brings.

Teachers of civic education vacillate between dependence on the curriculum-as-plan and independence from the curriculum-as-plan for the sake of their students' needs. In this place of tension erupts a "pedagogical situation," in that students are learning from each other (Dewey, 1916/2004). There has been a shift in dependence on the teacher to a state of interdependence on one another.

This experience in this study was not limited to that of the classroom teacher when in civic education students began to authorize their own learning. Most interesting, perhaps, is that the tension they experienced was at the hands of their peers and at their own hands. Many students perceived this as a time when the "teacher did not teach," or the teacher "let us go." In other words, it was a shift in control of authority and authorship from the teacher to the students. As the author reflected at the time:

> I am fading into the background of their learning, of their experience.... At this point, I think my work with my students becomes more authentic. I am giving them feedback on their writing, ideas, stances, positions. In reading their writing not for a grade but for their ideas, what they mean, how they will support them, why they have them, I feel like I know my students in a way that other forms of teaching do not allow. When students have to write for a grade it is different. But here they are writing in order to convince others, in a real-life setting. There is more at stake. It is not just a grade. In fact, there is no grade at stake. What is at stake for these students is themselves.... The tide is turning. After the rehearsals next week, it will turn again. Each turning brings a greater sense of urgency in the students. And a greater sense of autonomy. And a greater position. (Phillips, 2006)

Students' experience of authority, and in particular experience of free speech, is essential in civic education, for as citizens in a democracy they authorize the processes and use of power by the government. As such, students continue to name their experience in terms of the role of power, control, and authority in civic education. To capitalize on this inherent, constitutional moment, teachers need to lean into the tension created by the dynamic of learning democracy within the authoritarian setting and not be afraid to allow students to name it and call it out.

Let Students Name the Phenomenon

What if instead of teachers naming the phenomenon for the students, students are asked to describe what the activity of working with their classmates, independent of the teacher, was like for them? After this study, understandings gained from the students' descriptions of their work in civic education guided how the author subsequently organized the SCH preparation, designed districtwide curriculum, and created professional development for social studies teachers. Particularly, the author changed the way she named things for the sake of the students, using the lived language that emerged from conversations to describe to new students how they would engage in the curriculum. For example, the author understands now that to describe a learning situation as "hands-on" or "interactive" carries more phenomenological meaning for students than does "group problem-solving" or "partner work"—terms used in the past. How much more would teachers learn about their students if students were allowed to name their own experiences, especially those that engage them physically, socially, emotionally, and intellectually?

The naming of experience belongs to those who experience it. In modern American education, we have taken away this right from students and teachers. Clifford and Friesen (2003) declare it is not only a power but a right of the student to name and thus shape their experiences. The teacher *as* civic education not only allows but urges students to do just that. In extending the authority to the students to name their experiences, they in turn, may take ownership of their learning and subsequent transformation. Reconsideration of the authority dynamic opens the door to new possibilities for student-teacher relationships, pedagogy, curriculum development and policy.

IMPLICATIONS: A CALL FOR A NEW CRAFT

How do teachers create the conditions optimal for students to experience, express and fortify their access to expression of free speech? How do teachers balance the tension between the authoritarian setting of the school and the students' experience of that setting with the development of their constitutional sensibilities?

This study has shown that what students learn has very little to do with curriculum-as-plan. They learn from the teacher's actions and dispositions, in the classroom and toward the students, more than from any vinyl binder, handout, or colorful chart. How teachers relate to their students, how they portray justice, equality, freedom, civic virtue, responsibility, and the like, is more important that any conceptual construct of "how government works." The students' own experience of democracy in the classroom is their civic education. The simplified environment created by the teacher allows opportunities for students to fall into conversation around important civic and societal topics, to experience the tension between the authoritarian structure of the school and the expression of democratic sensibilities, and to experience the power to name these phenomena. All these serve to valorize students' experiences of free speech.

The research of VanSledright (2002), Wineburg (2006), and others has transformed the way teachers may approach the teaching of history, as it has named the way in which students may learn history not just as a set of inert facts, but rather as historical investigators. In the same way, civic education for the ultimate student experience of free speech and other rights must have a craft. Civic education is not "civics" education—the conservative notion that dictates that students need to memorize governmental organization and processes as well as historical facts about our nation's past. For a social studies teacher, there is no craft inherent to civic education in that case. The craft of the *teacher as civic education* begins with the teacher him or herself.

As inextricably linked as the teacher's own civic disposition is to the civic learning of their students, this necessitates a focused, intentional approach to teacher professional development. As highlighted earlier through the JMLP, effective teacher professional development that supports optimal student expression of free speech and other democratic experiences would engage teachers in role-plays, simulations, debates, conversations, and values-clarification exercises. Teachers would then reflect on their experiences during these activities and probe implications of them for justice, equality, participation, rule of law, order, security, liberty and other connections to democratic citizenship, including free speech and all of its continua and implications within their own classrooms and contexts.

For teachers to become teachers as civic education, they, too, need a chance to embody their civic education as well as reflect on their lived relation to their students. These experiences will serve as the basis for forming their orientation toward the curriculum-as-plan. The teaching of civic education and support for student free speech is not inherently present in every social studies classroom. It takes an attunement by the teacher to make the classroom the site of these and other democratic experiences. Thus, the goal of professional development for social studies teachers would be to guide teachers to become teachers as civic education. By engaging in conversations with one another about the implications of such experiences for students in the classroom, teachers as civic education can experience their own freedom of expression and carry those experiences into their own teaching to transform the democratic civic education of their students.

In our current schooling structures, teachers *as* civic education will always have to straddle the juxtaposition of developing democratic sensibilities of their students within the authoritarian setting of the school and even classroom. Among students who are experimenting with their own free speech and gaining authorship of their own processes, teachers who are agentic, active, and honest players can powerfully impact their students' development of essential civic dispositions, by crafting opportunities for free speech in conversations, supporting the experiences of freedom in classroom structures, and allowing for the transfer of authority. Most importantly, teachers can give students the time, space, and permission, to name and make meaning of their lived experiences. Once students recognize the sound of their own voices, they will never want to stop hearing them.

AUTHOR NOTE

Donna P. Phillips, PhD, currently is the director of academic innovations for DC Public School but was at The University of Maryland at the time of this research. The author expresses gratitude to Dr. Marcie Taylor-Thoma, director, Maryland Council for Civic and History Education, and Dr. Diana Owen, professor, communication, culture, and technology at Georgetown University whose JMLP research included in this paper was made possible through funding provided by a Supporting Effective Educator Development grant from the U.S. Department. Correspondence concerning this chapter should be addressed to Donna Phillips at doctorphillips236@gmail.com.

REFERENCES

Andolina, M. W., & Conklin, H. G. (2019). Fostering democratic and social-emotional learning in action civics programming: Factors that shape students' learning from Project Soapbox. *American Educational Research Journal, 20*(10), 1–37. https://doi.org/10.3102/0002831219869599

Branson, M. (1998). *The role of civic education: An education policy task force position paper with policy recommendations* (Research report). Center for Civic Education. http://www.civiced.org/promote-rationale/position-paper-with-policy-recommendations

Burch, R. (1990). Phenomenology, lived experience: Taking a measure of the topic. *Phenomenology + Pedagogy, 8,* 130–160. https://doi.org/10.29173/pandp15137

Clifford, P., & Friesen, S. (2003). Hard fun: Teaching and learning for the twenty-first century. In D. Jardine, P. Clifford, & S. Friesen, *Back to the basics of teaching and learning; Thinking the world together* (pp. 89–110). Erlbaum.

Comber, M. K. (2005). *Civic skills and civic education: An empirical assessment* [unpublished doctoral dissertation]. College Park, MD, University of Maryland.

Dalton, R. J. (2006). Citizenship norms and political participation in America: The good news is … the bad news is wrong. *Occasional Paper Series, 2006–01.* The Center for Democracy and Civil Society at Georgetown University.

Delli Carpini, M. X. (1999). In search of the information citizen: What Americans know about politics and why it matters. *The Communication Review, 4,* 129–164. http://dx.doi.org/10.1080/10714420009359466

Dewey, J. (1916). *Democracy and education.* http://en.wikisource.org/wiki/Democracy_and_Education#The_Democratic_Conception_in_Education

Ellsworth, E. (1997) *Teaching positions: Difference, pedagogy, and the power of address*. Teachers College Press.

Frantzich, S. (2005). *Citizen democracy: Political activists in a cynical age* (2nd ed.). Rowman & Littlefield.

Gadamer, H. (2003). *Truth and method* (2nd rev. ed., J. Weinsheimer, & D. G. Marshall, Trans.). The Crossroad Publishing Company. (Original work published 1960)

Giroux, H. (1980). Critical theory and rationality in citizenship education. *Curriculum Inquiry, 10*(4), 329–366

Goodman, J. (2005). The societal purposes of education. In D. Breault & R. Breault (Eds.), *Experiencing Dewey: Insights for today's classroom* (pp. 135–139). Kappa Delta Pi, International Honor Society in Education.

Gould, J., Hall Jamieson, K., Levine, P., McConnell, T., & Smith, D. B. (Eds.). (2011). *Guardian of democracy: The civic mission of schools*. Annenberg Public Policy Center at the University of Philadelphia.

Levine, P. (2007). *The future of democracy: Developing the next generation of American citizens*. Tufts University Press.

Li, S. (2002) Classroom conversation. In M. van Manen (Ed.), *Writing in the dark: Phenomenological studies in interpretive inquiry* (pp. 86–96). Althouse Press.

Owen, D. (2018). *Evaluation of the James Madison legacy project: Cohort II student knowledge* (Research report). http://jmlpresearch.org/research-1

Niemi, R., & Junn, J. (1998). *Civic education: What makes students learn*. Yale University Press.

Parker, W. C. (2003). Teaching democracy: Unity and diversity in public life. Teachers College Press.

Patrick, J. J. (2002, May). *Defining, delivering, and defending a common education for citizenship in a democracy* [Paper presentation]. Summit on Civic Learning in Teacher Preparation, Boston, MA. (ED464886). ERIC. https://files.eric.ed.gov/fulltext/ED464886.pdf

Phillips, D. T. Paoletti. (2006). *Fueling the fire: A phenomenological exploration of student experiences in democratic civic education* [Unpublished dissertation]. University of Maryland, College Park. https://drum.lib.umd.edu/handle/1903/4134

Phillips, D. (2014). Embodied civic education: The corporeality of a civil body politic. *Journal of Pedagogy, 5*(1), 90–114. https://doi.org/10.2478/jped-2014-0005

Quigley, C. (1999, February). *Civic education: Recent history, current status, and the future* [Paper presentation]. American Bar Association Symposium, Public Perception and Understanding of the Justice System. Washington, DC.

Sax, L.J., Astin, A. W., Korn, W. S., & Mahoney, K. M. (1998). *The American freshman: National norms fall 1997*. Higher Education Research Institute.

Soule, S. (2004). *Voting and political participation of We the People: The citizen and the Constitution alumni in the 2004 election*. Center for Civic Education. https://www.civiced.org/research/pdfs/AlumniReport2005.pdf

Torney-Purta, J. (2002). The school's role in developing civic engagement: Study of adolescents in twenty-eight countries. *Applied Developmental Science, 6*(4), 203–212.

van Manen, M. (2003). Researching lived experience: Human science for an action sensitive pedagogy. Althouse Press.

VanSledright, B. (2002). *In search of America's past: Learning to read history in elementary school.* Teacher's College Press.

Wineburg, S. (2006). *Historical thinking and other unnatural acts: Charting the future of teaching the past.* Temple University Press.

CHAPTER 10

REAL CHOICES TO ACT

Waking Up to Charlottesville and Testing the First Amendment

Elise Boyle
Bowling Green City Schools

Leo Bucks
The Ohio State University

Clay Kalaf-Hughes
Bowling Green City Schools

The editors solicited the help of a local high school teacher in collecting stories of student choices to act in the 2017–2018 context of events of the Charlottesville "Unite the Right Rally," ongoing National Football League player protests, and the Stoneman Douglas High School shooting. Students nationwide availed themselves of their rights of free speech and assembly in large numbers and in various ways over this year of polarizing controversies. The 2 vignettes that follow resulted from the trust 1 high school social studies teacher engendered in his students and were crafted by the students themselves through numerous conversations with their teacher. Ellie describes her transition from the private to the public school setting and how she learned through strong role models how to use her voice for

At the Schoolhouse Gate: Stakeholder Perceptions of First Amendment Rights and Responsibilities in U.S. Public Schools, pp. 195–212
www.infoagepub.com
Copyright © 2022 by Information Age Publishing
All rights of reproduction in any form reserved.

change. Leo describes his experience with school protests and offers the observation that students are unlikely to exercise their First Amendment rights of free speech and assembly in school due to a cycle of uncertainty about adult reactions and lack of familiarity with how to use their rights responsibly. The stories and reasoned actions of these 2 young people offer up the argument that high school students can indeed avail themselves responsibly of their rights and suggest that adults attend to the education of young people about their rights.

EDITORS' OPENING NOTE

The editors solicited the help of a local high school teacher in collecting stories of student choices to act in the 2017–2018 context of events of the Charlottesville *Unite the Right Rally*, ongoing National Football League player protests, and the Stoneman Douglas High School shooting. Students nationwide availed themselves of their rights of free speech and assembly in large numbers and in various ways over this year of polarizing controversies. The two vignettes that follow resulted from the trust one high school social studies teacher engendered in his students and were crafted by the students themselves through numerous conversations with their teacher. The school district is Bowling Green City Schools in Bowling Green, Ohio—a medium-sized district in a rural, university town. District administrators have given permission for the authors to use the school name, and the authors' names are their own as well. At the time of this writing, Ellie was in the 10th grade, and Leo was in the 12th grade. Their teacher has provided the introduction and closing.

Teacher Introduction

This fall of 2017 was my 32nd "first day of school." The first 12 were as a public K–12 school student, the next seven as a college undergraduate and graduate student, and the last 13 as a teacher. Each new year brings with it new hopes, new opportunities, and new realities. While I come from a suburban middle-class background, I have over the last 15 years taught in both inner-city and rural schools, in both public and charter school settings, and under a shifting national perspective on what types of skills and supports students need. Although students from these different contexts vary greatly in terms of their own hopes and fears, there are many commonalities.

As an educator in both social studies and English language arts, I have noticed a shift in the pedagogical philosophy guiding instructional practices. When I first started, the focus of the curriculum was on memorization (names, dates, established themes and analysis) and the student's ability to repeat those elements back to their instructor for assessment; however, the focus of instruction, at least from my perspective, has changed recently. Now students are given sources (often conflicting) and analysis and are tasked with giving weight and merit to the various points of view in order to render their own opinions. Students are no longer responsible for knowing the "right answer" as provided to them, but rather to sift through an ever-increasing amount of information in an effort to find their own voice. I believe that this better reflects the realities of the world into which these students are coming, and that as educators, we are providing them with the tools necessary to navigate the modern landscape of ideas. It has not been my experience, though, that this new approach includes taking these points of view and teaching students how to express them beyond the context of an assignment for a class. This chapter represents a unique opportunity in the unique context of the 2017–2018 academic year for me to explore the points of view of two students that have led them to take action outside the classroom.

Over the course of my teaching career, I have had the pleasure of working with many exceptional students, including Ellie and Leo. They are not only outstanding in their academic pursuits but also in that their personalities do not accept the status quo. They have worked both in their school settings and within their community to make changes and bring awareness to issues that they see as important, and each encountered various degrees of support and resistance for their efforts.

I want to thank both Ellie and Leo for taking time out of their busy lives to write about their experiences. It is greatly appreciated.

Ellie: Waking Up to Charlottesville

Today's circumstances make it important for all citizens to make their voices heard, not just for themselves, but for others. If you have the ability to stand up for important issues and do not, you are almost as responsible as those who are doing the thing you hate. I am currently a sophomore at Bowling Green (Ohio) High School. Bowling Green High School is an average high school, composed of students whose parents work at the college, people whose families have lived here their entire lives, and farming families. At school, I am a part of StuCrew (our student activities board), treasurer for French club, involved with the drama club, and on the tennis team. It is all a pretty normal high school experience, but I started high school at a not-normal time, in August of 2017, five days after the Charlottesville hate marches. I was starting a new chapter of my life, and with the recent events in mind, I knew that if we wanted a better world, we were going to have to work harder than many other generations of students have had to. I hope to take this and make it the foundation of a career in public service.

I did not wake up one morning and decide to be active in my community. When I was in eighth grade, during the 2016 election, a Clinton-for-President campaign office popped up in downtown Bowling Green. My dad and I had stopped in to pick up a yard sign and to see if they needed help. We ended up signing up for a shift to go door to door, making sure that registered democrats were going to go and vote in this important election. A few days later, Gloria Steinem came to the campaign office for a volunteer' rally. I went with my dad, and we listened to her speak. I had the opportunity to talk to her and take a picture with her. As an eighth grader, hearing her speak was so influential. We volunteered again on election night, working the phone banks with about twenty other people. With only about an hour before the polls closed, we were trying to reach as many people as we could.

Fast forward with the election over, and I went to high school. The Charlottesville hate marches took place in that first month of school, and I knew I wanted to do something, but I didn't know what to do. I wasn't involved with anything at that time, but I knew it was important to get involved at some point. That moment came in February 2018, when Marjory Stoneman Douglas High School in Parkland, Florida had just suffered a huge tragedy. A month after the shooting, our school was one of the many that organized a walkout in protest gun violence. At first, no one knew if there would be consequences for participating in the walkout. It was student-run and organized by upperclassman, and I wanted to be a part of it. We learned that our faculty and staff were supportive, assuring us that there would be no major consequence for walking out. We understood that this was different from the case with many schools across America. Some were warning students that they could be suspended for walking out. On March 14, a month after the Parkland school shooting, about 300 of my peers and I walked out for 17 minutes. I know that many of the students who made the choice to walk out were walking out so that they could get out of their class for seventeen minutes, but that was not the case with me and my friends.

The Saturday after the walkout, my friends and I decided to get up early to attend our city's rally against gun violence. We wanted to show that we weren't just doing it to skip out of class—we actually cared. We got to the rally, and we were some of the only young people there. This event was led by university students, and they opened up the microphone to anyone who wanted to speak. One of my old coaches encouraged me and my friends to go up and say something. We were all terrified. We went up, and I was handed the microphone with my friends by my side. It was definitely scary to be in front of many people you do not know, but we did it, and I am glad we did.

Several months later, I was asked to be part of something that has changed my role as a citizen. Each year, one high school student is selected to serve on Bowling Green's Human Relations Commission, which is a commission that strives to promote diversity and inclusion in our town and to represent the viewpoint of teenagers in our community. In May 2018, I was appointed to serve. It was an honor to be selected to represent my peers in making change. From my time on the commission, I have learned to not be fearful of stepping up, participating, and letting my voice be heard. People that I may never have had the opportunity to meet before became mentors for me. I had new opportunities. Most importantly, it is a small chance to help make change in Bowling Green.

Many of the people I have met through Human Relations Commission inspire and push me to keep moving forward and fight for what we want our city to be. They treat me like I am one of them. They place trust in me, so that I am empowered to take action now, when 2 years ago, I would have been afraid to engage in a debate with someone or be worried about backlash from peers. Now (for the most part!), I am willing to talk with someone that may share an opposing view and am not afraid to post or write about what I believe is right.

On November 2, I had a Human Relations Commission meeting in the morning, where we talked about the upcoming vigil for the lives lost at the Tree of Life Congregation in Pittsburgh and Jeffersontown, Kentucky shootings. It was at a local church in Bowling Green, and when the Human Relations Commission asked for people to read a short paragraph about each of the lives lost, I volunteered. I read the paragraph of Cecil Rosenthal, who died with his brother David Rosenthal in the shooting. It is important that they are being remembered around the country and don't just become "another guy." Twelve days later, I participated in the Bowling Green "Not in Our Town" Peace March. The peace march had a hope to stop hate, address bullying, and promote a safe and inclusive community. The march was at noon on a Wednesday, which meant that I would be missing school to take part in it. I hesitantly approached my principal—Mr. Jeff Dever—to ask him if I could participate, and he gave full support and allowed me to miss school to attend. It was amazing to see all of the different faces of Bowling Green—the police, the mayor, and many others—who were all there to make sure that people feel welcome in our town.

I have felt increasingly called to action because of people in public service who have become part of my life. In 2018, I met a long-time hero of mine, former Vice President Joe Biden. I had understood Biden to be a fun and engaging public servant since elementary school. It was pretty easy to love a guy who has been in "Parks and Recreation" and has thousands of memes about himself. In 2017, after his term ended, I found him to be a real hero, as he established the Biden Cancer Moonshot Initiative. It was important to me, because my dad has Stage 4 kidney cancer, and Biden's actions showed me how one can take their public service at any level and turn it into something literally life changing.

Through a whirlwind of events, my dad and I met Biden at the 2018 American Cancer Society Medal of Honor ceremony. He was talking to some of the other recipients and getting some photos with them, and once he had finished, he said, "You must be Ellie!" which added a personal touch to our interaction and helped me connect with him. I walked over, got a picture with him, and thanked him for all the work he had done. I saw in that night, between his work on cancer and his willingness to meet a high school student like me based on a letter I wrote him, just how much public service can change the world and change one person's life. Meeting him made me feel like anything was possible, especially after all of the hardships that he had to overcome—losing his wife, daughter and son. It also made me feel stronger about using my voice, not being as shy to things that I know are wrong, and it gave me a lot of hope for the future.

Now, as we are coming up on the 2020 presidential election, I see more and more the effects that one person can have. I also see the opportunities to learn. This last summer as candidates hit the campaign trail, my friend and I decided to see Elizabeth Warren when she went to Toledo. We found it interesting that we were some of the few, if any, young people who willingly drove ourselves there, without our parents offering, just because we found it fun. It was an amazing end to the summer, as we not only got to learn about different policies she hopes to share, but also, as we were waiting in line to meet her, it gave me just a hint of insight of what goes into being a politician, which is a lot! I saw all of this work, and it motivated me to want to pursue a career like that.

These experiences with finding my voice and meeting such leaders who serve as role models have shown me how important it is for young people to get informed and be active. I believe it is important at home, school and even out of the house to talk about current events, because so many are oblivious to what is happening in their own country and the world. Watching the news or following it on social media also can be beneficial. I think it is a good way for me and my peers to see not just what is happening nationally, but also globally, and it hopefully will spark discussion with others, too.

I am definitely not saying that you need to change your beliefs but recognizing the views of those with whom you may not always agree is very important. I have been in schools where not everyone's beliefs were necessarily being recognized. That school included a number of families who did not share my views, and therefore many of the students did not as well. I was afraid to share my voice with all of my peers, and the only time I would talk about issues was outside of school with one friend who I knew shared the same views. At my current school, I feel much more comfortable speaking my voice and talking with peers during the day. When we talk about current events, I am not scared of what people say. I know that students nationwide aren't as lucky to have supportive schools that work for all students, and that many still feel that they are trapped and can't share their voice like I can at my current school. I am incredibly grateful for what my school allows me to do, such as at the time of the Parkland walkout. Some students at public schools in our region were punished for walking out, even though they were just exercising their rights, just as my peers and I were doing.

I know that I am very lucky to now have an accepting school community, peers, and family. Most of my family agrees with my views, and I do not face much confrontation from them. However, those who may not agree with me on certain issues have never discouraged me from having an active voice. As for my friends, most of us also share similar views, and have attended events together, such as our city's gun violence march. Together, my friends and I talk about current events a lot, such as what we see on social media, and anything we can do to support it, we try to. I asked one of my friends if she thought our school and our community are safe places to speak out and be politically active and what she thinks keeps people from doing so if they are not comfortable with it. She responded with yes saying "because having the university here brings so many young people to Bowling Green, so I feel comfortable speaking out as a young person." As for why people may be hesitant, she said she thinks that people are afraid of the backlash, and she added that she thinks people are less afraid to address what they stand for on social media, because they don't have to face the confrontation.

Whether it be on social media, watching the news, or talking to people, I try to remember that it is good to hear from all sides. Many of my teachers also incorporate current events into teaching so that they help us better understand what is happening in our country, especially when we are living in a time when many of us do not understand everything that we hear in the news. Our teachers are also always available to engage in conversation we may have about current events, which leads to more active discussions of points of view in the classroom.

At my school, our administration and staff were supportive of the Parkland walkout, and they have let me take part in Human Relations Commission and many of their events, even during school hours. My school's principal has been nothing but supportive of me and my peers, and when you approach him with a question or a concern, he encourages us to use our rights. I also realize that many students like me were punished for doing this because they did not have a supportive school community. I am thankful our school will participate in the discussions and not ignore them.

Within the classroom, we have many group discussions about current events. My freshman year, I took a course called World Culture Studies, which is an integration of English and history, where we would have in-class discussions, and where our teachers would tackle big picture ideas like gun violence. It was different from what I had expected, because even though I knew not everyone had the same views, it was interesting to see sides debate. Since we were having this conversation after the Parkland shooting, it felt very close to home debating these issues in a school. Some students thought like me—that we needed to have more restrictions on gun laws. Others disagreed. A few of my peers thought that more guns in schools would protect us, and even some thought that arming teachers was a good idea, and I think that scared some of us. I think other people's views made me want to stand up for what I believed in, and I had the courage to speak out, because I felt that my teachers had created a safe environment. On such a divisive topic, it was probably the first time I felt comfortable sharing my views with more than just close friends or people I knew thought the same way I did about the subject. I am so grateful that I had teachers that worked to create a safe environment where we could share our opinions without retaliation from peers. However, I could see that if I were in a different classroom, with different teachers, I may not have been as comfortable. I don't even think I could have shared my views if it was me alone with my own peers at that time, and so I am grateful that that experience in my freshman year prepared me for more discussions that would come in later years, so that I had the courage to share my voice. I as a sophomore participated in many classroom discussions about current issues such as racism, the Holocaust, and gun violence in our English and social studies classes. With each new conversation we started, I began to feel more and more comfortable. The teachers and students made sure that we have respectful conversations, where everyone can let their own opinion be heard, instead of confrontation.

Outside of the classroom, we have a mostly tolerant student body. But I also haven't had a lot of attention drawn to me from my peers, and nothing that I have done has sparked controversy that I am aware of. In the classroom, I have many more peers from the county in my town who I tend to believe have a more conservative ideology then the more liberal ideology that I see within our city.

I am only 16 years old, and I don't know exactly what I want to do with my career, but right now I think I would like to go into a political science field. I do know that sometimes doing the little things to make my community a better place are the things that can make the world a better place eventually, no matter what I end up doing. I am thankful for the opportunities that I have had. These opportunities came to because of the support that I get from my heroes, my teachers, my school, my family and my friends. They all have shaped me for the better. I woke up to Charlottesville, but that is just where my role in democracy was getting started. I've learned that students' First Amendment Rights are important and need to be known, shared, and protected.

Leo: Testing the First Amendment

I am a senior at the same high school Ellie attends. My mom is a local middle school teacher, and my dad is a letter carrier. Since my mom teaches social studies, I grew up learning about American history and government and was familiar with parts of the Constitution from an early age. Politics were, and still are, a frequent subject for debate in my family. We have volunteered for political campaigns since I was in second grade, so I have always believed that political activism is not just for people who are able to vote.

In the fall of 2017, I decided that I wanted to take a knee during a high school football game. I supported professional athletes' justifications for peacefully protesting. It seemed like the perfect opportunity for me to show solidarity with the athletes, because I was already on the field performing the anthem as a member of the marching band. I knew that people in the audience would believe that I was disrespecting the anthem, the flag, and veterans, so I continued to play my trombone while I was kneeling. My goal was to make sure that my protest did not prevent me from playing in the band, which was a part of my grade.

I did not tell people that I was going to take a knee. I assumed that my band directors and parents would encourage me not to, and I didn't want to openly ignore their wishes. I decided to kneel and potentially face repercussions rather than risk consequences for protesting as well as insubordination. I knew that the First Amendment protected my protest. I was not certain, however, that I would not face additional scrutiny from school administrators because I chose a well-attended, public event after school hours. As students, we're frequently told to positively represent the school district when we're in public.

On the Monday after the football game, my band director and a principal each spoke to me about my decision to kneel. I was surprised that neither was critical of my decision. My principal told me that he couldn't punish me, and that he wouldn't even if he could. Both the teacher and the principal asked me if I considered the way my protest would impact my future. It seemed as though they were more concerned that I could have created a small controversy for myself within the conservative parts of the community. During both conversations, I was cautioned that many people misinterpreted my kneeling. The point of the conversations was to allow me to explain my side. I wasn't even punished for leaving "attention position" in marching band, for which my director could have punished me. In short, if I felt like protesting again, I knew there would be no official way to stop me. I'm happy with how my teachers and administrators handled my kneeling.

If more band members had taken a knee, I don't think I would have been as lucky. I trust that we wouldn't have been asked to stop, officially; however, I suspect that we would have been told to positively represent the marching band and the school district. It seems likely that adults would use the pressure of public opinion to encourage us to stop, because they'd want to avoid negative attention. The football crowd tends to be conservative. If other band members had joined me in taking a knee, it's likely that there would have been complaints from spectators. Kneeling would be seen as an attack on the football team's values. Both the band directors and the football coach emphasize the importance of the bond between the football team and the marching band. If the marching band had kneeled, we would have risked jeopardizing that relationship, and it would have made the school look divided.

I think that part of the reason my kneeling was met with so little resistance from the adults in charge was because of my reputation in school. I'm a responsible Honors student. I don't cause trouble, people trust me, and I'm only ever in the principal's office for good reasons. Also, many people know that I've been active in political campaigns. My protest was taken seriously, because my teachers and principals knew I wasn't just trying to cause trouble or get attention for myself. I can't speculate on whether students with a disciplinary record would receive a harsher talking to. It's possible that by questioning another student's actions and motivations and implicitly pressuring them to stop, this could have the same effect as prohibiting them outright. I think it depends on the student. I do know, however, that the conversations I had were fairly relaxed, because I'm trusted.

It would seem, then, that more students would exercise their First Amendment rights frequently, considering the lack of opposition from the school; however, protests have been rare at my school. Any policies regarding student speech seem to be infrequently tested, with the exception of beer shirt display. Within the last 4 years, I know of three protests: soccer players who took a knee, my own kneeling, and our successful walkout. In all of these cases, students have been motivated and pushed to act. The protests within my school seem to have occurred after the respective causes received significant media attention. While protest-worthy events happen monthly around the world, students' enthusiasm and focus determines whether students will protest.

It seems to me that the school is not officially preventing students from protesting; students are not taking action because they are unwilling to take advantage of their rights. Most of my peers know about the First Amendment. I would not say that a lack of knowledge is what's stagnating student speech. Rather, many of my classmates wonder how the First Amendment will be applied within our school. Students often feel like school is in a sort of legal limbo, where laws look slightly different and nobody knows exactly what to expect. A schoolwide drug search during my freshman year and years of debate over the dress code have shown us that our rights are different in school and at home. The limits on our other rights have led students to assume that our right to protest would be similarly limited. We know that adults can stand on the street, and provided they aren't impeding traffic, defaming someone, or disturbing the peace, tell passersby nearly anything they want, but because few people in our school actually test the First Amendment, many assume it can't be done.

I suspect that if students were told as freshman that the First Amendment applies to us in school, more students would be willing to assemble, speak, and possibly even write. By not telling us about our rights, we don't know what to expect. Currently, we have to risk testing our rights to learn about them, and I think many are doubtful that we will be protected. After I kneeled, at least five students came up to me and asked me if I was ready to be punished. I didn't know what to expect from my principal; I was surprised when he was as supportive as he was. If school officials were to explain what our rights look like in school, it would allow students to make their choice to take action based on their beliefs, rather than on a fear of punishment. It currently seems like First Amendment rights are a privilege for the few students who have found out the secret—that as long as a protest isn't impeding learning, it can't be stopped. In theory, this secret applies to the whole school. First Amendment protections in my school are like the rights of the accused before *Miranda v. Arizona*: they exist, but you've got to know about them to be able to take advantage of them. This is inadvertently exclusionary, and it's probably the most important factor preventing our school from having more protests.

In my experience, though, the right to assemble is protected. Last year, two students organized a successful walkout as a part of the National School Walkout. The walkout was unique, because it was carefully planned and meant to involve many students. Other protests had involved no more than three students, and the organizers aimed to have as many students walk out as possible.

While I was not involved in the planning of the walkout, I talked to the two students who were. One in particular told me about multiple conversations with administrators about the logistics of the protest. According to him, nothing was left to chance. Neither the administrators nor the students wanted any controversy, so every aspect was planned. The city police were informed. The superintendent was involved.

Thankfully, the walkout went as well as we hoped. Around 300 students took part, including middle schoolers. Nobody was rowdy. I didn't hear of anyone being harassed, whether they took part or not. The overwhelming feeling I got from the crowd was that participants were unsure of what they were supposed to be doing but glad they were taking part. The organizers were impressed by how many students walked out. We have less than 1,000 students at the high school, so having roughly 300 students take part was a success. We expected hostile community members to counterprotest, but there were none. Supportive community members did watch us, and they were kept removed from the students. Instead, the police watched around 300 very cold students stand around, listen to two speeches, chant a little, and then peacefully go back inside.

I attribute the success to two things. First, we were told that we would not face any punishment for skipping class during the protest, provided that we didn't break any rules as we took part. I think this was essentially an insurance policy for the school to guarantee that the students involved would be on their best behavior. It was a shrewd move. We did miss class, and while the protest itself would have been difficult to legally stop, the principals and teachers could have marked all participants absent during the time that we weren't in class. Thankfully, nobody had to risk getting marked absent due to the walkout, and this meant that each student got to freely decide whether they wanted to participate. The decision to participate rested solely on the students' opinions on the message of the walkout. If the principals had decided to punish participants for their absences, I think a significant number of students would not have wanted to risk the hassle of justifying their choice to walk out. I know I would still have participated, though. In this case, I think the administrators made the right decision. I think they were mostly just trying to minimize the number of complaints from parents, but the effect was that they gave every student the chance to join the walkout.

The other factor that influenced the success of the walkout was the media attention surrounding the issue. The walkout was meant to give students a chance to call for an end to school shootings. It's a hot button issue for high school students. We've all grown up participating in active shooter drills, and nearly every student has an opinion about how to stop school shootings. The walkout was planned for a month after the shooting in Parkland, Florida. In short, students were fired up about the issue. The walkout happened at the perfect time.

The organizers promoted the walkout on social media. They put up posters around school. Lots of people were talking about the planned protest. In many ways, I think the rarity of big protests like this contributed to its appeal. Nobody had ever taken part in something like it before. We were curious to see what would happen, and that caused people to become more interested. The buzz surrounding it made it too big to be ignored, and too big for anyone to want to risk it going poorly. As students, we needed the walkout to go smoothly or we risked losing our credibility, since many of us were not adults at the time. School officials faced worse risks. If the protesting students became violent, it would look like they allowed students to skip class and break the law. If counterprotesters showed up and caused trouble, it would look like they weren't protecting the protesting students. If they made it difficult for students to take part, they risked being accused of violating the protesters' rights. As a result, every aspect of the walkout was planned to avoid controversy.

The largest problem I see with the way the walkout was handled by the school was the police presence. There were multiple squad cars in front of the school before the protest began. The officers were fairly close to the students. At the time, it felt like we were being monitored to make sure we remained peaceful. The police presence led us to believe that the administrators did not trust us. We assumed that the police were there to stop *us*, if need be. This assumption was also based on the fact that we thought community members would come to heckle us. We thought that if students were going to cause trouble, it would be in response to counterprotesters.

It wasn't until later that I realized that the police were there to protect us. Nonetheless, having to coordinate police protection was not easy, according to the organizers. The difficulty of keeping the students safe (although it wasn't necessary) was the difficult aspect of planning the walkout, according to one of the organizers. Student behavior wasn't nearly as much of a concern, and rightfully so. We had no reason to break the rules; we wanted to be taken seriously, and acting immature would mean that we would not be able to organize a similar event. I remember talking with other students about how we hoped everyone realized that we had to behave respectfully so that we didn't reflect poorly on our cause.

I can't ignore that part of the reason why so many students participated in the walkout was probably because their friends were doing it, or because they were going to get out of class for 45 minutes. In some ways, part of the success of the walkout was due to peer pressure. Everybody knew that there were some students who were just there to get out of class.

Nobody really seemed to mind, though. In the future, if we hold more events like this, I suspect that people will claim that lots of students are just trying to skip class. I think school officials would be less likely to make it easy to organize mass protests if they happened frequently because they'd worry that instruction time would be wasted. These sorts of concerns show that adults doubt students' beliefs and think that our reasons for protesting are not as legitimate as adults. Even after I kneeled, I was asked to explain why I had done what I did, to confirm that I wasn't just trying to anger the football crowd.

Our school hasn't held another protest like it since. One reason is because the walkout was not easy to plan. It was the first protest of its size in recent memory and it required much more time than the organizers initially expected it would. Additionally, students are not motivated to be active about another subject in the way that they were after the Parkland shooting. There isn't a reason to go through the planning process again. I don't think that the difficulty in planning the walkout was meant to discourage the organizers. I think it was genuinely because the school wanted to make sure that the students would be completely protected. However, it seemed to the students that the administrators were trying to prevent the walkout from happening. The difficulty in organizing the walkout probably won't have any effect on the right to assemble in the future, though. Most students didn't hear about the details of planning the event; they just saw the end result. The lasting memory for the school, then, is of the walkout, not the organization.

While the walkout was successful, there's one student in my school who has tried to protest, and he has been stopped by the school. He likes to display the Confederate flag and wants to be able to do so in school. I don't support his opinion. I think the rebel flag is a symbol of White supremacy and I would be happy if nobody displayed it anymore. That being said, though, people frequently display the flag in public elsewhere in our town. Both the Confederate flag and kneeling during the anthem could have provoked roughly equivalent pushback within the community. Different people seem equally outraged by the two issues; however, when I kneeled, I was told by the school that I could continue to protest. The student with the flag was told to remove it, because the decision rested with the administrators. They said it wasn't within his right as a student. The justification was that the rebel flag is often considered a White supremacist symbol. The principal does have the right to prohibit hateful speech.

To complicate this issue, though, other students with rebel flag clothing haven't been asked to remove it. I've seen people wearing T-shirts, sweatshirts, and belt buckles with the rebel flag. Crucially, these students don't have a disciplinary record, but the one student does. He appears to be targeted because of his methods and his poor reputation. This student chose to criticize the principal during a meeting with the entire graduating class about the principal's order to remove the student's Confederate flag off the back of his truck. The student's goal was to pick a public fight. He wants to provoke people. The other students typically aren't in trouble, so the principals don't have an extensive, negative history with them.

The connotations of the flag are the same regardless of who's wearing it, yet some students are allowed to show it while one isn't. This difference in enforcement of the dress code shows students that they're more likely to have their rights respected if they have a good reputation. The fact that the principals enforced the hate speech policy in his case but ignored it for other students is unfair.

I don't think that the principals were deliberately trying to turn a blind eye to other students' rebel flags. It's likely that they would have made these other students remove theirs if they knew about it. The problem, though, is that they are actively monitoring the one student's behavior while essentially ignoring others' similar behaviors. What I object to, however, is that other students aren't immediately asked to remove their rebel flags. The rules are enforced inconsistently, and it's based on profiling.

I've benefited from the profiling. I get the benefit of the doubt when I decide to do something. Adults seemed to respect my decision to kneel, when they easily could have wrongly dismissed it as attention-seeking behavior. People trusted that I had put thought into my justification for kneeling. The difference in treatment between myself and the rebel flag student shows that my school respects the First Amendment when they are willing to trust the student. It sends a message that "bad" kids won't be protected like the other students. The school needs to respect the rights of all students.

One common theme between both protests I've been a part of was the concern over how the community would react. My principal asked me if I'd considered what people would say about me taking a knee, and the school went so far as bringing in police during the walkout in case community members got out of hand. Personally, I wasn't afraid of what people might say to or about me, but both of my parents heard their coworkers unhappily talking about "that band member who took a knee at the football game." I got asked by one classmate about why I was disrespecting veterans, but most were either supportive, or they didn't care. After the walkout, we heard about posts on social media about "students wasting taxpayer money" during the protest. I didn't have any negative interactions with students who didn't support the walkout.

Concern over how the community will react is what's driving the narrative around student speech, not what's actually being said. In effect, we're kept separate from the community. I believe that it's done with our safety in mind, but it sends a message that our speech is somehow different from every other citizen's. We need to be allowed to exercise our rights, but some people treat us like we can't think for ourselves. I think if the school were a separate ecosystem, and community members couldn't comment on what happened in school, we would be more willing to protest, and school officials would be less wary of our protests.

If more students were to protest, more students would understand their rights; but I think it is the rarity of protests in my school that ensures that they run smoothly. At this point, student speech is seen by the student body as unusual and, in effect, this carries weight. If more students were to try to exercise their First Amendment rights, it would unfortunately not be taken as seriously.

In my school, nothing officially prevents students from taking advantage of the First Amendment. My principal has made this clear to me. However, other factors shape the protection of free speech. The reputation of the student influences how adults view student speech. They are more willing to be sympathetic if the student is trusted and behaves maturely. A lack of knowledge about how the First Amendment is applied in schools may lead students to be uncertain of their rights. Students don't know that their rights are protected. These conditions both could be used to limit students' speech.

Today, protests are rare, and that means that there is lots of pressure for them to go well. The students want their message to be taken seriously, and we can't let foolishness impact people's opinion. The school can't risk mishandling student speech because it is so rare. The stakes are high for both the students and the school. In effect, student speech must be well-handled because it could reflect so poorly on both the student body and the administration. I was surprised that the school has, in my opinion, not been hostile toward students' right to protest.

Teacher Closing

Having worked in both urban and rural schools, both public and charter, in California and Ohio, I have noticed two trends in my classroom and in the broader educational community: (1) social media is changing the way students relate to the world around them, and (2) community perception of student interest and engagement has shifted from neutral to negative.

Increasingly, social media is becoming the new cultural sounding board for students to express their ideas, to take in information and make connections with like-minded individuals. These connections are not limited to a school district or community, and for many students with whom I have spoken, social media is not only an acceptable alternative to freedom of expression in the school building, but preferable.

For a large number outside of the school building, this online over in-person engagement can look like apathy. The perception for many in the community is of a younger generation defined by narcissism and detachment. While this characterization in no way describes Leo, Ellie, or many of their classmates, it does affect the community's belief in student efficacy and willingness to support student protests. Both Leo and Ellie were able to overcome this trend in part because of their additional engagement in nonschool community groups. However, this is not the case for most of their peers, who are in some ways victimized by an older generation too willing to cast their political and social engagement in a negative light.

Both Leo and Ellie encountered a variety of adults while endeavoring to express themselves. Some were supportive, some were concerned about upsetting "business as usual," and some felt that these students were too young, and therefore their voices were somehow less valid. I am pleased to report that neither was deterred, and both Leo and Ellie continue to advocate for what they believe in, both in local contexts and in state and national settings. For Ellie, the inspiration and support came from both her family and a prominent national figure spending a moment to acknowledge her by name and provide encouragement. As for Leo, she succeeded despite a lack of support and in several cases direct opposition. These two exemplify some of the best qualities students in a modern context can have, and I hope that by us sharing their experiences, we as educators can find better ways to nurture and support these qualities in future students.

EDITORS' CLOSING NOTE

The stories and reasoned actions of these two young people offer up the argument that high school students can indeed avail themselves responsibly of their rights and suggest that adults attend to the education of young people about their rights. Ellie argues that all citizens should practice using their voices to help themselves and each other. She woke up to Charlottesville. Leo tested out his First Amendment rights and made the strong argument that young people need more awareness of and practice with testing out their rights. The editors are grateful for the opportunity to hear their voices and applaud their courage and choices to act.

AUTHOR NOTE

Correspondence concerning this chapter should be addressed to Clay Kalaf-Hughes, Bowling Green City Schools, Bowling Green, Ohio, 43402. Contact: chughes@bgcs.k12.oh.us

ABOUT THE CONTRIBUTORS

Elise Boyle was a student at Bowling Green High School at the time of contributing to her chapter. She was involved in a number of school and community groups, including the Bowling Green Human Relations Commission and National Honor Society. She currently is pursuing a degree in political science at Bowling Green State University.

Diann Brown has spent the last 50+ years in classrooms from kindergarten through graduate school. Most of her teaching has been in middle school classrooms and teacher preparation at Bowling Green State University. Diann's calling is teaching, but she presently enjoys working as a teacher candidate university mentor in Bowling Green State University's College of Education and Human Development. She was on the data analysis team for the *At the Schoolhouse Gate* research project. She has spent the bulk of her career teaching social studies and language arts, coaching, directing and advising students. Besides teaching, Diann has enjoyed time with family, traveling, summer lake living and puttering at home in Ohio with her husband Bill.

Kristy A. Brugar is an associate professor of social studies education, at the University of Oklahoma in Norman, OK, where she teaches undergraduate and graduate courses in elementary and secondary social studies education. Dr. Brugar's research focuses on social studies and history education, interdisciplinary instruction involving social studies, literacy, and visual arts, and teacher development. Dr. Brugar is a recipient of the Oklahoma University Jeanine Rainbolt College of Education Junior Faculty Award (2017), the National Council for the Social Studies, College and University Faculty Assembly Early Career Award (2017), the Oklahoma University Robert L. and Nan A. Huddleston Presidential Professor of Education (2018), and the JRCOE Research Award (2020).

Leo Bucks is currently an undergraduate student at The Ohio State University studying history with a minor in Yiddish. Leo plans to specialize in modern American social and cultural history. At the time of writing his chapter, he was a senior at Bowling Green High School. In high school, Leo was involved in local political campaigns and served on the city's bicycle safety commission. An interest in current events, government, politics, and social justice issues led him to "take a knee" as a member of the high school marching band in solidarity with athletes protesting police brutality.

Prentice T. Chandler, PhD, is the dean of the Eriksson College of Education at Austin Peay State University (TN). From 2013–2017, he was the associate director of teacher education and leadership and an associate professor of social studies education at the University of Cincinnati. Prior to his time at Cincinnati, he was the department chair of secondary education and an associate professor of history and social science education at Athens State University from 2006-2013. Before joining the professoriate, Dr. Chandler taught middle and high school social studies in rural Alabama. Dr. Chandler's scholarship and writing interests are in the areas of history and social studies education, critical race theory, academic freedom, and authentic intellectual work. Dr. Chandler has authored or coauthored approximately 50 works, including 2 books on teaching about race and racism within the social studies curriculum. His latest book, *Race Lessons: Using Inquiry to Teach about Race in Social Studies* examines race and racism through the social science disciplines taught in social studies. In 2007, Dr. Chandler was named the Defense of Academic Freedom Award winner from the National Council for the Social Studies for his efforts teaching history in Alabama public schools. In 2018, he was named as the recipient the Notable Leader in Teacher Education Award from the Alabama Association of Teacher Education.

Sarah J. Kaka is an assistant professor of education in the Department of Education and Ohio Wesleyan University, and the director of the Adolescent to Young Adult and Multi-Age Licensure Programs. She is a former secondary social studies teacher. Her research strives to support teacher preparation programs in creating effective, long-term educators in all settings.

Mikayla Hernandez is an undergraduate student at The Ohio State University studying interior design. Prior to moving to Columbus to pursue postsecondary education, she participated in the research focus groups conducted by Dr. Nancy Patterson for *At the Schoolhouse Gate*, discussing her views regarding First Amendment rights with fellow classmates. She currently is studying in a collaborative environment to become a commercial interior designer, but still focuses on observing how her First Amendment rights apply to her daily life in the college setting while striving to exercise them and encourage friends and colleagues to do the same all over campus.

Clayton Kalaf-Hughes has been a classroom teacher for over 15 years. He has taught in both public and charter schools, in California and Ohio, for Grades 6–12 and continues in English language arts and social studies. In both states he has collaborated to create cross-curricular courses. He received his undergraduate from University of California at Davis and a masters of educational leadership from Bowling Green State University.

Cheryl Lambert is an assistant professor in the Eriksson College of Education at Austin Peay State University. Dr. Lambert teaches a variety of courses for the Department of Teaching and Learning and serves as the coordinator for Center for Rural Education at Austin Peay. She holds BS and MS degrees from the University of Tennessee at Martin, and an EdD from The University of Memphis. Dr. Lamber's previous work experience was in rural school districts in west Tennessee where she taught math, science, and social studies in elementary grades, served as a districtwide data coach, and held the positions of instructional supervisor and director of special education. Dr. Lambert's research interests include rural education, student ownership, and quality preservice education programs.

Jeffery D. Nokes is an associate professor in the History Department at Brigham Young University. A former middle school and high school teacher, his research focuses on history teaching and learning, historical literacy, preservice teacher development, and preparing young people for civic engagement. He is the author of *Building Students' Historical Literacies: Learning to Read and Reason With Historical Texts* and *Evidence and Teaching History, Learning Citizenship: Tools for Civic Engagement*, as well as several journal articles and book chapters. He has received teaching awards at the middle school, high school, and university levels and currently teaches historian's craft, methods of teaching, and literacy courses for prospective social studies and history teachers.

Nancy C. Patterson is a professor and the social studies content area coordinator at Bowling Green State University. Given her core commitments to global and local democratic education and social justice, her scholarly efforts are interdisciplinary and collaborative in nature and include perpetuating pedagogies that promote civic engagement as well as examining contexts, whether in schools in their larger communities at home or abroad, that foster democratic education and social justice. They have developed to include widening circles of stakeholders from students and the university community, to neighboring teachers and school districts, to state and national agencies as well as international partners. Dr. Patterson studied civic education curriculum as a Fulbright Scholar in Morocco. The themes of democratic education and social justice have also led her to opportunities for advocacy on the issue of educational and academic freedom in public schools, with particular attention to teacher and student First Amendment rights in public schools. Her work has been featured in *Theory & Research in Social Education; Social Education; The Journal of Social Studies Research; Social Studies Research and Practice; The High School Journal; Education, Citizenship, and Social Justice; and International Journal of Education Policy and Leadership*. She regularly presents at the annual meetings of the American Educational Research Association and the National Council for the Social Studies. She currently teaches undergraduate courses in secondary social studies methods and graduate courses in qualitative research at Bowling Green State University and is a past president of the Ohio Council for the Social Studies.

Donna P. Phillips is the director of academic innovations for District of Columbia Public Schools. She leads the work in assessments, interdisciplinary curriculum, global education, Advanced Placement, and computer science. Previously, she was the social studies curriculum manager spearheading the development of C3 inquiry and social justice aligned K–12 social studies curriculum. Prior, she taught secondary social studies in urban and suburban middle and high schools. Dr. Phillips's BA is in history from Columbia University with a concentration in psychology. Her MA is in leadership in teaching from Notre Dame University of Maryland. Dr. Phillips has a PhD from University of Maryland in education policy and leadership, curriculum theory and development where she researched the lived experience of democratic civic education.

Dalton C. Savage is a public school teacher at Edmond Memorial High School in Edmond, Oklahoma where he teaches courses in social studies, including AP Human Geography and Oklahoma History. He received his B.A in Political Science and his M.Ed. in Instructional Leadership and Academic Curriculum from the University of Oklahoma. His research focuses on social studies educators and professional learning. Dalton is a recipient of the Charles Redd Center Teaching Western History Award (2016), Jeannine Rainbolt College of Education Outstanding Intern Award (2017), and the Oklahoma Council for the Social Studies Clara Luper Memorial Rising Star Teaching Award (2019).

Michael D. Simpson was the assistant general counsel of the National Education Association and the former executive director of the Student Press Law Center. His specialty was defending the constitutional rights of public school employees, with an emphasis on the First Amendment.

Ryan Suskey serves as director of professional development and programs at the Ohio Center for Law-Related Education, a civic education nonprofit in the Buckeye State. He holds a bachelor of philosophy in French literature from the University of Pittsburgh, a master of arts in teaching from Johns Hopkins University, and a Juris Doctor from The Ohio State University. His primary professional and academic interests include authenticity in civic education curricula and inquiry models of instruction.

Wesley Wagner is currently an undergraduate student at Duquesne University in Pittsburgh, PA, where he is enrolled in a 4+1 master of science in forensic science and law program, with an undergraduate focus in biochemistry, along with minors in biology and mathematics, and a prelaw certification. On campus, he is a member of the executive board of Phi Sigma Lambda and Habitat for Humanity, along with being a member of the Duquesne Honors College. Upon receiving his master's in forensic science, Wesley plans on furthering his education by attending law school.

Jeanne Vidoni grew up in northeast Ohio and attended Kent State University, earning a bachelor of Music and MEd in school counseling. While she thoroughly enjoyed teaching choral and general music for ten years, she returned to university to obtain certification to teach Grades 1-8. For the next 22 years, she taught language arts and social studies to fifth and sixth graders in Ravenna City Schools. She participated in several innovative curriculum and teacher development programs including the Classroom of the Future and the International Leadership in Education Program. After retirement, she earned a TESOL certification and helped adults pass the written and oral sections of the U.S. Naturalization Test. Since 2018, she has worked as a University Mentor in Bowling Green State University's College of Education and Human Development. She was on the data analysis team for the *At the Schoolhouse Gate* research project.

ngramcontent.com/pod-product-compliance
ng Source LLC
ne TN
52313200926
1LV00002B/545
8 1 6 4 8 0 2 7 2 4 6 *